Strategising Industrial Development in Jammu and Kashmir

About the Book

The state of Jammu and Kashmir is one of the least developed states of India. It exhibits all the characteristics of an underdeveloped economy, viz. low per capita income, poor quality of life, widespread unemployment, fiscal imbalance and excessive reliance on the Indian Union.

In the past, numerous initiatives were taken to transform the economic landscape of the state through industrialization. However, the balance-sheet of shortcomings and achievements of industrialization so far presents a rather gloomy picture. Given a situation like this, an earnest attempt has been made in this book to address the following questions: (a) How has the state faired in terms of industrialization so far? (b) What is the state of business environment in the state? (c) What is the industrial potential of the state and where does it lie? (d) What factors are inhibiting the growth of industrial sectors? and (e) What specific strategies are needed to achieve meaningful industrial development?

No detailed study has been made so far to address the above questions. The present book is an attempt to fill this vacuum. The book, it is hoped, will make a valuable addition to the existing body of literature on industrial development. It provides valuable insights into the challenges, opportunities and the strategies necessary to achieve sustainable industrial development of the strategically located state of Jammu and Kashmir of the Indian Union. The policy formulations offered in this book, if implemented, will to go a long way in placing the state on a high growth trajectory.

About the Author

Dr. Khursheed A. Butt obtained his Ph.D. from the University of Kashmir. He specializes in corporate finance and management of small-scale industries. He has also served in reputed American Universities in United Arab Emirates (UAE). Besides teaching, he is actively involved in research and training. Dr. Khursheed has authored two books and published numerous research articles in reputed business journals. Presently, he is an Associate Professor in the Department of Commerce, University of Kashmir.

Strategising Industrial Development in Jammu and Kashmir

Khursheed A. Butt

New Century Publications
New Delhi, India

New Century Publications
4800/24, Bharat Ram Road,
Ansari Road, Daryaganj,
New Delhi-110 002
Tel.: 23247798, 55396605
Telefax: 011-51017798
E-mail: indiatax@vsnl.com
www.newcenturypublications.com

Editorial office:
34, Gujranwala Town, Part-2,
Delhi - 110 009
Tel.: 27247805, 27464774

First Published 2005

ISBN: 81-7708-095-4

Published by New Century Publications and printed at Singhal Print Media, Delhi -110 007

PRINTED IN INDIA

FOREWORD

It gives me great pleasure to write foreword for this book. The book provides a comprehensive framework for understanding the different aspects of industrialization in the state of Jammu and Kashmir. It is undoubtedly a scholarly book which is rendered readable because of the vast original source material that the author has used. What makes it commendable is the illuminating light that it throws on the hitherto hidden aspects of the state. The approach used in this book is simple, analytical and explicit. The book seeks to examine the causes of industrial backwardness in the state of Jammu and Kashmir. The study in fact gives a panoramic view of what went wrong with the state policy vis-à-vis the rapid industrialization in the state. The introductory chapter gives a summary of the business environment in the state aptly. In the next chapter, an honest endeavor has been made to identify the areas where industrialization can be seriously thought of. In the subsequent chapters, the author has critically examined the development of industrialization in the state and has also deliberated upon the factors that are inhibiting it. In the last chapter, the author has analytically identified the strategies required to be adopted by the state for undertaking a purposeful industrialization synchronizing with geo-economic advantages.

Dr. Butt's book is a valuable contribution to the field of industrial development and an eye opener for organizations, scholars and state planners. The book would serve as a useful guide for the state planners to formulate suitable strategies for attaining sustainable industrial development in the state. I appreciate the efforts and the commitment of Dr. Butt in attempting this comprehensive work.

05/06/05

(Professor Abdul Wahid)
Vice Chancellor
University of Kashmir
Srinagar

Preface

The state of Jammu and Kashmir is one of the least developed states of India. It exhibits all the characteristics of an underdeveloped economy, viz. low per capita income, poor quality of life, widespread unemployment, fiscal imbalance and excessive reliance on the Indian Union. Agriculture, though leading sector of the state's economy, is constrained by low land-man ratio and other structural limitations. Yet, development of agriculture alone is not enough for taking the state's economy to a higher growth path. The lasting solution to fight the twin formidable problems of poverty and unemployment lies in the expansion of industrial base of the state. The pace of industrialization in the state can be stepped up by mobilizing the hitherto under-utilised human and material resources of the state.

However, the peculiar physical conditions of the state like topography, extreme location in the national setting, absence of railway link for a major portion of its areas, and long distances from main markets limit the scope for industrialization. Still, on the positive side, the state is well endowed with some proven resources of great importance which offer vast potential for industrialization in selected areas. The state is also gifted with scenic beauty, world famous health resorts, fascinating landscape and also historical legacies in crafts of various kinds. Hence, the state enjoys a distinct and an important place in tourism and handicraft industry.

The small-scale industries dovetail well with the economic imperatives of the state. However, the development of small-scale industries alone is not sufficient to free the state from age-old stagnation and economic backwardness. Therefore, the development of large and medium enterprises is also called for. There is scope, though limited, for large-scale manufacturing in areas where the state enjoys comparative advantage in resource endowments.

In the past, numerous initiatives were taken to transform the economic landscape of the state through industrialization.

Contents

Dedicated to My Parents

For Whom

The Holy Quran Orders to Mankind

That you be kind to parents. If one of them or both of them attain to old age in their life, say not to them a word of contempt nor repulse them but address them a gracious word in terms of 'Honour'. Allah Almighty also teaches us to pray for them; say "May Allah have mercy on them; as they cherished me mercifully when I was little."

1

Jammu and Kashmir: A Profile

Introduction

The state of Jammu and Kashmir exhibits all the characteristic features of an underdeveloped economy. It suffers from low per capita income, large scale unemployment, poor quality of life, problems of poverty and pre-dominance of agriculture. The agricultural sector itself is beset with multiple problems like, severe agro climatic conditions resulting in mono cropping, low land man ratio, inadequate agricultural inputs and uneconomical size of holdings. In such a scenario, the agricultural sector can not be expected to free the state of its age old stagnation and economic backwardness. This fact was reinforced by various expert committee reports from time to time for example L. K. Jha committee (1977) and NCAER Study group (1969). The classical remedy to the under-development of the state's economy is that the developmental priorities should emphasize more on the development of modern industries. This is because that the industrial sector possesses relatively a high marginal propensity to save and invest thus, can contribute significantly to the eventual achievement of a self-sustaining economy with continued high levels of investment and a rapid rate of increase in income and industrial employment. It is in view of this fact that the industrialization on sound lines is accepted an appropriate means to the attainment of rapid economic development as being amply demonstrated by the industrially developed countries while as, negatively by the less developed countries which are industrially under-developed and whose people live in poverty. However, the development of agriculture in any scheme of development needs to be given due attention because of its complementary relationship with the industry.

There is no denying the fact that industrialization is of utmost importance to the developing economies like ours for solving the problems of economic backwardness. Establishment of wide variety of industries, however, alone is not important but what matters most is their survival and growth. To achieve sustainable industrial development, there is a need to seek an answer to the question "How to Industrialise"? This would require to thoroughly scanning the environment in which the industrial entities will have to operate. This is highly warranted because an industrial enterprise is like any other organism which inherits its strengths and weaknesses from the environment in which it operates. Just as the success of an individual depends on his innate capabilities similarly, the growth prospect of an industrial enterprise depends on the innate strengths that it inherits from its environment. The industrial environment is a blend of internal and external environs. An industrial enterprise can have control on the internal environment, therefore it can change or modify it to suit its changing requirements.

However, an industrial enterprise in no way can influence the forces of external environment. It is, therefore, the external environment and not the internal environment that determines the pattern and the type of industrialization that can be promoted successfully in a given area. The external environment does not guarantee greater productivity but certainly proves a decisive factor. To derive maximum out of conducive external environment, it is equally important to create and maintain healthy internal environment. The external environment consists of micro and macro dimensions of an industrial environment. The micro environment consists of the actors in the immediate environment of an enterprise like, suppliers, competitors, customers etc. while as macro environment include demographic, economic, technological, legal, political and socio-cultural forces. Micro environmental forces may affect only few firms but macro forces shape opportunities and threats for the entire industrial economy although with varying degrees for different industries.

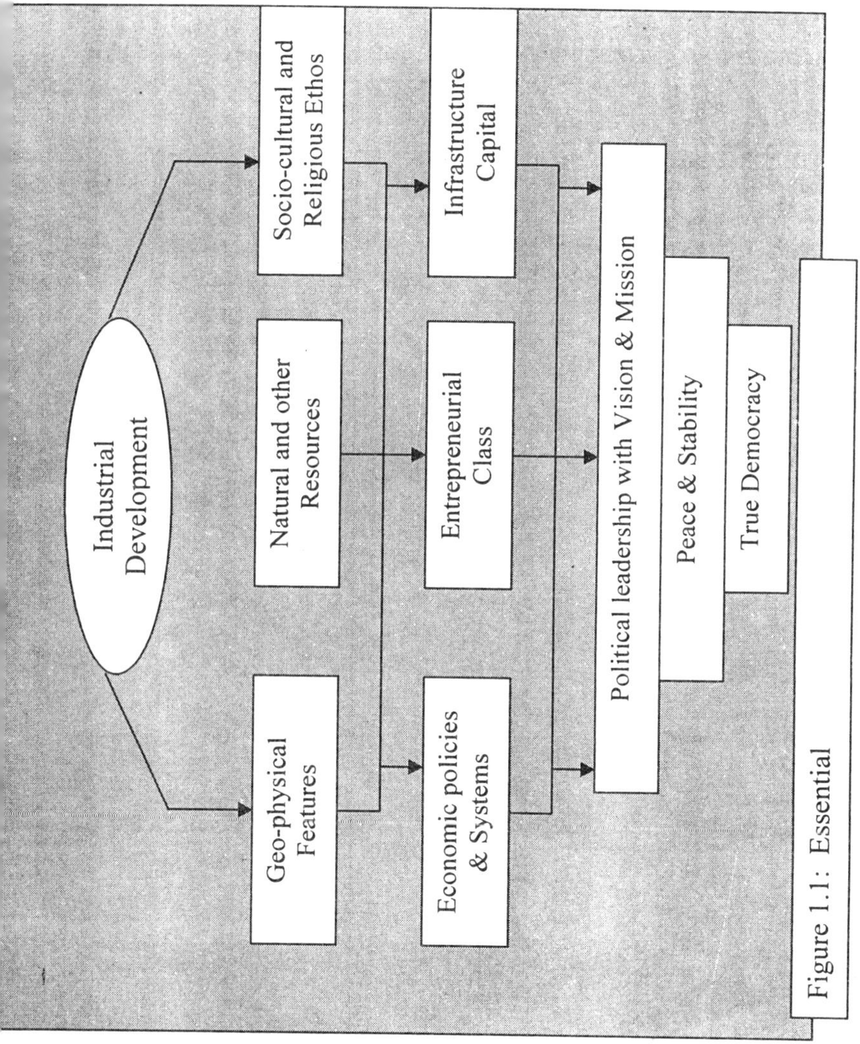

Figure 1.1: Essential

The micro and macro dimensions with which the state of Jammu and Kashmir is bestowed with is being thoroughly analysed in the subsequent sections of this chapter with the purpose to capture the picture of the state's industrial potential – the thrust areas, the optimum size of different industries and to unveil the environmental bottlenecks so that the same can be improved upon. To draw a total and candid picture of the state's industrial potential, it will be obviously essential to have a close view of resource endowments, infrastructural capital, geo-physical feature, political compulsions, religo-cultural realities, socio-economic features and lego-competitive conditioning of the state. The natural resource base and the industrial potential in the state have been discussed in the next chapter.

Geo-physical Features

Industrial orientation of a given area is also determined by its location in the national context, climatic and topographic features and physical conditioning. Location and certain physical factors determine accessibility to the markets and competitiveness of the firms.

The state of Jammu and Kashmir is situated in the extreme north of India between latitude 32.30 degrees and 37.0 degrees north and longitude 72.50 degrees and 80.20 degrees east. The borders of the state touch Pakistan, Kazakhstan, Afghanistan and the states like Punjab and Himachal Pradesh. The total area of the state is 2, 33,800 sq kms and on this side of the line of control is 1, 38,992 sq kms, larger than Tamil Nadu and more than twice of Haryana. However, major portion of the state is mountainous with a height from sea level varying from 1000 feet to 28,500 feet. The southern side of the state has a strip of plains connecting the state with the rest of the country.

The geography of the state is divided into three constituent units- Jammu division, Kashmir division and Ladakh division. Jammu division falls on the southern side, has a strip of plains but major part of this province is hilly. Jammu and Kathua districts consist of plain area while as Doda, Udhampur, Rajouri and

Poonch districts of the division are mostly mountainous. The climate of Jammu division varies from tropical heat in the plains of Jammu and Kathua districts to temperate cold in other districts of the region. Further, Kathua and Jammu districts are gateway to the rest of the country and are connected with all sorts of transport with the rest of the country.

Kashmir, the largest division of the state with regard to population is mostly mountainous and the climate of this important region of the state is far from extremes of tropical heat and artic cold and has a temperate and salubrious climate. The entry and exit points to the valley are covered with mountains and winter season lasts for more than six months. This division is devoid of any rail link and is connected with the rest of the country by 300 km road which passes through Pir-Punjal Range and travel is treacherous. However, Kashmir division is rich in scenic beauty, forest wealth, horticulture produce, handicraft skills and some mineral resources, thus leaving enough scope for the related industries.

Ladakh is the largest division of the state with regard to area, covering 70 percent of the total area of the state. But, with regard to population it is smallest with 2.5 percent of the total state's population. It is all hilly without vegetation. It is experiencing severe winter which lasts almost for 8 months and is mountain locked hence, difficult to reach in and out. The Ladakh division of the state is characterized by extreme cold weather, lack of resources, skills, necessary infrastructural facilities and worthwhile market base but, is a place of attraction for the tourists world over. In view of the peculiar features of the Ladakh division, except tourism related activities like Hotels, there is very little scope for any other industrial activity for the time being. There is a need to develop and promote the tourist potential of this division.

Population Growth: The state has witnessed a big leap forward in population growth as becomes clear from the perusal of data contained in Table 1.1 The population of the state as per census 1951 was 32.53 lakh persons, has increased to 100.70 lakh persons in 2001.on an average annually the population of the state is growing at the rate of more than 4 percent which is highest in the country. During the decade of 1991-2001, the population of the state has increased by 29.04 percent. The big leap forward in population growth in the state poses some major implications to the future of the state. Though more population means more market size for industrial and other commodities but at the same time it will cause more pressure on land, forests and other scarce resources in the state which in turn will have its impact on the developmental process in the state. So there is a need to curb this population explosion for the better future of the state.

Table 1.1: Population Growth in J&K State: 1981–2001

Census	Total population	Decadal growth	Change in growth
1981	59,87,389	29.69	
1991	78,03,900	30.84	1.15
2001	1,00,69,917	29.04	-1.80

Source: *Digest of Statistics*, Planning & Development Department, Govt. of Jammu & Kashmir, 2002-03.

The density of population in the state as per census 2001 works out to 99 persons per Sq. Km. While it is 324 persons as per census 2001 for the Indian union. Of the three regions, Kashmir region is having more density of population while as, Ladakh region is the most sparsely populated region in the state. The density of population is much lower than most of the states in the country. However, low density of population in the state would be misleading owing to the fact that major part of the state is mountainous and inhospitable thus providing little scope for extension of cultivation.

As can be seen from Table 1.2 that as on 2000-01 the net area sown is 30.96 percent of total reporting area only which does not compare favorably with the net area sown in the rest of the country. The net area under cultivation which was 657 hectares in

1960-61 has grown to 748 hectares in 2001-02 in 45 years period, recording a growth of 2.77 per cent only.

Table 1.2: Percentage Decadal Variation in Population in J&K State

Decade	Kashmir region	Jammu region	Ladakh region	J&K state
1901-11	7.05	4.14	12.01	7.16
1911-21	9.47	4.58	2.31	5.75
1921-31	13.54	10.16	6.13	10.14
1931-41	10.73	10.89	5.83	10.36
1941-51	12.58	8.20	8.81	10.42
1951-61	11.45	7.86	7.86	9.44
1961-71	28.93	29.63	19.96	29.65
1971-81	29.25	31.97	27.66	29.69
1981-91	32.44	27.42	32.51	30.34
1991-01	31.58	25.90	30.70	29.04

Source: *Digest of Statistics*, Directorate of Economics and Statistics, Planning and Development Department, J & K Government, 2002-03

It can also be seen from Table 1.3 that during the last two decades, the net area sown in the state has stagnated at 30 percent of the total area. This low growth in net area sown in the state can be mainly attributed to the geography of the state which offers little scope for extension of cultivation. This means that the major breakthrough by sizeable increase in agriculture production is ruled out. Against a background such as this, the state has no option but to emphasize on industrialization to accelerate the process of economic development.

Land-man Ratio: Among other things, agricultural sector in the state is constrained by the uneconomical size of landholdings. Added to this even these small size holdings are not in one compact block but largely fragmented. In 2002-03, the average size of land holdings in the state is 0.999 hectares as compared to

2.9 hectares in the country. The number of agricultural holdings in the state as on 2002-03 are 10,35,376 covering a total area of 10,29557 hectares. Of the total number of holdings, about 70 percent holdings are of the size of less than one hectare (for more details see Table 1.4). The per capita cultivable land is as low as 0.17 hectares which is much lower than the per capita cultivable land in most of the other states in the country.

Table 1.3: Net Area Sown in J&K State

Year	Total area (000 hectares)	Net area sown (000 hectares)	net area sown as %age of total area	Decadal %age growth
1960-61	2416	657	27.19	-
1970-71	2417	706	29.20	7.45
1980-81	2414	715	29.62	1.27
1990-91	2416	731	30.25	2.23
2000-01	2416	748	30.96	2.32
Cg				**1.29**

Note: Cg Stands for Compound growth

Source: *Digest of Statistics*, Planning & Development Department, Govt. of Jammu & Kashmir, 2002-03

Of the three divisions, Kashmir region is having much smaller size of land holdings as compared to Jammu and Ladakh regions of the state. The average size of land holdings in Kashmir region is 1.7 acres while as it is 3.08 acres in Jammu division and 3.78 acres in Ladakh division. The average size of land holdings in Kashmir division is not only lower than Ladakh and Jammu divisions but also less than the state average of 2.29 acres. The main reason for smaller size land holdings is due to break-up of joint family system and the peculiar laws of inheritance which provide division of ancestral property (Nisar, 1987). This is also attributed to the increasing pressure of population on land on account of lack of alternate employment opportunities in the rural Kashmir.

Table 1.4: Average Size of Land Holdings in J&K State (in hectares)

Size of Holdings	Number	Percentage
Total Area Total No of Holdings Average Holding Size	10,12,530 13,35,770 0.76 hectares	
Holding below 0.5	6,96,151	52.12
0.5 – 1.0	3,45,339	25.85
1.0 – 2.0	1,86,590	13.97
2.0 – 3.0	64,153	4.80
3.0 – 4.0	24,406	1.83
4.0 – 5.0	10,694	0.80
5.0 – 7.5	5,845	0.44
7.5 – 10.0	1,650	0.12
10 – 20	752	0.06
20 and Above	199	0.01
Total	13,35,770	100.00

Source: *Digest of Statistics*, Planning & Development Department, Govt. of Jammu & Kashmir, 2002-03

The serious implication of small size holdings in the state is that such holdings are uneconomical to undertake agriculture activities on commercial lines. It is due to this that the rural youth in the state are pushed to seek jobs in the secondary sector. However, the secondary sector in the state has not expanded and grown to the extent needed to create sufficient jobs. Instead of absorbing the ever increasing workforce in the state, the secondary sector has further pushed them towards government sector which in turn has constrained the state government with more wage bill. This explains why the overall picture of the state's economy is one of backwardness.

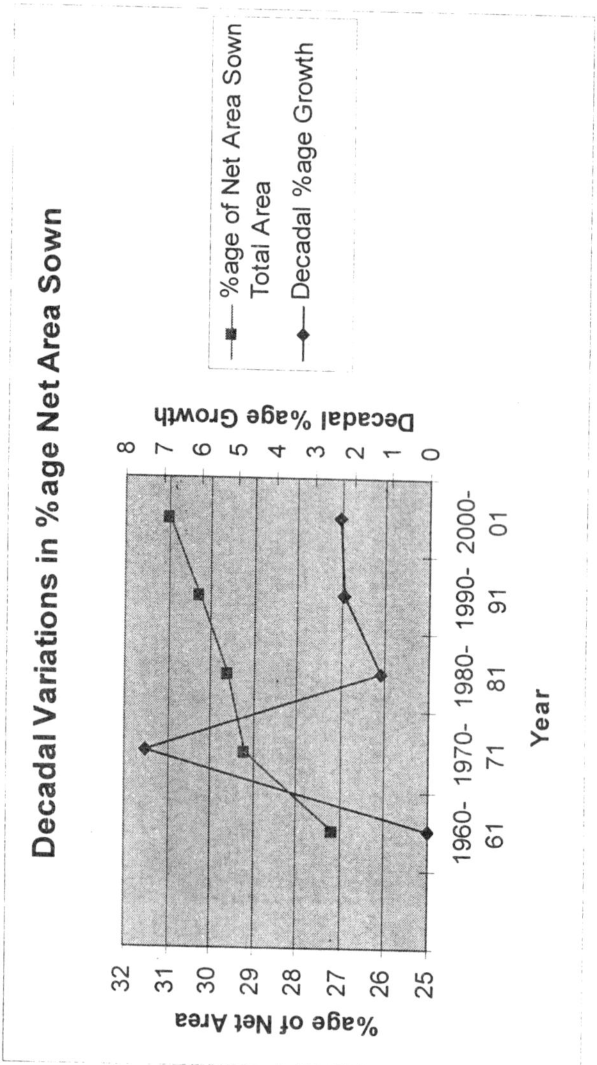
Decadal Variations in %age Net Area Sown
%age of Net Area Sown Total Area
Decadal %age Growth
%age of Net Area
32
31
30
29
28
27
26
25
Decadal %age Growth
8
7
6
5
4
3
2
1
0
1960-61
1970-71
1980-81
1990-91
2000-01
Year

Peculiar geo-physical features of the state in general and of the Kashmir division in particular, like mountainous terrain, isolated location, extreme climatic conditions are some of the deficiencies to the conducive industrial environment in the State. The extreme location with poor accessibility to the market has limited the size of industries where state does not enjoy definite advantage in resource endowments. Severe climatic conditions make Kashmir division unsuitable location for certain industries, like ceramic industry, silk printing industry etc. Absence of any railway network and mountainous terrain makes the transportation arduous, time consuming and costly, which further adds to the poor industrial environment in the state in general and of Kashmir division in particular. Comparatively, Jammu division is locationally and climatically well placed and hence, enjoys some advantage for industrial take-off.

The adverse Geo-physical features do not stop the state from the race for industrialization, but certainly limits the extent and scope of industrialization. Forest based industries, Handicrafts, some agro-based industries and some mineral based industries have enough to offer to the state's economy. The state enjoys huge potential for hydro electric power generation. However, surprisingly the said natural resources remain grossly under-utilised. Further, the tourism has much in stock for the state. The exploitation of tourism potential could supplement the smallness of state's market to some extent. However, much remains to be done by the state in the development and promotion of tourist potential, particularly, winter and adventure tourism. But all this needs to focus on the development of tourism related infrastructural facilities on priority basis.

Political Environment

Politics is deep rooted into the social fabric of modern communities. The attitudes and perceptions of the people are dictated by the political realities surrounding them. Political stability is an essential ingredient for industrial prosperity. The State of Jammu and Kashmir has been quite unfortunate with regard to political stability right from 1947. This has acted as a recurring parasite to the state's economy. The state remains a bone of contention between India and Pakistan. Three wars have been fought so far over J&K State. People of the country in general and the people of Kashmir in particular are uncertain about the future of Kashmir right from the beginning. With the return of late Sheikh Muhammad Abdullah as the state's Chief Minster in 1986, the political stability of the state was considered as restored. However, these predictions proved wrong as in the recent past the state has witnessed uprising with a different face which has pulverized the political stability to the dust. The youth of Kashmir have taken to arms against India. The present uprising with gun culture has alarmed the whole world and has shattered peace and stability in the state.

Today the state in general and the Kashmir region in particular is characterized with security bunkers, crackdowns, identification parades, bomb blasts, cross firing, very frequent dusk to dawn strikes and working days shrinking to 6 hours only. All these unfortunate events are coming in the way of the normal functioning of the industries in the state.

Political instability in the state is being considered as one of the main reasons for underdevelopment of industrial sector. It is perhaps due to political insecurity in the state, the government of India did very little in the development of industrially important infrastructure. In- spite of having definite potential for hydro-electric generation, the state still remains chronically deficient in electric power which is essential for putting the wheels of industrialization on run. Industrialists from outside are also reluctant to invest in the state due to number of inhibiting factors, one major factor is political uncertainty with which the state is suffering. People of Jammu and Kashmir are passing through political turmoil and uncertainties since 1947 and have now learnt to live with such undesirable conditions. They have resolved not to wait but to start the race for industrial development. However, they are anxiously waiting for the overdue permanent settlement of the Kashmir problem to the satisfaction of the people of the state so that there are no bottlenecks to them for achieving economic development in general and industrial development in particular. Looking at the present changing global scenario on the political front, it looks that now time is nearing for the permanent settlement of all the political miseries of the public in the state.

Socio-cultural Environment

Every living being, whether actual or artificial is tied into a socio-cultural fabric in one way or the other. The attitudinal perceptions and actions of people are governed by the socio-cultural beliefs. Customs, traditions, taboos, motives, value systems, preferences, work culture, work ethics and alike are included in socio-cultural environment. Although the study of socio-cultural ethos is not that important in shaping the industrial landscape but the study into the socio-cultural imperatives certainly would help in unveiling the socio-cultural inefficiencies that are impeding the industrial performance and in identifying the social stigmas that come in the way of promotion of certain industries. The industrial policy that reflects the socio-cultural realities would result in minimum of wastes and social complexities.

The state of Jammu and Kashmir is characterized with socio-cultural diversity. Jammu is Hindu majority, Kashmir valley Muslim majority and Ladakh Buddhist dominated region of the State. The three regions differ in language, customs, taboos, value systems, consumption patterns etc. To the people of Jammu and Ladakh any type of industry is acceptable while as, to the religious beliefs of Kashmiri's some industries, like wine and wine allied industries, pig rearing etc. are not acceptable. After the recent uprising, the industrial units manufacturing alcohol in the valley have been made to shut down because such industries were established in contravention to the religious principles of the majority community. Further excessive meat eating is deep rooted in the socio-cultural ethos of the Muslim brethren of Kashmir division, while as most of the people in Jammu division are herbivorous. During festivities in the Kashmir division, almost all the dishes are meat based. Such a unique food habit of the people in Kashmir division provides enough market base for different varieties of meat, which in turn promises industrial potential for poultry farming, sheep farming, and allied industries.

"Culture the sum total of social behavior, which includes knowledge and beliefs refer to prevailing notions of reality, ideals to societal norms and preferences to social definitions of those things in life which are attractive or unattractive as objects of desire" (Cherunilam, 1997). The preferences of the people in the state vary from region to region. The Kashmiri are heavily oriented towards government jobs and give little preference to industrial entrepreneurship. While as, the average Jammuites have high preference for industrial entrepreneurship. Most of the entrepreneurs in Kashmir region have been found not by choice, as such, lacking commitment and motivation. People in the state also suffer from the misconception that there is no potential for modern industries. The main reason behind this misconception is more industrial failures and absence of any worthwhile initiative by the government in the creation of better industrial environment and awareness. However, on account of more exposure to the developments taking place on the industrial scene in the country, the preferences of youth towards industry has started giving its roots. The role of non-governmental organizations in educating and helping the youth of the state towards this important sector is called for.

The most disturbing and intriguing feature about the state's socio-cultural side is its undesirable work culture and work ethics which has added to the already poor industrial environment in the state. Redtapism and corruption, though a national phenomena yet, it is more widespread and acute in the state and has reached to alarming proportions. People working in different departments and agencies including those concerned with the development of industries in the state are not conscientious in their duties, helpful, and committed but most of them are insincere, rigid with bureaucratic attitudes and open to bribery. It is an open fact that red-tapism, favoritism and nepotism are rampant in the state which has given birth to corruption at all levels and cadres. "Procedural wrangles, and inordinate and willful delays have become a part of the formal system and the most intriguing aspect is that there is no one to check these malpractices even at the highest levels". All these things have made the genuine entrepreneurs to suffer a lot and has given birth to those entrepreneurs who are there to pocket-away subsidies and defraud financial institutions. The undesirable work culture in the state has given crippling blow to the industrial scene and continues to impede purposeful industrialization. To put the state on right path on all fronts including socio-cultural front, the society in general and the intellectuals in particular has a definite role to play. For the purpose they need to be alarmed of the dangerous consequences of the socio-cultural inertia from which the society is suffering.

Economic Environment

Industries partly draw their substance from the economic environment in which operating. The economic environment which subsumes economic conditions, economic policies and economic systems has a profound impact on the pattern industrialization. Economic conditions are important determinants of the type of industries that are well suited while as, economic policies and economic systems determine the scope of public and private enterprises and the areas within the private sector which fall within the priority sector. The priority sector is generally being offered number of fiscal and non-fiscal sops to see its accelerated development.

Economic conditions like, level of income, nature of economy, economic resources etc. in the state of Jammu and Kashmir are not rosy enough. Although the per capita income of the state is less than the national average yet, there has been steady growth in the State Domestic Product and per capita income. As on 2001-02, the per capita income of the state is Rs. 7,841 (at constant prices) while as the per capita income of the country as a whole is Rs. 10,254 at constant prices (Digest of

Statistics, 2002-03). The important feature about the growth in the per capita income in the state is that in recent years there has been marked growth. In the first two decades since 1950, the growth rate has hovered around 1.5 per cent per annum. However, in the eighties the growth rate has increased to 2.4 per cent per annum. During nineties when every thing in the state got paralysed due to insurgency, the growth rate in per capita income has declined to 1.9 percent. But during the last few years there has been more than sufficient growth in per capita income of the state which is a healthy sign for the future of the state.

The steady increase in per capita income in the state offers bright business prospects and for further investments in different businesses. However, in a low income economy like ours, it would be highly important for business enterprises in the state to continuously make efforts to reduce cost of production and to develop new low cost products to suit the low income market. A positive aspect about the distribution of income in the state is that the people living below the poverty line are less as compared to other states in the country. More important aspect of the state's economy is that it has developed some resilience. It is showing signs of rebound after it took heavy beating during nineties due to out break of militancy.

The State of Jammu and Kashmir is characterized by relatively low, slow and halting economic growth. The state still remains one of the industrially and economically backward states in the country. Its backwardness can be judged from its sectoral break-up of State Domestic Product. As on 2001-02 agriculture contributed more than 36.34 percent to the State Domestic Product and employed 50.10 percent of the total work force as per census 2001, which does not compare favourably with the national averages (Digest of Statistics, 2002-03). However, the positive aspect about the state's economy is that there has a steady increase in the share of non-agricultural sector thus falling in line with the desired economic transformation. The primary sector which was contributing 47.4 per cent in 1980-81 has declined to 36.34 per cent in 2001-02.

However, the shift has been more pronounced towards the tertiary sector whose contribution to the State's Domestic Product has increased from 39.70 percent in 1980-81 to 49.51per cent in 2001-02 (Digest of Statistics, 2002-03). The fact is that the secondary sector has not expanded to the level required to take the state on high growth path. The industrial sector in the state though consists of all the three sectors yet, most of the private investment has come in the small scale sector. This is due to the fact that the peculiar feature of the state are well suited to the development of small scale industries. This is true that the future of the state lies in small and medium enterprises but modern rather than traditional enterprises.

Industrial Policy, 1991: Industrial policy which forms a part of an economic system invariably determines the pace and direction of industrialization. India which was dominated by planned economic system right from 1947, came-up with the new industrial policy in 1991 which marks a big departure from the *'Nehruian Model of Socialism'*. The new policy has to a great extent transformed the sluggish Indian economy into progressive economy through the means of Globalisation, Liberalisation and Privatisation. The role of direct foreign investment and privatization has been emphasized under the various new policy measures announced since 1991. To have an idea about the things to come, let us look into the important features of the path breaking industrial policy of 1991.

- Marketization of Indian industrial economy with minimum of controls and regulations is at the heart of new industrial policy. Under the current economic system, entrepreneurs enjoy freedom in their commercial decisions. Now it is the market and an entrepreneur and not the bureaucrat who will govern the industrial development.
- Globalization of Indian economy is emphasized in new Industrial policy. To integrate the domestic economy with the global economy, the approval of direct foreign investment without any limit in 34 sectors including hotel and tourism industry and all food processing industries and also in respect

of foreign technology into priority sectors is automatic. In fact, the promotion of economy for foreign investment stands at the top in the agenda of the present economic system.

- Privatization is the heart throb of the new policy initiatives. Under new policy, industrial licensing has been abolished for all projects except A few specified groups which pertain to the industries related to security and strategic concerns, hazardous chemical etc. The space for the private sector to operate now has been widened by limiting the fields for exclusive operation by public sector.
- The new industrial policy guarantees more freedom to the private entrepreneurs in shaping the fortunes of their enterprises. Under the new policy, the industries are not required to register with the government, however, need to fill an information memorandum on new projects and for substantial expansion projects with the government. Further, the inspector Raj, the long standing problem of the industries has been reduced considerably.
- The restrictions on the functioning of monopolies embodied in the Monopolistic and Restrictive Trade Practices Act in operation since 1970 have been removed and new policy puts emphasis on tackling undesirable Monopolistic activities.

The piece meal changes in the economic system through the process of Liberalisation, Privatization and Globalisation have significantly changed the economic environment in which the industrial enterprises will have to operate. The new economic system that has emerged since 1991 has increased the competitive intensity of the Indian markets. A *'sellers market'* has gradually transformed into *'Buyers Market'*. The emerging new economic environment is not only throwing open great challenges but innumerable opportunities as well. Aggarwal (1999) has observed that the opening up of an Indian economy has unfolded vast opportunities for growth in the from of technology transfer, flow of funds etc. The critics of the new economic system argues that it lead to the dominance of multinationals and large business houses much to the disadvantage of small and medium enterprises.

However, the outcome of the last decade or so has proved critics wrong.

As a matter of fact, the small and medium enterprises have thrived side by side with multinationals and large industrial houses. It is due the new economic system as well that the India is emerging as a major hub for outsourcing. The propounders of the industrial policy of 1991 have held that the globalization, liberalization and privatization of Indian economy is in fact a struggle for social and economic justice, to end poverty and unemployment and to build a modern, democratic, socialistic and forward-looking India. The new policy promises result oriented provisions and resources for achieving growth with efficiency in the form of foreign investment, foreign technology and much needed capital from varied sources. In fact, Globalization, Privatization and Liberalisation have become the universal policy planks and India tried to just to keep a pace with the changing world scenario. However, new industrial policy at the same time gave birth to a number of apprehensions like, more concentration of economic power and over-dependence on foreigners.

New Industrial Policy of the State: The state's industrial sector which overwhelmingly consists of small scale industries is beset with a number of problems which in fact, have zeroed its performance. The various problems confronting the industrial sector have resulted in large scale industrial sickness, which has vitiated the entire industrial fabric with serious psycho-socio-economic costs. It has lead to an unhealthy notion in the minds of youth that no industrial activity can be taken successfully in the state, particularly in Kashmir division. It is because of this undesirable psycho-social behavior, that the youth of the state are heavily oriented towards government jobs rather than industrial entrepreneurship. Given this fact, the need in the state is to battle-out this unwanted behavior. The role of the government and its sponsored agencies in this regard is great. As a first step, the government and its sponsored agencies have to come up with some bold policy initiative towards outward and forward looking economy, essential features of which are an ambitious entrepreneurial class adaptive to changing market initiatives, modern managerial cadre, latest technological back-up, improved infrastructural index and efficient and sufficient support system. The policy initiative should focus more on promotion than regulation: improving competitiveness than protection; be popular than political; be specific than general in nature. Moreover, the policy should be long-term in perspective, identifying the core competencies of the state and based on these facts evolve right strategies to promote thrust areas.

Ever since the new government took over the reigns of the state administration, it has shown its resolve to revive the industrial economy which took heavy beating since 1989.After a long wait and much publicity, the government came-up with the industrial policy 2004 to set a direction and pace of industrialization in the state. Earlier governments have also announced policy initiatives at various stages, but such policy initiatives have failed to make much difference due to host of factors, the prominent factor being the political disturbances. The industrial policy 2004 consists of broad objectives, strategies and the package of incentives to achieve the goal of rapid and meaningful industrialization.

Approach and Strategy of New Policy: The strategy for achieving the objectives and the main elements of the industrial policy, 2004 are: (Full text of the new policy document is given in Annexure I).

- Providing improved infrastructure and support services, with emphasis on regular and uninterrupted power supply.
- Provide attractive incentives of the government of India and of the state.
- Introduce Single Window Clearance system for power, pollution control, land allotment and registration of industrial units.
- To have closer interaction with financial institutions and commercial banks to ensure regular and adequate flow of credit to the industrial sector.
- Rehabilitation of potentially viable sick industrial units.

- Improving competitiveness of existing industrial units by facilitating modernization aimed at enhancing productivity, energy efficiency and better management of environment.
- Enabling manufacturers of quality consistent products to augment their sales within and outside the state by brand promotion.
- Reorienting Industries and Commerce Department.
- Export promotion measures to augment export of products outside the country.
- Permanent Grievance Redressal System to remove bottlenecks in import and export of products to and from the state.
- Environment protection to conform to state, national and global regulations.
- Emphasize on entrepreneurship development in the state to provide opportunities to educated unemployed.
- Encourage research and development.
- Focusing on thrust areas with natural advantages in the state and facilitating large investments in prestigious projects.

Fiscal Incentives: The new policy offers the following fiscal incentives to new industrial units and for substantial expansion of existing units:

- New industrial units and existing industrial units on their substantial expansion are entitled to 100 percent excise duty exemption for a period of 10 years from the date of commencement of commercial production.
- All new industries in the notified locations would be eligible for capital investment subsidy @ 15 per cent of their investment in plant and machinery subject to a ceiling of Rs. 30 lakh. The existing units will be entitled to this subsidy on substantial expansion, as defined.
- An interest subsidy of 3 per cent on the working capital loan would be provided to all new industrial units in notified locations for a period of 10 years after commencement of commercial production. This benefit is also extended to existing units in notified locations on expansion projects.

- The insurance premium to the extent of hundred percent on capital investment for a period of 10 years would be extended by the Central Government to all new units and to existing units on substantial expansion.
- The existing and new units are exempt from the payment of general sales tax and central sales tax.
- Subsidy to promote brands within and outside the state is offered for a period of three years at the rate of:
  - ✓ 50 per cent of expenses incurred in the first year subject to a limit of Rs. 20 lakh
  - ✓ 30 per cent of expenses incurred in the first year subject to a limit of Rs. 15 lakh
  - ✓ 10 per cent of expenses incurred in the first year subject to a limit of Rs. 10 lakh.
- 100 per cent subsidy on the expenditure incurred on the preparation of project feasibility reports subject to a limit of Rs. 2 lakh.
- 100 per cent subsidy on new DG Sets from 10 KV to 1000 KV capacity purchased from reputed companies to a maximum limit of Rs. 25 lakh.
- Up to 15 per cent price preference is made available on the landed cost of the product to the local SSI units in all government purchases.

Other Incentives: Exemption from the payment of stamp duty, additional toll tax on the raw-materials fuel and consumables

- 100 per cent subsidy on the installation of testing equipment subject to a maximum amount of Rs. 25 lakh.
- 50 per cent subsidy on air freight on finished goods and raw materials to any destination subject to a maximum amount of Rs. 5 lakh.
- 30 per cent subsidy on the purchase of pollution control equipment subject to a maximum amount of Rs. 20 lakh. This will be in addition to the entitlement of Central investment subsidy.

- 5 per cent interest subsidy on term loans to technocrats, 50 per cent on research and development and 50 per cent subsidy on the cost of training of employees is also available

Industrial policy 2004 is somewhat different from the earlier policy initiatives. It is for the first time, there is a mention of transparency in supporting agencies and re-orientation of Industries and Commerce Department. In fact there is a great urgency to restructure and rewrite the promotional methodologies of all the agencies involved in the promotion of industries in the state. Unless this is done, it is very much unlikely that the industrial policy 2004 will make any worthwhile change in the industrial landscape of the state. There is no denying the fact that all the promotional agencies suffer from wide spread red-tape and corruption which had the most dampening effect on the process of industrialization. The other pleasing factor of the new policy is that among other things it emphasizes on improving the competitiveness of existing units so as to enable them to withstand the shivers of competitive onslaughts caused due to globalization and liberalization of the national economy. To improve competitiveness, the new policy offers incentives for modernization and for brand positioning. The most important silver lining in the cloud is that the new policy has identified thrust areas for development on priority basis. On the basis of existing resources whose potential has been assessed so far, the areas classified as thrust areas in the new policy hold good prospects for establishment and further development. However, the list is not complete and it misses some other potential areas.

The new policy initiative offers number of incentives. Such incentives if delivered in time and with ease to the genuine entrepreneurs will go a long way in improving the management of logistics of the local units. The strategies of establishing a single window clearance system, setting-up of permanent grievance redressal system, encouraging research are some of the important steps of the new policy. Such strategies if implemented properly would go a long way in pushing the pace of industrialization in the state.

The important missing link in the new policy is that it has failed to attend to the problem of the rehabilitation of sick industrial units. It has offered a casual and half hearted approach to this serious socio-economic problem. The new policy offers nothing concrete. The new policy mentions that government will separately announce a debt relief package. Unfortunately policy makers view rehabilitation of sick industrial units in term of finance only but it has other aspects which need an equal attention. Preparation of detailed blue print of the reconstruction programme is much called for; detailing out policy decisions of *"What to Nurse and What to give a Mercy Killing"? What Revival Package is needed? And Whose Responsibility is it"?*

The other important missing link in the new policy is that it has failed to offer suitable strategies to address the problems of red-tapism, corruption and procedural wrangles rampant in different promotional agencies. The various organizations looking after industrial development in the state suffer from various form of administrative ill health which had the most dampening effect on the industrial development in the state (Bhat, 1999). Steps to improve the role performance of these organizations should be at the top of the agenda aiming at the acceleration of industrial growth in the state.

Competitive Environment

Globalization, Privatization and Liberalisation have become universal slogans, sweeping large number of economies including India which in turn is resulting in rapid technological innovations, changing government policy initiatives, fluctuating economic trends as well as changes in organizational patterns, such as, size, geographical dispersion of industries and intense competition. Transformation of Indian economy from planned to market economy has turned industrial economy into a highly competitive one with a catalytic impact by multi-nationals and foreign companies. In its resolve to eliminate unfair competition and to dilute monopoly power, the government of India enacted MRTP Act in 1970, which continues to regulate fair competition in the country. Competition which often acts as a 'change agent' is certainly going to change the outlook and approach of entrepreneurs, determine the scope and extent of industrialization in any given area and alter the approach to the area of marketing. Fair competition in an economy is a healthy sign. It reduces wastes, facilitates efficiencies and expands industrial horizons through innovations of new trade, products, services etc.

Indian industrial economy is not highly competitive yet, however, the competition with varied competitors is growing at a significant rate. The effects of growing competition in the Indian economy can be felt everywhere. The markets in the state are open to all products manufactured within and outside the country. There is no protection against outside competition to the goods manufactured by the local industries. However, certain incentives are available to the firms located in the state which are sufficient enough to compensate for not being located at an ideal place. The growing competition both within and outside the state is further going to limit the already smallness of markets available to the local industries. Despite the growing competition, the industries using net raw materials even though not available in the state can be successfully run in the state. However, the size such units have to be small as their market will be confined to the four walls of the state only.

However, the industries where state enjoys comparative advantage in natural resource endowments and in historical legacies, like, silk, leather, wood, some agro and mineral based industries would enjoy cost competitiveness and thus have much to offer to the industrial economy of the state. Further, there are number of schemes in operation in the state aimed at improving the competitiveness of the local industries. There is nothing as such that could hamper the competitiveness of the local firms. To be highly competitive, the local entrepreneurs are required to design optimum plant capacities, install modern technologies, evolve efficient management practices, a strong commitment to quality and cost reduction, change in outlook and approach to marketing, resort to continual innovations and keep pace with the changing world.

Above all, the support of the government is essential on account of unique geo-physical conditioning of the state. Small scale industries are presumed to fit in to the realm of state's industrial economy, which are being offered secure berth and also helped to grow out of its infancy, through protection from large scale industries, and by considerable latitude in respect of taxes etc. At present more than 800 products are reserved for exclusive production by small scale industrial units thus making it a protected sector. In addition to the number of organizations that have been created both by the central and state governments to help the small scale sector to improve competitiveness, various incentives are provided to the small scale industries to help them to improve their competitiveness significantly. In spite of a clearly demarcated field of production between small and large scale sector and official watchdog agencies, "there has been an inter-penetration by large scale industrial houses and multinationals in the small scale sector".

Human Resources

Automisation of industrial world has not been able to replace human completely. In today's hi-tech world, labour particularly skilled still continues to occupy a central place in the process of industrialization. In fact, any meaningful industrialization is not possible in the absence of competent technical and managerial skills. It has been seen that modern technologies produce miracles only when used properly which in turn demands positive mind and well trained hands. In view of the precious role the human plays in achieving business objectives, modern industrial entities continuously emphasis on the development of human resources. A region with sufficient technical skills of varied nature enjoys a definite advantage for industrialization.

However, today labour does not have that much influence on industrial location as it used to have in the past. Now-a-days people go to far away places for better jobs, but still the areas endowed with sufficient technical and other skills at less cost certainly would enjoy some leverage for industrialization. Foreign investors are interested to invest in India more due to availability of cheap and competent human resources. Sufficient labour supply alone is not important, but the labour with commitment, dexterity, steadiness, ingenuity, self discipline, etc makes a difference.

The state of Jammu and Kashmir is not deficient in industrially important man power. The growth rate in population during 1991-2001 was 29 per cent as against 24.00 per cent at the all India level. However, under unique Indian conditions, increase in labour supply is not desired as there are already surplus workable hands.

As a result, any further increase in labour supply will only aggravate the problem of unemployment. Further a mere increase in labour supply is not important but the more important thing is to have competent, skilled and committed people with strong determination. In the field of education, Jammu and Kashmir has made some note worthy performance. The literacy rate which was 11 per cent in 1961 had gone to 54.46 per cent in 2001 (Tables 1.5 and 1.6). The government is making all out efforts to achieve significant growth in literacy and in the 10th five year plan, a sum of Rs. 35.57 crore has been allocated to the education which accounts for 8.89 percent of the total plan outlay (Digest of Statistics, 2002-03).

Table 1.5: Growth in Literacy Rate in J&K State, 1981–2001

Census	Literacy rate (%age)	Change in growth
1981	26.67	
2001	54.46	27.79

Source: Digest of Statistics, Planning & Development Department, Govt. of Jammu & Kashmir, 2002-03

Table 1.6: Literacy Rate in Different States (Census 2001)

State	Literacy rate (%)	Rank
Andhra Pradesh	61.11	23
Arunachal Pradesh	54.74	26
Assam	64.28	19
Bihar	47.53	29
Chattisgarh	65.18	18
Delhi	81.82	4
Goa	82.32	3
Gujarat	69.97	10
Haryana	68.59	15
Himachal Pradesh	77.13	6
Jaharkhand	54.13	28
Jammu & Kashmir	54.46	27
Karnataka	67.04	17
Kerela	90.92	1
Madhya Pradesh	64.11	20
Maharashtra	77.27	5
Manipur	68.87	14
Meghalaya	63.31	22
Mizoram	88.49	2
Nagaland	67.11	16
Orissa	63.61	21
Punjab	69.95	11
Rajasthan	61.03	24
Sikkim	69.68	12
Tamil Nadu	73.47	8
Tripura	73.66	7
Uttranchal	72.28	9
Utter Pradesh	57.36	25
West Bengal	69.22	13
All India	**65.38**	

Source: *Digest of Statistics*, Planning & Development Department, Govt. of Jammu & Kashmir, 2002-03

Today in the state, there is no deficiency of accountants, administrators, professional managers, office clerks, marketers and engineers, however, still there remains some deficiency of machine operators which are important for smooth functioning of modern manufacturing industries.

Much has not been done in the development of technical skills required by the modern industries. At present, number of institutions, like, Regional Engineering College, Polytechnic Colleges and Industrial Training Institutes are actively engaged in imparting technical training. Further the private polytechnics which are mushrooming in the state have also joined in the pursuit of imparting technical training. However these institutes largely produce technocrats in traditional fields like Civil, Electric, Mechanical, Electronics etc. Most of them seek jobs in government departments only. The Industrial Training Institutes which were established with the aim to develop technical manpower especially for the local industries are doing their bit in this regard. Small Industries Services Institutes (SISI) which is conducting training courses in Turners and Fitters course, Machine shop practices, Management etc is proving of some help to the industries in the state but could not make state self-sufficient in these and other trades and skills. The need in the state is to identify the technical skills needed by the industries and involve different training institutes to train in the same skills. The deficiency of some technical skills in the state in no way is coming in the way of industrialization. The Industrial units are facing no difficulty in hiring the manpower from other states (Table 1.7).

However, to meet the growing demand for technical skills, there is an immense need to formulate a comprehensive long term industrial policy in the state, identifying thrust areas and other activities that will be promoted and developed and this will enable to match the training endeavors of different training institutes with the requirements of these industries. Further, the private polytechnics among other trades should impart training in modern industries oriented trades like fabricating, designing, information technology, electronics etc.

Table 1.7: Number of Polytechnics and ITIs in J&K State

Year	Number of polytechnics	Number of ITIs
1970-71	2	7
1980-81	5	18
1990-91	7	35
1994-95	11	37

Source: *Report of the Godbole Committee on Economic Reforms for Jammu and Kashmir, 1998.*

Craftsmanship Skills

The state of Jammu and Kashmir is famous throughout the world as much for its craftsmanship skills as for its physical charms and natural beauty. "It was during the reign of Sultan Zain-ul-Abidin, popularly known as Budshah or the great king who ruled Kashmir from 1420-1470 AD that handicrafts were introduced in Kashmir"(Sadhu & Singh, 1984).The king Zain-ul-Abidin hired skilled craftsmen from Central Asia to train local inhabitants in a number of handicraft arts which were till then altogether unknown to the people of the state (Bamzai, 1979). Since then historical legacies continued and got encouragement and patronage from different rulers, princess, visitors to the valley thus skills remained passing on generation to generation. Kashmir artisans are still famous throughout the world for their artistic work. Carpets, Shawls, Paper Machie, wood carving, Embroidery and Namdahs have achieved both national and international acclimation and continues to be the attraction of millions of tourists visiting the state. In the state, it is the Kashmir Valley which is home for world famous craftsmanship skills. Handicrafts in Kashmir valley form an important part of the economic life of the people. It contributes significantly to the state's exchequer, and provides employment to nearly 3.454 lakh people as on 2002-

03. The production of handicraft goods has gone-up from Rs. 57.82 crore in 1980-81 to Rs. 775.00 crore in 2002-03 and direct exports went-up from Rs. 39.92 crore to Rs. 549.20 crore during the same period (Table 1.8).

Knowing that tremendous potential lies in handicraft industry, the state has been attaching great significance to the promotion and development of this age old industry. Different promotional agencies were created to help the development of this industry to its fullest potential. However, despite of having definite comparative advantage in these historical legacies and a favourable market for different handicraft products, the development of handicrafts in the state has not been commensurate with its potential. In fact this age old industry of the state, which was enjoying prestige and unique place in the market, is loosing its grip. The industry is suffering from many problems which are eating the vitals of this crucial industry of the state. This industry is lacking proper organization and at the same time Merchants/producers do not practice businesses on modern lines and are working on high margins. Study team for Industrial Potential Survey (1972), observed that the statism in the industry has not only retarded the growth of this sector, but worse it has begun to discourage the sons of the artisans from taking-up their traditional vocation (Industrial Potential Survey, 1972).

There are many unscrupulous merchants cheating customers on many counts which have really eroded the credibility of Kashmir handicrafts in the market. In fact, this prestigious industry is marred with number of inefficiencies and there is an immense need to put it on the track of growth and prosperity. If a corrective action is not taken at an earliest, there is every probability of loosing this potential earner. The industry still has a lot to offer to the states industrial economy. Reports of the delegations sent to different foreign countries by the state government and surveys conducted by the All India Handicrafts Board revealed that there exists a tremendous demand for Kashmiri fine woolen carpets, wood carving, Paper Machie, Namdahs, Embroidery, Chain-stich etc.(Bhat, 1997). The industry

Table 1.8: Employment and Direct Exports of Handicrafts in the State of J&K

(Employment, lakh Nos; Exports, Rs. crore)

Year	Employment	Absolute growth	%age growth	Exports	Absolute growth	%age growth
1980-81	1.44	-	-	39.92	-	-
1985-86	1.85	0.41	28.47	40.00	0.08	0.20
1990-91	2.25	0.40	21.62	34.60	-5.40	-13.50
1995-96	2.78	0.53	23.55	293.5	258.90	748.26
1996-97	2.90	0.12	4.32	88.14	-205.36	-69.96
1997-98	3.01*	0.11	3.79	197.26*	109.12	12.38
1998-99	3.10	0.09	2.99	247.00	39.74	25.21
1999-00	3.20	0.10	3.23	556.99	309.99	125.50
2000-01	3.29	0.09	2.81	439.90	-117.09	-21.02
2001-02	3.87	0.58	17.63	504.25	64.35	14.62
2002-03	3.454	-0.416	-10.74	549.20	45.00	8.92
Cumulative growth			**4.6**			**17.4**

*Estimated Figure

Source: *Digest of Statistics*, Planning & Development Department, Govt. of Jammu & Kashmir, 2002-03.

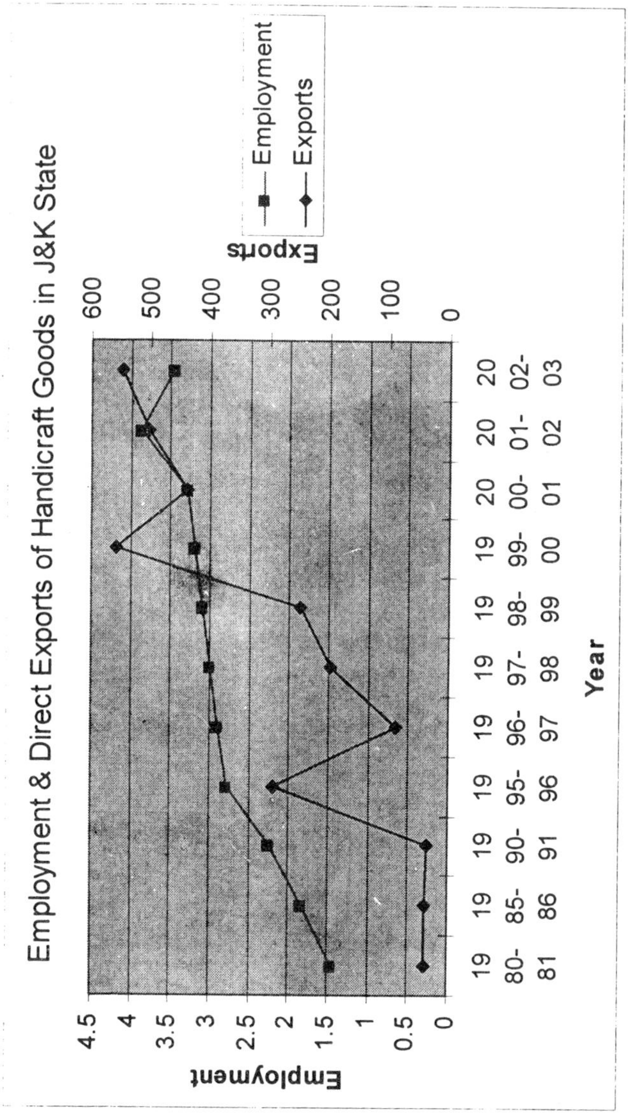
Employment & Direct Exports of Handicraft Goods in J&K State
Employment
Exports
Year
4.5
4
3.5
3
2.5
2
1.5
1
0.5
0
600
500
400
300
200
100
0
1980-81
1985-86
1990-91
1995-96
1996-97
1997-98
1998-99
1999-00
2000-01
2001-02
2002-03

can pay full dividends only if the industry is organized on modern lines, artisans are guided in product designing, raw-materials and other resources are made readily available, the products are subjected to strict quality controls, malpractices in the marketing are eradicated and due attention is paid on the promotion of this industry. Above all, the patronage and encouragement of artisans through adequate returns and cheap and adequate credit are must.

Enterpreneurial Competence

Entrepreneurs who are the frontline actors in the process of economic development belong to a different social breed with a conflux of desire, goal, motivation, vision, strong determination, caliber, and venturesomeness. Theoretically, an entrepreneur is one who carries out new combinations, which are influenced by personal psyche and certain environmental forces. It has been revealed that the formal education is the facilitator and not the ultimate decider. Experiments conducted all over India as also in the Asia Pacific Region brought out that the right personality, caliber, motivation, willingness to learn and venturesomeness are more important for entrepreneurial success than mere formal educational attainments" (Singh, 1989).

The globalization of Indian economy has transformed the Indian business scene into highly competitive which preaches the principles of 'Survival of the fittest'. Under the changed business scenario, entrepreneurs lacking essential entrepreneurial traits will have to make a way for others. The State of Jammu and Kashmir is not fortunate enough with regard to right type of entrepreneurial class. The youth of the state in particular of Kashmir province lack spirit for Industrial entrepreneurship and are oriented more towards government jobs, this is because that no effort has been made to create an inducing industrial culture in the state. It has been seen that majority of people who fail to seek jobs in other fields assume industrial entrepreneurship. However over the past several years, there has been some positive change particularly among the youth. Youth of the state with strong determination, caliber, motivation, venturesomeness have started developing interest in industrial entrepreneurship but unfortunately these are made to entangle in the maze of complexities of red-tapism, favoritism and nepotism which the socio-political and administrative system has set-up for them. Lack of right guidance, patronage and encouragement to the prospective entrepreneurs has severely retarded the growth and development of entrepreneurship in the state. In fact, entrepreneurship development has received very little attention of the policy-makers in the state.

The State of Jammu and Kashmir due to certain inherent features is mainly suitable for small scale industries, where manager-ownership relationship exists. On account of this fact, the small entrepreneurs are required to continuously upgrade their information, knowledge and skills. Small Industries Services Institute (SISI) is conducting management appreciation courses in the state, however, these courses are marred with number of serious deficiencies.

There is unawareness among the entrepreneurs of the need of financial discipline, maintenance of books of accounts. They have failed to appreciate the utility of modern business practices and overlooked the role of organized selling agencies. To develop entrepreneurs befitting the changed industrial scenario, there is a vital role for the recently established Entrepreneurship Development Institute in promoting sustainable industrial culture by propounding industrial planning methodologies, organizing research to identify the problems and provide plausible solutions thereof; and conducting entrepreneurship awareness and development programmes on continuous basis. The institute should also provide back-up support to the entrepreneurs to the extent possible. Encouragement and patronage of different agencies is must to sustain and supplement the entrepreneurship development efforts of the institute.

Capital: "Capital is wealth which yields an income or aids in production of an income or it intends to do so. (Kuchal, 1989). Deficiency of capital seriously affects the optimum utilization of other resources. An entrepreneur with adequate capital would be able to achieve better integration of different economic resources for greater profitability. Under the changed business situations it would not be possible to think of an economically viable enterprise in the absence of adequate capital. Industries require two types of capital, viz. Equity Capital and borrowed capital to finance long term and short term assets. Equity capital which enables in obtaining external finances is to be provided by the promoter himself. The International Planning team was of the opinion that "the borrowed capital should not exceed 50 percent of the total capital requirements of the enterprise".. Normally an entrepreneur should invest itself an amount which will enable him to start the industry at some scale and then apply for credit. (Butt, 2000).

The deficiency of capital has been reported as one of the factors that has hindered industrial development in the state. Many of the units in the small scale sector are reported to have suffered from lack of capital. The new industrial policy recognizes that the procedure presently followed in providing financial assistance to industrial units in the state have not withstood the test of time. The new policy acknowledges that there have been glaring instance of delay and under financing of projects resulting in cost and time overrun. Accordingly, the new policy initiative emphasized to strengthen the state owned Financial Institutes. In this regard, the government has decided to:

- Actively monitor credit flow through State Level Bankers Committee (SLBC) and State Level Inter Institutional Committee (SLIIC).
- Orient and help the state owned Developmental Financial Institutes in availing refinance from national level institutes
- Set-up Division and District level Coordinate Committees to monitor expeditious settlement of loan cases.

There is no dearth of capital in the state. In fact, there is a flight of capital from the state and there is a fervent need to reverse this trend which among other things calls for promoting sustainable industrialization. The state has a network of bank branches and two states owned Developmental Financial Institutes namely, J&K State Financial Corporation and State Industrial

Development Corporation. The Jammu and Kashmir State Financial Corporation which was set-up in the year 1960 is the premier industrial financial institution in the state. Till 2002-03, it has sanctioned loans aggregating Rs. 423.15 crore, and disbursed an amount of Rs. 355.88 crore since its inception. As on 31st March 2002-03, the loans outstanding are to the tune of Rs. 688.01 crore including interest liability, account for 98 percent of the total disbursements (Table 1.9). The Corporation is suffering from poor recoveries which in turn have reduced its loaning capacity. The corporation is accused of taking lot of time in sanctioning and disbursing of loans thereby causing the problem of under-financing. To ensure smooth industrialization in the state, there is an immediate need to cure this premier finance corporation so that the industries will in no way suffer from the lack of timely and sufficient finances.

Table 1.9: Sector-wise Loans Outstanding Advanced by J & K State Financial Corporation (Rs. lakh)

Sector	2000-01	2001-02	2002-03
Industries	34152.44 (64.22)	40,092.66 (66.26)	49,786.82 (72.36)
Tourism	5557.13 (10.45)	5786.86 (9.56)	5571.03 (8.10)
Transport	13,469.84 (25.33)	14,631.45 (24.18)	13,443.36 (19.54)
Total	**53,179.41** **(100.00)**	**60,501.97** **(100.00)**	**68,801.21** **(100.00)**

Note: Figures in Parenthesis Indicate Percentage to the Total.
Source: *Digest of Statistics*, Planning & Development Department, Govt. of Jammu & Kashmir, 2002-03.

The requirements for working capital of the industrial units in the state are met by commercial banks. There are as many as 14 banks operating in the state with branches covering whole of the state. In terms of population per bank, the state ranks 19th among 29 states of the country (Table 1.10).

Table 1.10: Population Per Bank in Different States in the Country as on 2001-02 (in 000s)

State	Population per Bank	Rank
Andhra Pradesh	14.61	15
Arunachal Pradesh	15.89	13
Assam	21.62	4
Bihar	23.25	3
Chattisgarh	20.09	6
Delhi	9.48	26
Goa	4.12	29
Gujarat	13.26	17
Haryana	13.61	16
Himachal Pradesh	7.74	28
Jaharkhand	18.46	7
Jammu & Kashmir	12.22	20
Karnataka	11.04	23
Kerela	9.06	27
Madhya Pradesh	17.46	10
Maharashtra	15.34	14
Manipur	31.01	1
Meghalaya	12.88	19
Mizoram	11.42	22
Nagaland	28.41	2
Orissa	16.49	12
Punjab	9.51	25
Rajasthan	16.96	11
Sikkim	11.50	21
Tamil Nadu	13.07	18

Contd...

Tripura	17.73	9
Uttranchal	10.08	24
Utter Pradesh	20.32	5
West Bengal	18.11	8
All India	**15.47**	

Source: *Digest of Statistics*, Planning & Development Department, Govt. of Jammu & Kashmir, 2002-03.

The unfavourable position with regard to the population per bank is to a great extent being attributed to the militancy which has affected most of parts of the state. As a result of disturbed conditions in the state, most of the banks have closed many of their branches in the valley. Although the per capita deposit of Rs. 165.9 is highest in the country yet, the credit-deposit ratio of 12.9 and per capita credit of Rs. 69.2 is lower in the country (Godbole Committee, 1997). This indicates that either the banks are strict in granting credit or there are very few asking for credit. Banks in the state are being accused of creating working capital problems by the entrepreneurs, so there, is a need to unfold the truth in this regard. Banks which are profit-making organizations consider lending to small scale units highly risky due to lack of information to judge about the credit worthiness of the borrower and lack of suitable security.

To ensure the smooth flow of credit to the industries, there is a need to develop a mechanism which will allow more safety to the banks and simultaneously adequate credit to the genuine entrepreneurs at ease. Banks are being suggested to create a data bank and credit inquiry agency on the pattern of Japan for speedy and sound decisions. To mitigate the financial problems in particular of working capital of industrial units, there is a proposal to set-up Jammu and Kashmir Developmental Financial Corporation by the central government with one time provision of Rs.50 Crore on the lines of North-East Development Financial Corporation. This Corporation shall provide term loan, working capital and other infrastructural support. It would also be designated as the Nodal agency for routing the subsidies and incentives under various schemes. It will go a long way in promoting industrial development if managed on sound lines.

Infrastructural Facilities

Adequate infrastructural facilities are necessary to exist to fully capitalize on natural resource with which an economy is endowed. If infrastructural facilities are in a desired shape, the economy progresses, but puts breaks in the wheels of an economy, if these are in bad shape. Infrastructural capital creates a third wall of defense around the industry and is more important to allow the smooth flow of production processes. It is the infrastructural handicaps which are forcing under-developed countries to keep their economic activities to a very minimal size. Industrial infrastructure is defined as the social overhead-capital that embodies in such forms that help in the smooth conduct of productive activities. The industrially important infrastructural facilities include; power, fuel, transport, communications and industrial accommodation. Some of these are more important like power, fuel and transport. The state of Jammu and Kashmir in general and Kashmir and Ladakh divisions in particular suffer from poor industrial infrastructure particularly electric power and railway transport.

Power and Fuel: Modern industries which are characterized by mechanization and automation require adequate supply of quality power and fuel to put the wheels of production in motion. The State of Jammu and Kashmir which for the last two decades or so is striving to industrialize its economy still suffers from the deficiency of electric power. Shortage of power in the state is being considered as one of the serious impediments to any meaningful industrial activity. The installed capacity of various power stations in the state sector is 537.76 mega-watts. It also includes the installed capacity of power houses that are not in operation and the total capacity of these power houses is 240.81 MWs, thus leaving the operational capacity to 296.95 MWs only which is meager given the total power required in the state. It can be seen from Table 1.11 that the installed capacity of power in the state has grown 5.6 per cent only from 1980-81 to 2002-03 while as, in most of the other states in the country has witnessed a big leap forward in power generation. Since 1999, there has been no addition to the installed capacity of power in the state whereas during the same period the demand for electric power has grown considerably.

Table 1.11: Installed Capacity of Power in the State of J & K

(Capacity Mws)

Year	Installed capacity	Absolute growth	%age growth
1980-81	208.56	-	-
1985-86	208.35	-0.21	0.1006
1990-91	285.62	77.27	37.08
1995-96	391.49	115.87	40.57
1996-97	396.63	5.14	1.31
1997-98	401.22**	4.59	1.15
1998-99	405.48*	4.26	1.06
1999-00	537.76*	132.28	32.62
2000-01	537.76*	0	0
2001-02	537.76*	0	0
2002-03	537.76*	0	0
Cumulative growth			5.6

P: provisional.

*Includes installed capacity of power houses not in operation. The total capacity of these power houses is 240.81 Mws.

** Estimated Installed Capacity.

Source: *Digest of Statistics*, Planning & Development Department, Govt. of Jammu & Kashmir, 2002-03.

The electricity generated from operational power houses varies between 289-183 mega-watts, while as the total demand for power is estimated at more than 1200 mega-watts, thus leaving big gap between the power produced in the state sector and the power required in the state. As much as 75 percent of the power is

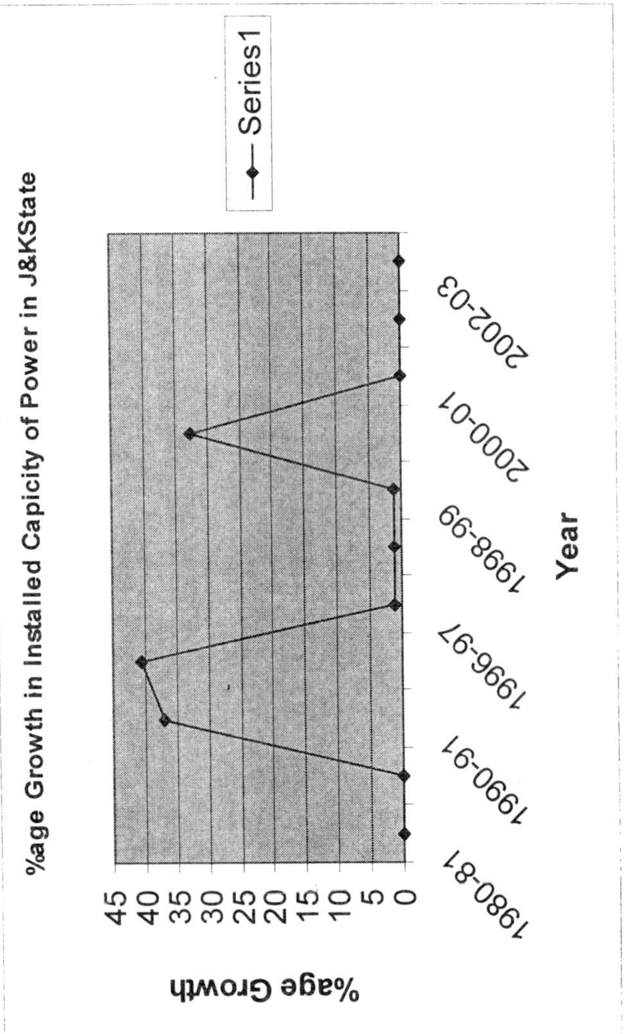
%age Growth in Installed Capicity of Power in J&KState
%age Growth
45
40
35
30
25
20
15
10
5
0
1980-81
1990-91
1996-97
1998-99
2000-01
2002-03
Year
Series1

met by the purchases from the central sector. It is unfortunate that state has to buy high cost thermal power from the central sector when cheap power could have been made available in the state in adequate quantities if only the hydel potential had been harnessed in time (Godbole, 1997). The generation of electricity is not only quite insufficient in the valley but very erratic and the industries are frequently disturbed by sudden breakdown in power and low voltage. During winter which lasts for more than 6 months, in a week out of 180 hours there remains electricity approximately for 90 hours only. In summer the power supply remains almost regular but the industries suffer from low voltage and fluctuations in voltage.

It is amazing to see that despite of having immense potential for the development of Hydro-power generation, the state is deficient in electric power. The state is also well endowed with lignite deposits found at Baniyar not suitable for industries but can be utilized for thermal power generation that also remains un-utilized. In 60's there was a plan to commission Lignite based Thermal Power project at Handwara, but so far could not come-up for unknown reasons. A team of experts from Germany on the invitation of State government studied the prospects of Hydro-Power generation and suggested that instead of installing big projects, the better would be to commission mini-hydro electric power projects which are best suited to the state and are also cost-affective. It seems that the state has miserably failed to make best use of this natural economic resource partly due to political instability and partly due to policy failure on the part of the government.

It is clear that the Industries in the state have to live with insufficient power supply, low voltage etc. for some more time. Much of the problem of electric power in the state is also due to the fact that the National Thermal Power Corporation (NHPC) has failed miserably in harnessing the huge potential that the state enjoys in hydel power. So far it could commission only two projects in the central sector and has failed to execute Dulhasti (390MW), Baghlihar (450MW), Kishenganga (330mw) and

Savalkote (600mw) projects. The state government has already taken back Baghlihar project and is intending to take back other projects as well. The state government is also contemplating to undertake a number of mini hydel projects. If the proposed projects are undertaken then not only the state will be able to meet the demand for electric power from its own generation but will be able to export as well. But given the amount of investment that will be needed and the poor state of financial health of the state, it would be very much unlikely that the state will be able to undertake all these projects at its own.

Transport and Communications: Transportation creates time and place utility and extends the horizons of trade, commerce and industry. Industrialization calls for the presence of all means of transport, however, places more emphasis on rail transport. On account of unique geo-physical conditioning, the state in general and Kashmir and Ladakh divisions in particular are unfavorably placed so far as the different means of transportation are concerned. Kashmir and Ladakh provinces of the state still remains to be connected with the rest of the country by the rail link, however Jammu division is linked by rail, air and road transport with the rest of the country, thus enjoying a comparative advantage in the race for industrialization over Kashmir province. Means of water transport are limited because Jehlum and Chinab are navigable only over small length. The work on the rail link extension up to Udhampur is in-progress, however, such an extension is not going to make any difference to the industries located in Kashmir valley unless it is taken up to Qazigund. The deficiency of rail transport which is being felt in the valley can be improved upon only when the rail head is extended right up to Srinagar. Air transport is not a problem in the valley, but it cannot facilitate the transportation of industrial products as being costly.

Lack of railway transport and very limited scope for water transport, leaves the state in particular Kashmir province with roads as the only means of transport. Jammu province where different districts remain without any rail connection also depends largely on road transport. The Kashmir valley is connected to

Jammu rail head by National Highway "1A" which passes through Karakorum mountainous range. The mountainous terrain and extreme climatic conditions during winter makes transportation difficult. So far as the internal roads are concerned, which are not that important for industries are nearly sufficient. There is a network of roads some in good condition and some in bad condition connecting different parts of the state with one another and other parts of the country. As on 2002-03, the total road length surfaced and unsurfaced is 12,109 kms and 2,749 kms in 2002-03 respectively in the state, which gives an average of 341.34 kms of all types of roads per 1000 sq kms as against the all India average of 779 kms (Tables 1.12 and 1.13). The outlay of Rs. 45.42 crore for the development of roads in the state has been provided in the 10th five-year plan which is expected to improve the condition and length of roads.

Table 1.12: Road Length Per 1,000 Square kms in the State of J&K (Road length in kms)

Year ending	Total surfaced	Total unsurfaced	Total surfaced and unsurfaced	Road length per 1,000 Sq. kms
1980-81	5,624	2,582	8,206	101.94
1985-86	7,808	2,458	10,266	133.26
1990-91	9,379	2,459	11,838	199.76
1995-96	10,577	2,440	13,017	222.39
1996-97	10,683	2,218	12,901	231.25
1997-98	NA	NA	NA	NA
1998-99	11,211	2,210	13,421	260.37
1999-00	11,260	2,279	13,539	277.54
2000-01	11,335	2,325	13,660	298.73
2001-02	11,843	2,351	14,194	312.99
2002-03	12,109	2,749	14,858	341.34

Source: *Digest of Statistics*, Planning & Development Department, Govt. of Jammu & Kashmir, 2002-03.

Table 1.13: Average Road Length Per 1,000 Sq. Kms of Area in Different States of the Country as on 1997

State	Road Length	Rank
Andhra Pradesh	647	14
Arunachal Pradesh	168	26
Assam	872	10
Bihar	508	17
Chattisgarh	NE	-
Delhi	876	9
Goa	2313	2
Gujarat	464	19
Haryana	637	15
Himachal Pradesh	542	16
Jaharkhand	NE	-
Jammu & Kashmir	212*	25
Karnataka	751	13
Kerela	3749	1
Madhya Pradesh	451	20
Maharashtra	1176	7
Manipur	490	18
Meghalaya	378	22
Mizoram	230	24
Nagaland	1107	8
Orissa	1687	13
Punjab	1278	6
Rajasthan	379	21
Sikkim	258	23
Tamil Nadu	1588	4

Contd...

Tripura	1405	5
Uttranchal	NE	-
Utter Pradesh	868	11
West Bengal	850	12
All India	**779**	

Source: *Digest of Statistics*, Planning & Development Department, Govt. of Jammu & Kashmir, 2002-03

The absence of railway transport in the state continues to work to the disadvantage of industries particularly those located in the Kashmir province and some districts of Jammu province. To overcome this limitation to the local industries, the state government is providing transport subsidy on import of raw-materials as well as on export of finished goods to the industries located in the state so as to improve upon their competitiveness. Further, the government is seriously planning to take the railway head right up to Srinagar and if the said project comes into shape, it will benefit the industrial economy of the state significantly.

Telephone, posts and telegraphs, etc are the modern means of business communication. Privatization of Indian economy has expanded the field of communication in the country with modern means like, internet, mobile phones etc. Better means of communication enables business men to operate from a distance and in extending the area of operation. Different means of communication, like, telephone, posts and telegraph and courier services are available in the state, but not efficient and sufficient enough. The total strength of telephone exchanges and telegraph and post offices in the state in 2001-02 stand at 35,402 connections and 1947 respectively. (Digest of Statistics, 2002-03). As against all India average of 1 phone per 72 persons, the one phone per 166 persons in the state is far from satisfactory. The industrial units in the state are being provided telephone connections on priority basis. There is also a direct dialing between Srinagar, Jammu Delhi and other parts of country. Grossly the means of communication are available to the satisfaction of the industrialists in the state.

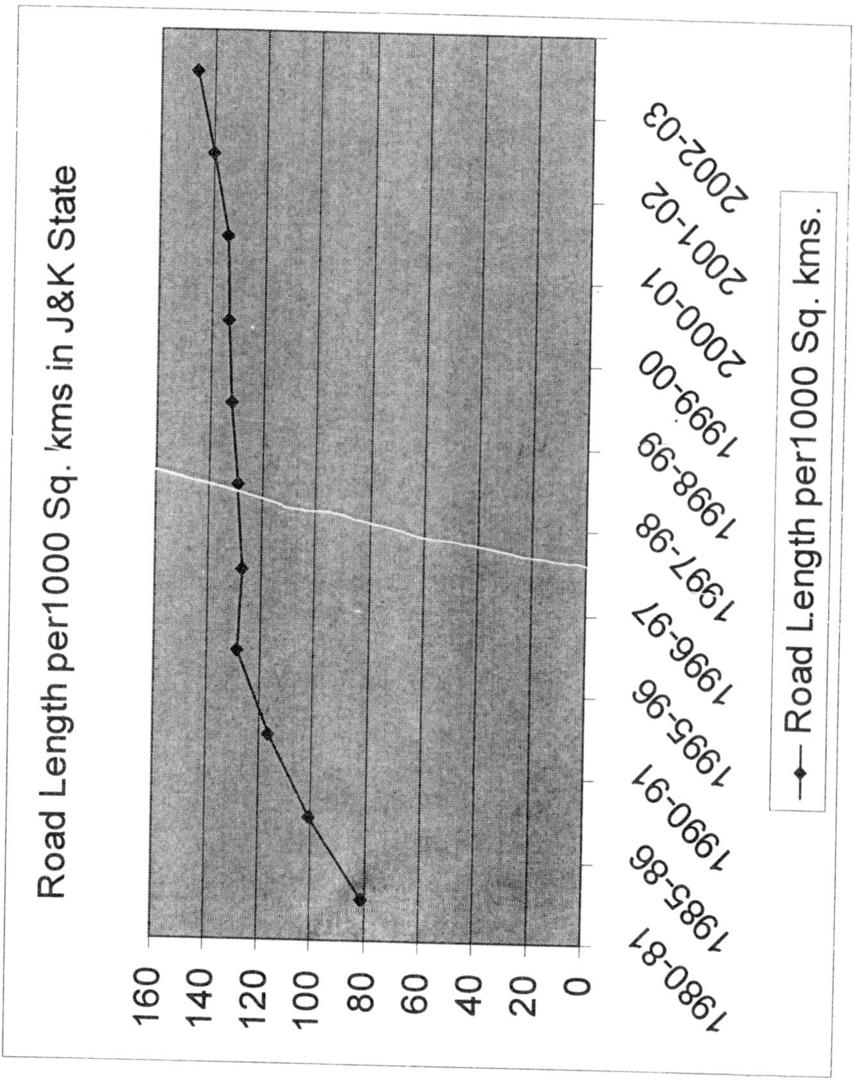
Road Length per1000 Sq. kms in J&K State
160
140
120
100
80
60
40
20
0
1980-81
1985-86
1990-91
1995-96
1996-97
1997-98
1998-99
1999-00
2000-01
2001-02
2002-03
Road Length per1000 Sq. kms.

Industrial Accommodation: The cost of land and the availability of suitable size of industrial plot influence location decision and choice between urban and sub-urban locations. The availability of land for setting up an industry is not a problem in the state. As an extension of the central scheme, the state of Jammu and Kashmir from the second Five Year Plan started establishing industrial estates with the purpose to provide suitable site for establishing industrial units and also to provide different services and facilities at one place like water, gas, steam, compressed air, railway siding, common testing facilities etc. It was also aimed that the estate would in effect become a complex of interdependent and inter-related industries. At present there are 40 industrial estates in the state and the work is in-progress in the development of three more estates in the State. On an average one to two Kanals of land is being provided to entrepreneurs on lease for a period of 90 years with a provision for revision of rent after every 10 years. The rent charged per sq ft is Rs. 5 which in fact is less by all standards. The entrepreneurs enjoys freedom in designing their factory structure and are also given priority in the supply of building materials like cement by the government or semi-government agencies. When the shed is constructed by the entrepreneur himself he is entitled to investment subsidy @ 15 percent and if the construction has been made outside the estate in any backward area or by an Engineering graduate irrespective of place, in addition to capital investment subsidy, he is provided loans at subsidized rates of interest.

Work on Industrial Growth Centres at Lassipora and Samba has been completed in the very recent past and allotment is going on in these estates. Further, work is in progress in the development of two food parks at Jammu and Sopore. Also the Software Technology Park at Jammu with 7500 Sq. feet fully developed area has been thrown open for IT industry. The park is equipped with Digital Microwave Network and broadband connectivity with a gateway capacity of 8 to 20 mbps that could cater to the requirements of around 4000 units in small scale sector. There is a plan to establish Artisans Estate in the valley of

Kashmir so as to provide the healthy and better working conditions to the artisans who presently are working in unhygienic conditions. Such an estate would enable to provide different facilities to the artisans at one place. Before contemplating any new investment in the development of new estates, it would be appropriate for the government to take necessary steps to utilize the closed/ abandoned units. Such a policy would enable the state to put the idle capital assets into productive use and simultaneously save precious capital resources. "It is displeasing to note that most of the estates in the state are lacking different facilities such as proper drainage system, dispensaries, raw-material depots, post offices, street lights, common testing facilities, etc"(Bakal, 1989). The backwardness of industrial estates with regard to different facilities is against the very principle objective of estates programme in the country.

Environmental Change

Change is permanent in nature and those who keep pace with the change, come out as winners. Many elements of an industrial environment are dynamic in nature thus, subject to change. Recent changes in industrial policy in fact have metamorphosed the industrial environment in the country throwing open innumerable opportunities but with unnerving challenges. The new economic landscape emerging fast in the country requires a change in the outlook and approach of local industrialists. On the political front, good news is that the state is braving for a political settlement. India and Pakistan seems to have now realized the futility of sticking to their age old positions regarding dispute over Kashmir and are showing some sort of flexibility. The developments taking place between the two countries and on ground in Kashmir are pointing to the fact that the solution to this vexed problem is imminent. But how much time it takes is difficult to guess. So far the government of India has followed a policy crosinisation which in fact has only aggravated the problem and made it more difficult to solve. The state will continue to suffer due to the lack of political stability till this issue is resolved to the satisfaction of the people of Kashmir.

Summary

The state of Jammu and Kashmir, located on the extreme of northern India is famous for its scenic beauty and landscape all over the world. Agriculture is the main sector of the state's economy. Due to the limited cultivable land and serve agro-climatic conditions, the development of agriculture at large scale is ruled out in the state. Large scale industrialization is the only way out to take the state out from age old stagnation and economic backwardness. However, the peculiar physical conditioning of the state, like extreme location, difficult mountainous terrain, transportation bottlenecks, and extreme climatic conditions which cannot be improved upon except transportation to some extent, limits the scope for industrialization. Where state does not enjoy the comparative advantage in natural resources, industries in such areas can be taken-up somewhat at a small scale to cater the local demand. On the positive side, the state is well endowed with some proven large mineral resources like, agricultural, forest mineral and other resources which provide better prospects for industrial development in the related lines. State is also gifted with scenic beauty, world famous health resorts, fascinating landscape and historical legacies in craftsmanship skills, thus enjoying a distinct and important place in the hotel industry and handicrafts. The state has not been able to develop these industries to their full potential so far.

Number of incentives /concessions and supporting services are available to the industries in the state which are sufficient enough to help the units located in the state to help in the management of logistics. The legal, economic and competitive environmental forces in the state are favourable to conducive industrial environment in the state. But, the greatest weakness to the conducive industrial environment in the state is the inadequacy of role performance of various organizations created to promote industrialization in the state. People looking after industrial development in the state lack commitment, understanding, motivation, accountability and are not conscientious to their duties, helpful, vigilant and complaint with the rules and regulations. All these problems have resulted into rampant corruption, nepotism, favourtism and red-tapism, which are impeding the smooth conduct of an industrial activity. Added to this, the industrially important infrastructural facilities in the state are far from satisfactory particularly in the valley of Kashmir. Electric power is in short supply, railway networking is missing, some technical skills are not available locally and political stability and peace essential for smooth functioning of industries is missing in the state. However, the silver lining in the cloud is that the developments taking place between India and Pakistan are hinting towards the resolution of the Kashmir dispute according to the wishes of the people of the state. Once the political uncertainties looming over the state right from the beginning are removed, the investment climate will improve at its own.

References

Aggarwal, M. L. (1999), "Market Freedom in India and Action Agenda" The Business Review, Vol. 5, No. 1 & 2.

Bakal, G. M. (1989), "Role of DICs in the Industrial Development", Ph. D. Thesis (Unpublished), Department of Commerce, University of Kashmir.

Bamzai, P. K. (1979), 'A History of Jammu and Kashmir', Metropolitan Book Company Ltd., Delhi.

Bhat, K. A. (2000), 'Modern Small Scale Industries and Industrial Sickness', Anmol Publications Pvt. Ltd., New Delhi.

Cherunilam, F. (1997), 'Business Environment', Himalaya Publishing House, Mumbai.

Digest of Statistics, (2002-03), Directorate of Economics & Statistics, Planning & Development Department, Govt. of Jammu & Kashmir.

Report of the Godbole Committee on Economic Reforms for Jammu and Kashmir, (1997).

Industrial Potential Survey of Jammu and Kashmir, 'Report of a Study Team sponsored by the IDBI, RBI, ICICI & IFCI, (1972).

Kuchal, S. C. (1989), 'The Industrial Economy of India', Chaitanya Publishing House, Allahabad, India.

Nisar A. (1987), 'Problems and Management of Small Scale and Cottage Industries', Deep and Deep Publications, New Delhi.

Sadhu A. N. and Singh A. (1984), 'Jammu and Kashmir Economy', Trikuta Publishing House, Jammu.

Singh N. P. (1989), "Entrepreneurship Development: Some Thoughts", MDI Management Journal, Vol. 2, No 1.

2

Industrial Potential and Natural Resource Base

Introduction

Natural resources influence not only economic growth but also its economic structure. The type of resources available their quantities and the scale of their exploration determine to a considerable extent the type and scale of industrialization that can be taken up with ease. However, the quantity and type of resources that a particular region is endowed with depends on the effort and knowledge applied to discover various resources. It is in view of this fact it passionately being argued that the economic greatness of nations is not a result of mere natural resource base but of other factors in particular science and technology. The fact of the matter is that natural resource base could only provide a comparative advantage to the nations concerned for industrialization. The most glaring examples in this regard are some of the industrially developed nations of the world especially Japan, Taiwan, Hongkong etc. which have achieved phenomenal growth not because of natural resource endowments but due to other factors.

"A natural resource is anything found by man in his natural environment on, above and under the surface of the earth" (UN study). The industrially important resources provided by the nature includes; mineral resources, agricultural resources and forest resources. These resources are a source of raw–material to various types of industries. Lack of raw–material acts as a strong barrier to intensive industrialization. In fact, the difference in the progress of industrial development between different parts of the country is also due to its variations in range, quality and quantity of raw–materials. Since raw material constitutes a major component of total cost of the product, as such it influences the choice for locating an industrial enterprise. However, the extent of influence on the choice of location would depend upon the nature of raw–material needed for an industrial activity. Industries using net raw–material enjoy freedom in their plant location decision as their location near the centre of raw-material or near the market make no difference on their operating efficiency. The industries using gross raw–materials would enjoy economy in their production cost only near the material centres. The objective based assessment of various natural resource endowments of the state is discussed hereunder to decide about the type and extent of industrialization that can be taken up in different regions of the state given the various natural resource endowments.

Agricultural Resources

Complementary relationship exists between industry and agriculture and one can not prosper without the proper development of the other. In general, the contribution of agriculture to the economy can be judged from the point of its Product Contribution, Market Contribution and Factor Contribution. The agricultural sector of the state still remains under developed and has a very little to offer to the meaningful industrial activity in the state. Although, the agriculture sector of the state offers raw–materials like, cotton, sugarcane, maze, oilseeds etc. Yet it can benefit industrially only from the cultivation of 'Asparagus', oilseeds, mushrooms, maize and to some extent from the by-products of paddy. The sugar-cane and cotton is grown at a very low scale in the state.

Asparagus: On account of soil features and climatic conditions, the Kashmir valley has been found highly suitable for the cultivation of this commercial crop. The cultivation of this crop has been taken-up by a good number of farmers in the valley. More returns from this crop at a minimum of effort and risk is expected to attract further land under its cultivation. Canned Asparagus enjoys good country-wide market mostly among the higher strata of the society and also in the international market where it fetches very good price. At present in the country there is a wide gap between supply and demand of Canned Asparagus and to meet the deficit in supply the country is importing from Japan. The state in this segment of the canned industry enjoys a definite industrial potential due to comparative advantage in the availability of raw-material. However, this industry in the state remains largely under-utilized. At present there is only one unit canning asparagus and most of this crop is imported outside the state without any value addition. To exploit this resource industrially to the maximum, the government has to play an important role in the promotion and development of this industry by bringing more land under its cultivation, developing this industry on most modern lines in the state and expanding market base through export promotion.

Mushrooms: The other nature's gift to the state of Jammu and Kashmir is its suitability to the cultivation of mushrooms which is a fungus and forms a tasty and nutritious diet especially for diabetic patients. Number of people in the valley with the assistance of agriculture department is engaged in the cultivation of mushrooms and one canned unit at present is operating in the valley. The state has failed to capitalize on this natural advantage. In fact, there is a lot of market potential for mushrooms and mushroom based Jams both within and outside the state, which if made into an active demand, could give a big push to this industry. To realize due potential out of this natural resource, the government has to come forward and play an active role in the development of this resource. Proper marketing with aggressive promotion and better quality at minimum possible cost would certainly explore new markets for this product and provide source of income to many.

Oil Seeds: The area under oil seeds and production of oil seeds has shown an upward trend since the last decade. During the last decade, the area sown under oil seeds and the production has increased from 67.62 thousand hectares and 365 thousand quintals in 1990-91 to 78.31 thousand hectares and 422 thousand quintals respectively (Table 2.1). It can also be seen from the above mentioned table that both area sown and the production has not recorded steady growth but witnessed fluctuating trend. It can also be seen from the above table that although the area sown under oil seeds has increased yet, the oil seeds production has declined from 548 thousand quintals in 1980-81 to 422 thousand quintals. This sort of mismatch hints perhaps at the fact that the yield per hectare has decreased. Such a disturbing state of affairs calls for an immediate action.

Table 2.1: Production and Area Sown Under Oil Seeds (Area sown, 000 hac.) (Production, 000 qtts.)

Year	Area sown	%age growth	Production	%age growth
1980-81	52.74		548	
1985-86	72.91	38.24	708	29.19
1990-91	67.62	7.25	365	-48.45
1995-96	68.2	0.857	440	20.55
1996-97	71.02	4.135	480	9.09
1997-98	69.39	2.295	471	-1.875
1998-99	70.64	1.801	510	8.28
1999-00	75.92	7.474	535	2.803
2000-01	73.91	2.647	282	-47.289
2001-02	78.31	5.953	422	49.645
Cg		**1.29**		**1.9**

Cg Stands for Compound Growth

Source: *Digest of Statistics*, Directorate of Economics and Statistics, Planning and Development Department, J & K Government, 2002.

People in general in the state have high preference for mustard oil than any other vegetable oil. The oil expelling units located in the state using local supply of oil seeds will have an edge with regard to cost competitiveness in the local market over the firms located outside the state. The deficiency of mustard oil coupled with the advantage of cost competitiveness and the ambitious program undertaken by the state government to increase oil seeds production in the state promises better future for the development of mustard oil extraction industry in the years to come under the roof of small scale sector. So far as the current state of oil expelling industry in the state is concerned, number of expelling units exists in the state. But majority of such units are not being organized on modern lines. It is because of this fact, that barring a few units, none has been able to create a brand name of its own. There is a scope for many more units. But to realize the due industrial potential from this useful crop, there is a need to organize new units on most modern lines and at the same time the government has to make all-out efforts in increasing the production of oil seeds in the state by bringing more land under its cultivation and by introducing high yielding oil seeds.

Other Agricultural Resources: Maize is the second largest agricultural produce in the state and staple diet of the people living in the higher reaches of the state. On account of intensive cultivation of maize in the state, "the study team for Industrial Potential in J&K (1972) had suggested the establishment of a maize milling plant to process maize into Maida, Suji and Rawa". The milling plant will supplement the cattle and poultry feed units, starch, glucose units by providing certain ingredients. Further, two or three units could be established to manufacture "Straw Board" from the paddy husk which is available in large quantities in the state, particularly in the valley of Kashmir.

Vegetable Dehydration-cum-Tomato Juice Plant: The agro-climatic conditions of the state in particular of Kashmir valley, Ladakh division and some parts of Jammu are extreme which does not allow to maintain the adequate supply of different types of fresh vegetables internally during the winter. Also the supplies to such areas during winter come from outside which, however, remain uncertain, inadequate and costly. Further, the people in these areas, aver the time have developed a habit for dried vegetables. All these facts make the prospects bright for one or two small dehydration-cum-tomato juice plants in each district to cater the local demand. Such units can Dehydrate vegetables and extract tomato juice during summer when vegetables are available in abundant quantities at cheap rates and market them during winter. Such plants could find easy market both in the valley and in Ladakh divisions of the state which remains cut-off from the rest of the state for almost 6 months. Tomato juice can be marketed during summer in other parts of the country as well. However, it may take one or two years to penetrate deep into the different segments of market. Good quality at reasonable price supported by effective promotion and marketing strategies could bring many laurels to this industry. It is suggested that the canning units as a part of expansion and diversification should install such operations along with canning activity.

Horticulture: The state of Jammu and Kashmir is also famous for its delicious fruits throughout the country. In the state, both temperate and sub-tropical fruits are grown. The important fruits grown in the state include apples, walnuts, almonds, pears, apricots, peaches, plums, cherries, citrus, mangoes and guava. Of these fruits, apple is the only fruit which promises definite industrial potential of great importance to the state.

Apple Produce: The vale of Kashmir is considered as the home to delicious apples. Wide variety of apples each having different taste, size and colour are grown in the Valley. The apple production in the state accounts for near about 47 per cent of the total the production of apples in the country. Customers in the national market give preference to the apples from Kashmir over the apples from other parts of the country because of its taste. Most of the apple produce is sold in the national market. Before transporting to different markets in the country apples are properly graded. This process of grading leaves huge quantity of substandard apples and culls. The availability of culls, substandard apples and pre-falls provide enough scope for apple juice industry.

Given the abundant supply of apples and the potential market base, this industry can be taken up at a large scale to cater the demand both in the national market and international market particularly in gulf and other Asian markets. In fact, there is a tremendous market potential for apple juice which remains under-taped and the improvement in the standard of living will further add to the demand base of this product. At present there is wide gap between demand and supply in the country. The potential of this industry has not been fully utilized in the state as yet. At present there are around five juice units operating in the small scale sector, four in private sector and one in public-sector run by Jammu Kashmir Horticulture Produce and Marketing Corporation (JKHPMC). This natural resource has much to offer to the state's industrial economy, however, the need is to organize this industry on most scientific lines on all fronts.

Also concerted efforts are needed to be made to promote the apple juice in foreign countries in particular in gulf countries and other Asian countries where lot of demand for this product lies. Good quality at comparable price with effective sales promotion would certainly help to compete against the established brands. The industry in the state would enjoy sufficient and regular supply of apples at reasonable price. The industry would be able to produce juice of different tastes and at different rates by using different variety of apples available in the valley. Further the industry can provide market to the inferior quality apples. Further, from the pulp that is left after extraction of juice "pectin" can be obtained which enjoys sufficient demand in Pharmaceutical industry?

Fruit Jam is the other area where some industrial activity can be taken-up. There is a very good market lying under the cover, which needs to be aroused into an active demand. In fact, market is no problem but the problem lies with the outlook and approach of the enterprises towards the marketing of these fruit jams. In this era of globalization, we should not look into the local and national market only, but look for the potential international markets as well. Collaboration with foreign companies, in particular, in the areas where state enjoys definite comparative advantage in resource endowments could give a big push to such industries. Culled fruits which are available in abundance in the state could be utilized by the food processing industry, thus providing a ready market to culled fruits and at the same time canning units will be able to get basic raw-materials at cheap rates. Jams and fruit slices particularly apple slices can be the possible products of fruit canning units. Availability of different types of fruits, like, pear, peaches, apples etc. could enable them to produce Jams from different fruits and also mixed Jams.

However, such units will need government assistance in the supply of sugar at subsidized rates and tin containers till the industry is out of its infancy. The growth in this industry will then itself solve the problem of the availability of tins through ancillerisation of tin manufacturing right in the valley. With the government support, the future of fruit preservation and canning industry is quite bright in Kashmir, provided the product is of comparable quality and cost and fully backed by effective and regressive market promotion which in turn calls for entrepreneurs to be adaptive to changing market forces.

Livestock

From time immemorial livestock has been best companion of human. Livestock has contributed to human development by providing nutritious food, means of transport, helping hand in cultivation and many more services. Although the mechanization of agriculture has limited their role in cultivation, however, their role in industrialization has widened. They are a source of raw-material to many industries and at the same time provide market to many industrial products. The state of Jammu and Kashmir is rich in livestock wealth which offers scope for number of industrial activities. Hides and skins, wool and bones are found in sufficient quantities in the state. The availability of such materials provides sufficient scope to the state to industrialize in the lines based on these resources. Large scale efforts are on to achieve the all-round development of Animal Husbandry in the state particularly in sheep, dairy and poultry farming. The number of cattle in the state which were just around 18.08 lakh has grown to 31.75 lakh in 1997. The population of other animals like Buffaloes, sheep and goats has also a registered a significant growth over a period of time as can be seen from Table 2.2.

Table 2.2: Live Stock Population in J&K State (in lakh)

Year	Cattle	Buffaloes	Sheep	Goats	Yaks	Horses & ponies
1961	18.081	4.012	11.626	5.774	NA	0.694
1972	20.569	4.926	10.724	5.692	0.124	0.6
1977	21.385	4.995	12.161	6.92	0.147	0.691
1982	23.252	5.631	19.087	10.039	0.209	0.973
1988	27.657	5.953	24.934	13.96	0.214	1.04
1992	30.55	7.325	29.469	17.655	0.336	1.215
1997	31.754	7.878	31.695	18.095	0.33	1.412

Source: *Digest of Statistics*, Directorate of Economics and Statistics, Planning and Development Department, J & K Government, 2002-03.

Skins and Hides: Meat particularly red meat is one of the daily items of the kitchens of average Kashmiri homes. Marriages and other festivities of Muslims in the state are marked by a variety of meat dishes. In fact, people of Kashmir have developed a strong appetite to non-vegetarian dishes. To cater the huge demand for meat in the state it is estimated that more than 3.4 million sheep's and 1500 cattle are slaughtered every year. Thus providing sufficient base for the development of leather tanneries and leather based industries in the state. This figure is being worked out @ 100 gms. of red meat per person per week for a total population of 100.699 lakh people as per census 2001 and the average weight of sheep is taken equal to net 15 kgs. The estimated output of hides in the state is 10,500 per annum which is being worked out at the standard mortality rate of 6 percent of total cattle population in the state. The total population of cattle as on 1997 stands at 31.75 lakh. However, the figure has been shown on a lower side as most of the people have given-up the collection of hides from dead cattle. The number of hides and skins available in the state are estimated to feed 4 big tanneries.

Leather as a basic input is used in footwear industry and Leather garment industry. There is a tremendous scope for leather

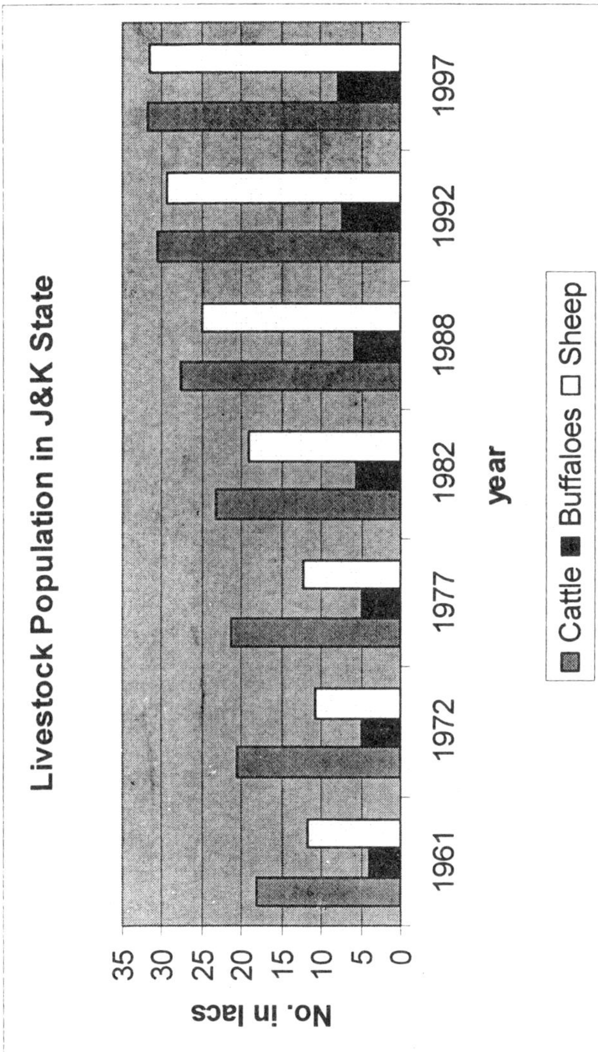

Livestock Population in J&K State
No. in lacs
35
30
25
20
15
10
5
0
1961
1972
1977
1982
1988
1992
1997
year
Cattle
Buffaloes
Sheep

and leather products nationally and internationally. The leather tanneries located in Kashmir would enjoy enough competitiveness and can find its market both within and outside the country, Leather tannery industry in the state can give birth to leather footwear industry and big boost to leather garment industry. There were two tanneries in the public sector and two in the private sector in the Small Scale Sector. However, these have stopped their manufacturing operations since, thus leaving this resource of great use grossly under-utilized. If state wants to develop its industrial economy, the leather is the one industry which has a sufficient potential to contribute to the state's industrial economy. To develop this potential industry of great magnitude, the government is required to play a catalytic role by:

- Conducting a study to know what specifically needs to be done to develop the leather industry in the state.
- Banning export of Skins and Hides from the state.
- Seeking help from the institutes specializing in leather industry in the development of leather industry in the state.
- Developing a separate estate for leather tanneries at some isolated place with all the requisite facilities.

Wool: Sheep rearing has been the age old activity of the state's peasants. To increase the meat and wool production in the state, Sheep Husbandry Department, Jammu and Kashmir Government has drawn ambitious plans and so far some headway has been made through cross breeding of local stock with Russian and Australian Marino known for finer varieties of wool with more counts and more output of wool and meat. The data about the wool production of both the government livestock only is available in the state. However, it is being reported that the total wool production in the state would be around 600 quintals.

However, the wool production of government livestock which in 1980-81 was 448 quintals, has declined to 256.36 quintals in 2002-03 as can be seen from Table 2.3. Although some progress has been made in wool production yet, there is still to go a long way. The available wool in the state is processed into woolen fabrics. The manufacture of hand spun and hand woven woolen fabric is carried on a fairly large scale in the state. Khadi and Village Industries Commission, the Gandhi Ashram, Handloom Development Corporation, Dastkar Anjuman and Bemina Woolen Mills, Government Spinning Mills, Nowshera and Knitting Factory Jammu are engaged in the manufacturing of woolen fabrics, worsted suiting and shirting, tweeds serge, blankets, Raffal yarn, and Jerseys, socks, hand gloves by knitting unit Jammu for state government departments like police.

Table 2.3: Wool Production of Government Livestock (qtts.)

Year	Wool Production	Absolute Growth	%age Growth
1971-72	128		
1980-81	448.35	320.35	250
1985-86	388.34	60.01	13.38
1990-94	373.81	14.53	3.74
1995-96	235.53	138.28	36.99
1996-97	254.09	18.56	7.88
1997-98	261.21*	7.12	2.80
1998-99	273.07	11.86	4.54
1999-00	284.39	11.32	4.145
2000-01	260.31	24.08	8.467
2001-02	254.38	5.93	2.278
2002-03	256.36	1.98	0.778
Cumulative growth			**11.5**

*Estimated Wool Production.

Source: *Digest of Statistics*, Directorate of Economics and Statistics, Planning and Development Department, J & K Government, 2002-03.

There are few units operating in the private sector which are engaged in weaving and spinning of woolens. Except a few units working under the banner of Jammu and Kashmir Industries ltd, the spinning, weaving, dyeing and finishing of woolen fabrics by other manufacturers is "carried on in a age old traditional way resulting in inherent handicaps like maintenance of uniformity, quality and finishing of products" (Nisar, 1987). The Woolen Mills Shireen Bagh Srinagar is closed on account of obsolete plant and machinery. The different woolen mills working under the banner of JKI including Bemina Woolen Mills which was equipped with modern technology which was established to capitalize mainly on medium and high value market available within and outside the state are constrained with different operating inefficiencies, like limited product range, poor design and quality, poor marketing efforts. In fact, the state has failed to exploit this industry to its fullest potential in spite of being a traditional industry of the state; having an advantage in resource endowments and easy access to the markets. The industry has still a lot to offer to the state's Industrial economy.

The markets for woolen products particularly for knit wares. are expanding both in length and breadth. Improvements in standard of living of the people would be continuously supplementing to the market base for woolen products. In fact, the future of this industry seems to be bright. Privatization of this industry in the state would be a step towards right direction. Private investment should be encouraged particularly in the manufacturing of worsted fabrics, woolen blankets, knit wares, hand gloves, mufflers etc. However, there is a definite role for the government to play in the development of this industry in the state. Among other things the government is required to make efforts to increase wool production in the state.

Sheep and Dairy Farming: The state of Jammu and Kashmir, in particular Kashmir division is highly deficient in meat and milk production. It depends largely on the imports from other states particularly for meat. The annual requirements for meat are estimated at more than 40 lakh kgs. While as, the annual production in the state stands at above one lakh kgs only. Such a large imbalance in local demand and supply provides enough scope for sheep farming in the state. Although sheep rearing has been the age old activity of the peasants in the state, however, in general farmers rear just a few mostly local breed and not on commercial basis. Educated rural youth with sufficient landholding can benefit from sheep and diary farming tremendously.

However, the farming activity should be taken fairly at a large scale with the best breed and on most scientific lines. Orchardists enjoy a definite advantage of having sufficient grazing space, thus can go for sheep and diary farming along with the fruit production without any difficulty. Unfortunately, the rural youth in the state has hardly any preference for diary or sheep farming as their full time jobs. They are heavily oriented towards government jobs which are scarce. Therefore, it is highly essential to defeat this undesirable behaviour on the part of the rural youth. The state will not be able to achieve self-sufficiency in meat and milk production through cross breeding only. There is a need to educate and encourage rural youth to take-up farming on large scale and on commercial basis by providing credit on easy terms, imported breeds and other facilities without much official complexities. To boost this trade, the farming in the state should be treated as an industry for the purpose of availing different incentives which are offered to the other industries in the state and its development taken on priority basis.

In poultry farming, some beginning has been made in the state, however, still needs to go a long way. At present there are two hatcheries, some feed factories and number of poultry farms over and above the government hatchery and farms. However, the supply is still quite less than the demand for broilers and eggs. Most of the farms in the state are located in congested areas and farming done on unscientific lines and with uneconomical size which is resulting in more costs, less profitability and losses to many farmers thus leaving unhealthy impression about the poultry industry in the state. The data about the egg production in government farms only is available (Table 2.4). The egg production in government farms which was 2.65 lakh eggs has gone to 5.76 lakh in 2002-03. The egg production in the state is reported to be minimal standing at 7.41 lakh eggs per annum as on 2002-03 where as total demand for eggs in the state is estimated to be around 7.25 crore eggs per annum (estimated @ 1 egg per 50 persons per day for a total population of 100.699 lakh persons as per census 2001). The estimate has been kept on a lower side in view of the poor standard of living in the state.

Table 2.4: Egg Production in Government Farms (in lakh)

Year	Egg Production	Absolute Growth	%age Growth
1980-81	2.65		
1985-86	10.16	7.51	283.39
1990-91	6.42	-3.74	-36.81
1995-96	5.10	-1.32	-20.56
1996-97	6.74	1.64	32.15
1997-98	7.25*	0.51	7.03
1998-99	7.47	-0.22	-2.94
1999-2000	6.72	-0.75	-10.04
2000-2001	5.19	-1.53	-22.76
2001-2002	7.18	1.99	38.34
2002-2003	5.76	-1.42	-19.77
Cumulative growth			**10.7**

*Estimated Egg Production.

Source: *Digest of Statistics*, Directorate of Economics and Statistics, Planning and Development Department, J & K Government, 2002-03.

There is a lot of scope for organizing poultry farming purely on scientific lines around Srinagar and Jammu cities and in other district headquarters to fulfill the wide gap in demand for both fresh eggs and dressed broilers. People in the state have developed interest in poultry farming but need encouragement from the government in the form of financial support etc. It is unfortunate to note here that the government so far has done very little to develop poultry industry in the state on desired lines like other industries. The prospective farmers should be provided land and loans for the construction of sheds etc. It may be stated that it has been found that the farmers of the state are not able to compete with the competitors from outside the state. So there is a need to investigate into the causes of poor competitiveness so as to come out with suitable strategies to help the local farmers to improve upon their competitiveness.

Feed Industry: The total population of live stock in the state as on 1997 stood at 31.75 lakh cattle, 7.87 lakh Buffaloes, 49.79 lakh sheep and goats and 42.66 lakh fowls respectively. The livestock wealth in the state has grown at the rate of 14.5 percent annually (see Table 2.2) and the uptrend in livestock population is expected to continue in the years to come as more and more people are turning to the farming. The commercialization of farming in the state has caused a great demand for cattle and poultry feed. It is being reported that the total demand for cattle feed stood at 263.7 lakh quintals and of poultry feed at 153.57 lakh quintals as on 2001-02. the data presented in table 2.4 brings to fore that the egg production in government farms has witnessed a fluctuating trend which is not a healthy sign about the government farms. However, the total production within the state is quite insignificant as compared to the total demand. The demand for livestock feed in the state is going to increase further in the years to come as the state has yet only made a beginning in the farming sector.

In fact, the future for this industry in the state seems to be very rosy. To meet the demands for feed in the state, the number of units in the small scale sector were established, however, most of them remain closed not because they could not find the market for their products but for other reasons. The deficiency in feed production presently is being met from the imports from Punjab and other neighboring states. To put, the feed industry on the wheels of prosperity in the state, there is a need to investigate into the dismal performance of feed industry in the state so as to come up with the turn around strategies for the large scale development of this industry on sustainable lines.

Silk Industry: Cocoon rearing had origin in ancient China from where it traveled to other parts on the famous silk root which was passing through central Asia to Kashmir from China. However, according to Khan (1982) that basically silk originated from Kashmir. "The references in Mahabharta and Ramayana in the two old great epics establish that sericulture was being practiced in Kashmir from times immemorial" (industrial potential survey, 1973). Whether originated in China or in Kashmir, the silk industry has a very long tradition in Kashmir. The industry came into limelight during the reigns of Zain-ul-abidin, AD 1420-1470 (Gani, 1988). However, the industry in its present form was organized in 1897 in Kashmir valley with the cooperation of Sir Thomas Warde, President Silk Association of Great Britain who was impressed by the immense potential possessed by the state for silk industry (Kesar, 1980). Maharaja Ranbir Singh also did a lot for the development of silk industry in the state. He had provided number of concessions and facilities to the people engaged in silk industry like, no *'Beggar'* for those working in silk industry, imported plant and machinery for silk reeling units and built number of rearing houses.

It was once the main revenue earning industry in the state and also played an important role in the movement for political rationalization in the state. Silk industry was considered as one of the largest concerns of its kind in the state, providing employment to about 5000 people (Bamzai , 1973). Kashmir was famous for quality silk throughout the world and enjoying distinction for producing mulberry, Tasser, Cri and Muga varieties of silk in the country. During the French–British Exhibition held in 1908, Kashmir silk received the highest awards by bagging both gold and silver medals (Khursheed, 1982). Customers both local and foreign used to give preference to silk made in Kashmir over other manufactures. In fact, it was the major and prime industry of the state contributing significantly to industrial production. However, it is disheartening to note here that the state has lost its glory and charm in silk industry despite of being only state in the country suitable for rearing Tri-voltine/ Bi-voltine silk worms, having long experience in silk industry, and only state with hundred percent reeling capacity. In fact, the industry is in deep shambles. The production of raw silk in the state has declined from 88 thousand kgs. in 1954-55 to just 30.41 thousand kgs in 2002-03 and the production of green cocoons from 9.62 lakh kgs to just 8.32 thousand kgs. in 2002-03 (Table 2.5).

Contrary the production of raw silk in other states has increased significantly which enabled the country to become the second largest producer of silk in the world after China. Jammu and Kashmir which was holding third position in the country in silk production in 1954-55 slipped down almost to the last position in 2002-03. Andhra Pradesh and Tamil Nadu whose contribution to the silk market was negligible in 1961-62, emerged major contributors in 2002-03 after Karnataka which has witnessed a big leap in silk industry. However, the fact of the matter is that such a gloomy picture of state's-silk industry is not due to the lack of market or poor quality. In fact, the industry in the state suffered partly due to lack of well conceived direction and partly on account of role failure of Sericulture Development Department, J&K government, the effects of which have surfaced in insufficient cocoon production, low productivity, low plant utilization, thus allowed every opportunity to the competitors to gain and establish their Rit in the market. Decline in cocoon production, the basic raw-material for silk industry has been partly due to un-remunerative price to the rears, inferior seeds, insufficient and poor quality of mulberry leaves and poor management of rearing (Shah, 1989) and partly due to the shift of some rearers to other jobs. After 1990, the decline in cocoon production in Kashmir has also been attributed to ongoing disturbances in the state, in particular in the valley.

The silk industry which continued to be a state's monopoly since 1892 was demonopolised in 1988 with the aim to give a new direction to this declining industry so as to regain the lost glory in the industry. Further, the price of cocoons was raised in the year 1986 and the World Bank funded project for the development of Sericulture in the state was launched. At present, there are two

Table 2.5: Sericulture Development in the State of J&K

Year	No. of Sericulture Villages (000s)	No. of Sericulture House owners (000s)	Production of Cocoons (In 000 qts)	Utilisation of Cocoons for Rearing (000 qts)	Production of Raw silk	
					Quantity (000 kg)	Value (000 lakh)
1980-81	2.70	38.50	10.36	7.70	75.85	234.98
1985-86	2.26	32.50	6.42	4.51	33.70	291.28
1990-91	2.59	29.19	7.00	2.39	20.74	55.35
1995-96	2.36	23.53	6.66	0.51	9.50	140.16
1996-97	2.24	25.52	7.67	7.33	85.10	1076.00
1997-98	NA	NA	NA	NA	NA	NA
1998-99	2.307	22.737	8.29	8.10	92.10	1288.00
1999-00	2.15	25.28	8.25	8.04	80.00	960.00
2000-01	2.166	26.052	8.90	8.68	21.00	---
2001-02	2,164	20.249	7.07	6.92	37.00	---
2002-03	2.179	23.138	8.489	8.329	30.41	---

Source: *Digest of Statistics*, Directorate of Economics and Statistics, Planning and Development Department, J&K Government, 2002-03.

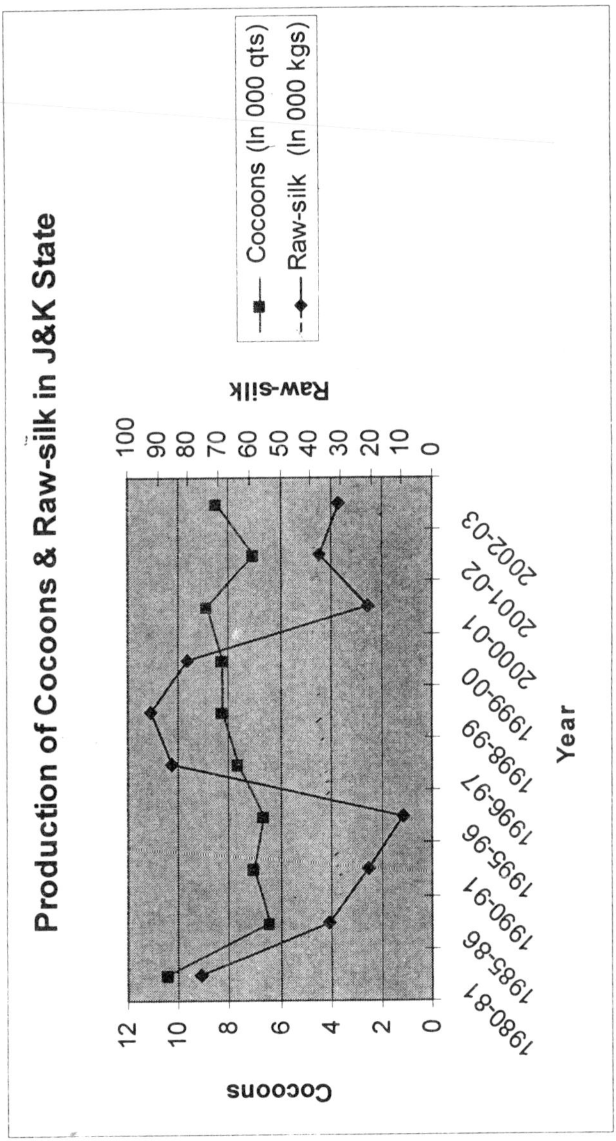
Production of Cocoons & Raw-silk in J&K State
Cocoons (In 000 qts)
Raw-silk (In 000 kgs)
Cocoons
Raw-silk
Year
1980-81
1985-86
1990-91
1995-96
1996-97
1998-99
1999-00
2000-01
2001-02
2002-03
0
2
4
6
8
10
12
0
10
20
30
40
50
60
70
80
90
100

government filatures with 584 reeling basins and six private filatures operating in the state. In silk weaving, there are two government owned weaving factories namely Rajbagh Silk factory and Handloom Weaving factory at Ram Bagh, weaving most of the silk output in the state and 126 power looms and 100 handlooms engaged in silk weaving in the private sector (JKI Status Report). The performance of all silk producing units particularly government runs units is well below the mark. The growth in government filatures was marred by obsolete technology, insufficient and poor quality of cocoons, low labor productivity and management inefficiencies. It is surprising to note that World Bank funded project which started in 80's for the development of Sericulture in the state so far could not make any dent into the sagging performance of the silk industry.

The silk industry in the state has a lot to offer to the state's industrial economy. Kashmir silk still enjoys market credibility, figuring in the preference list of most of the customers. The market for silk industry would be expanding both in length and breadth in the country with the growth in the national economy. On account of having an advantage of being the only state in the country suitable for rearing Uni-voltine and Bi-voltine races of silk worms, which are known for high quality and more silk; better market credibility and better expertise and experience in the industry, the state has got a definite comparative advantage and could regain the lost glory in the industry. However there is need for a sincere and well thought out long term and coherent policy measures reflecting the changing economic scenario.

On the basis of research findings, Shah (1989) suggested that production of improved seeds, proper maintenance of mulberry gardens, production of improved varieties of mulberry plants, scientific rearing of cocoons, developing double cropping pattern, financing of Seri-culturists, modernizing existing units of silk reeling and weaving and reducing silk waste can put the industry on the track of growth and prosperity. In fact, there is an immense need for the encouragement of cocoon rearers through different facilities and incentives. They need to be helped in improving productivity, reducing cost and protected from powerful buyers so as to enable them to produce more. Demonopolisation of silk industry is a step towards right direction which is expected to give some boost to the industry in the state. However, genuine entrepreneurs only should get encouragement. Government should assume the role of a developmental agency only.

Mineral Resources

Exploration and proper utilization of mineral resources with which the state is endowed, can provide some vitals for achieving meaningful industrial development. Minerals have greater role in building the productive capacity of economies by providing raw-materials. Realizing the importance of mineral resources in the process of economic development, the state government in 1955 had set-up a full-fledged Directorate of Geology and Mining to supplement the activities of the Geological Survey of India and Indian Bureau of Mines in the exploration and development of mines in the state. For the exploitation of mineral resources in the state, the state government in 1967 also established J&K Minerals Ltd. which at present is running a cement plant, pre-stressed concrete and spun pipe factories and also engaged in mining of different minerals in the state. Jammu and Kashmir has many, though not all types of minerals. The minerals found in the state include lignite, quartzite, limestone, gypsum, Sulphur, bauxite, iron ore, oil and natural gas, mica, borax etc. However, the state has large proven reserves of coal, lignite, limestone, gypsum, quartzite and stones only. Reserves of copper, lead, bauxite, Sulphur and borax have been reported in sufficient quantities but stated to be economically not-workable. The existences of different minerals brighten the prospects of state's industrial economy by promising industrial potential in the related lines.

Coal and Lignite: Conventional energy like coal and lignite etc. also plays an important role in keeping the wheels of an industrial economy moving. The state of Jammu and Kashmir is fortunate to have some coal and lignite-deposits. Coal in the state is found in Jammu province and the coal belt runs from Jangalgali to Jigri over a distance of 60 km (Table 2.6 for important coal fields with estimated reserves in the state). The coal found is semi-anthracite coal. Among all, Kotli coal fields possess good quality coal. The coal production from these fields which was 34,000 tonnes in 1962-63 has gone up to 67,000 tonnes in 2001-02. On an average, 56,000 tonnes of coal is mined from the coalfields in the state annually (J&K Minerals Ltd. Status Report). Almost 90 percent of the total coal mined meets the requirements of the Kalakote Thermal Power Plant and the balance partly meets the requirements of brick making industry in the state.

Table 2.6: Coal Fields with Estimated Reserves in J&K State as on 1995-96

Area	Reserves (000, tones)
Jigri-kura Coal Field	184.20
Kalakote Coal Field	461.80
Metka Coal Field	2270.00
Mahogala Coal Field	N.E
Chinkah Coal Field	3900.00
Jangalgali Coal Field	4790.00

Source: Sadhu A.N. and Singh A. (1984), 'Jammu and Kashmir Economy', Trikuta Publishing House, Jammu.

Lignite, another form of coal is also found in the state in Nichahome–Chowkibal, Adur and Raithan-Lanyalok areas of Kashmir province with total reported reserves of about 72.6 lakh tonnes. However, the lignite found in the state has high ash-content which does not warrant its use as a source of energy in the industrial sector. Initially some quantity of lignite was mined for a briquetting plant established by the State Government for the manufacturing of coal briquettes. The plant was later on shut down as the demand for briquettes could not pick up due to poor burning characteristics. With the closure of briquetting plant, the mining of lignite was stopped in the year 1965-66. The government earlier had planned to commission lignite based thermal power plant, however, that did not come-up for unknown reasons.

The state is chronically deficient in much needed electric power. The state has mostly hydel-based power generation system. Due to low discharge in winter months, the generation level falls significantly aggravating the problem of power shortages. The problem is further accentuated due to the increasing demand during winter. The presence of coal and lignite can be used to supplement the energy needs by commissioning thermal power plants to support the falling capacity of hydel power projects during winter when there is low discharge of water from the rivers. At present coal deposits are commercially exploited to meet the energy needs of brick-making industry in the state, however, lignite deposits in the state remain un-taped. Lignite in the state can be utilized in the generation of electricity for which industries have suffered a lot especially in Kashmir region. In view of the fact, that the position of power generation is far from satisfactory, it becomes necessary to take appropriate steps to utilize this natural resource for power generation.

Limestone and Gypsum: Limestone and gypsum are industrially most important minerals. Gypsum is used in the manufacturing of cement, chalk crayons, surgical plaster, plaster of Paris and building plaster. The limestone is used in the manufacturing of cement, iron and steel, fertilizers etc. Fortunately, the state of Jammu & Kashmir is well endowed with huge reserves of limestone and gypsum of high quality. Huge reserves of cement, chemical and flux grade limestone is available in sizable quantity of standard quality in all the three provinces of the State. In Jammu it is found in different parts of Udhampur, Doda, Kathua and Poonch districts and in Kashmir province it is found in Pulwama and Baramulla districts. In Kashmir valley, the lime stone deposits are found over an area of almost 5 sq. km. running from Khanmuh to Khrew and the limestone found in Kashmir is of better quality than the deposits found at other places both in the state and outside. The total deposits of lime stone in the state have been estimated to be of the order of 360 lakh tonnes which are sufficient to meet the requirements of many large cement plants (see table 2.7 for the estimates of lime stone reserves at different places in the state).

Table 2.7: Estimated Reserves of Limestone in J&K State

(in lakh tonnes)

Province	Estimated Reserves
Kashmir Province	
• Wuyan	1.00
Jammu Province	
• Basohli-Bani Area	50.00
• Jangalgali – Sukhwagali Area	53.00
• Bangalagala	94.00
• Salal	60.00
• Kalakote – Kurajigni Area	120.00
Ladakh Province	
• Ladakh – Khalsi	2.00

Source: Industrial Potential Survey of Jammu and Kashmir, 'Report of a Study Team sponsored by the IDBI, RBI, ICICI & IFCI, (1972).

Gypsum which along with limestone is used in the manufacturing of cement is also found in all three regions of the state. In Kashmir it is being found in Buniyar, Baramullah district along the Jehlum River and in Jammu division it is found in Batote of Doda district. The gypsum found along River Chinab is of high grade comparable with the best quality gypsum found at any other place in the country. The total reserves of gypsum in the state are estimated at 100 million tonnes. Presently, gypsum is quarried only from the deposits found in Jammu province.

Realizing the industrial potential lying beneath these natural deposits, the state government in 1960 started exploiting this potential wealth. J&K Minerals Ltd., in 1962 has set up a cement plant with 60 TPD based on Lurgis Dry sintering process to manufacture cement at Wayun, Kashmir. Besides J&K minerals has established two pre-stressed concrete cement plants one each at Kashmir and Jammu to manufacture PCC poles. Later on in

1969, J&K Cements Ltd. a Public Sector Company was floated by the state government to utilize quality limestone available at Krew with an authorized capital of Rs. 105 crore. The corporation has set up a cement plant at Khrew to manufacture Portland cement with a capacity of 600 tonnes per day based on most modern technology. From 1986 private investment was also allowed to exploit this useful natural resource to its fullest potential. Accordingly number of cement plants in the private sector came into existence.

All the cement plants in the state are operating almost at their full capacities. The Wayun cement plant which remained closed for some time on account of the difficulties caused by old designed 6th grade bed, non availability of coal with ash content of 13 percent and calorific value of about 6000 kgs, power problems is also now operational. But the plant is not operating at full capacity in spite of the fact that the product has ready market. It may be stated here that the gypsum used in cement factories located in Kashmir province comes from the gypsum mines of Jammu and not from gypsum found at Buniyar, Baramulla. Efforts need to be made for mining gypsum from Buniyar so that the transportation cost is minimized for the units located in Kashmir valley. The cost of production of local cement industry does not compare favourably with the cement plants located elsewhere in the country.

These natural resources still have much in their stock to offer to the industrial economy in the state, however, it is unpleasing to see that the state has failed to fully capitalize the industrial potential lying in these natural deposits. In spite of having a definite comparative advantage in the availability of limestone and gypsum, the state had failed to meet the growing demand for cement in the state internally. The total demand for cement in 2003 was estimated at 12.7 lakh tonnes, while as, the total production of cement in the state stood at around 4.55 lakh tonnes during the same period. The demand for Portland cement is expected to increase significantly both within the state and outside as the construction industry is booming and is expected to keep the same pace in the future as well.

The cement industry in the state not only enjoys active and growing market within the state, but its market extends beyond the state boarders, however, there is a need for the state's cement industry to be efficient in all respects. There is a sufficient scope for the expansion of this industry in the state. The industry is full of promise and if properly planned and developed, it could become one of the major industries in the state. The government should encourage private investment in the industry and itself assume the role of a facilitator only. The state government should accelerate the pace of development of minerals, ensure easy availability of various resources to the mineral based industries and help them to exploit the market potential falling beyond the state boarders.

The state is also suited to the manufacture of chalk crayons, surgical plaster, plaster of Paris and building plaster as state is well endowed with large reserves of fairly high grade gypsum. Gypsum constitutes a major input for the manufacture of these products which enjoy sufficient market in the fast expanding construction industry and orthopedic hospitals for surgical plaster. Presently there is no such unit in the state manufacturing above products thus, providing scope for the commercial exploitation of gypsum in these related lines of activity. The manufacturing units located in the state would be enjoying sufficient competitiveness on account of availability of raw-material. With the coming up of a bridge on the river Jehlum near the gypsum deposits at Baramullah, now the gypsum mining there would be easy and less costly affair.

Quartzite: Quartzite, a non-metallic mineral found in different forms is another industrially important mineral. It forms a basic raw-material in glass industry in the manufacturing of glassware. Jammu and Kashmir is fortunate enough to have sufficient reserves of quartzite suitable for making glassware. Two brands of quartzite have been found in Anantnag district in the area of Gugaldar-Hapatnar. Huge reserves of quartzite have also been reported from Batal Hill area of Poonch district. "Tests carried out by the Central Ceramic and Glass Research Institute, Calcutta, have shown that quartzite found in Batal Hill area is suitable for manufacturing "B" grade glass and after magnetry it can suitably be used to manufacture high class glass even crystal glassware"(Industrial Potential Survey, 1972).

According to Geology and Mining Department, J&K government, the quartzite found in Hapatnar area is well suited for glass industry except for the manufacture of optical glasses. But, the quartzite found in Kashmir province is in rock form which would need to be crushed before it can be used for making glassware. The total reserves at Hapatnar are estimated to be of the order of six lakh tonnes. It is unpleasing to see that the industrial potential lying in this natural resource remains totally un-taped. There is a good scope for the manufacture of glassware except optical glasses and the units to be located in the state would be enjoying cost competitiveness in local markets on account of the availability of basic raw-material i.e. quartzite and the absence of any transit breakage and transportation costs. The glass industry in the state is full of promise. The market for the products of this industry is expanding manifold. However, to draw maximum dividends from this natural economic advantage, the government is required to facilitate the manufacturing of glassware from the quartzite available in the state by developing mines, encouraging genuine entrepreneurs for exploration of this natural resource and by providing technical support.

Bauxite and White Clay: Bauxite an important metaliferrous mineral is required in aluminum industry, regractory, abrasive industry etc. Gibbsitic and diasporic type of bauxites are mostly found in India, the former finds its use in aluminum industry etc. While as, the latter can be used in aluminum industry but not in abrasive industry. Sizeable deposits of bauxite are found around Reasi and Poonch in Jammu province. However, the bauxite found in Jammu province, apart from being diasporic is highly siliceous, thus restricting its use in aluminum industry, but the deposits can be used in regractory and abrasive industries.(Sadhu

& Singh, 1984) The total reserves of bauxite are estimated to be of the order of 8.69 million tonnes (see Table 2.8 for the total reserves of bauxite at different places with mineral characteristics). This metaliferrous mineral provides some scope for abrasive industry in Jammu Province. At present, there is only one abrasive manufacturing unit in the state located at Gangyal industrial estate, Jammu, which caters to the demands of the local market only. In fact, the market for abrasive industry located in Jammu province extends beyond the state boarders.

Table 2.8: Estimated Reserves of Bauxite in J&K State as on 1995-96

Characteristics	Reserves (in Mt. Tonnes)
• Pisolitic/ Semi Pisolitic bauxite	2.84
• Aluminous Bauxite	3.15
• Kaslinite Bauxite	2.70
Total	**8.69**

Source: Industrial Potential Survey of Jammu and Kashmir, 'Report of a Study Team Sponsored by the IDBI, RBI, ICICI & IFCI, (1972).

White Clay: The deposits of white clay suitable for utilization in ceramic industry have been found in Jungle-Gali, Panhasa and Salal areas of Jammu province. According to the studies conducted, the clay has been reported to be suitable for the manufacturing of ceramic ware, high tension electric pole insulators, sanitary wares and potteries. The total reserves are estimated to be around one lakh tonnes. At present, there is no industrial unit in the state manufacturing ceramic wares. One unit namely M/s Kashmir Ceramics Ltd. was set up in the private sector at Kathua to manufacture ceramic ware using white clay from the Jungle-gali area. But, the unit could not do well reportedly partly due to poor quality, competition from big names in the industry and partly due to inefficient marketing effort and poor sales network. The factory then has shifted to the manufacturing of high tension electric pole insulators and sanitary ware.

Later on the unit was completely shut down. It is unfortunate to note here that no concerted effort has been made in the state to develop ceramic ware industry. The units to be located in the state would enjoy definite cost competitiveness at least in the local markets, however, there will be stiff competition from big houses which calls for total commitment to the quality and needed to evolve better marketing strategies. There is sufficient demand of ceramic ware, potteries and sanitary wares and the same is expected to grow with the increase in the standard of living of the people. In fact, the future for this industry in the country is quite promising.

Forest Resources

Forests constitute an important renewable resource serving the society in a number of ways. Forests confer many benefits on to the economies both in material and non material form and the magnitude of benefits are ample quality wise and quantity wise. Forests contribute to ecology, ensure soil conservation thereby reducing intensity of floods, regulate moisture and stream flow, supply variety of raw materials to industries, like timber to wood based industry and fuel wood, revenues to government. Forests, which are also the home for green pastures and flora and fauna, form a vital element for achieving a congenial natural environment for the economy. Jammu and Kashmir is fortunate enough to have sufficient forest wealth. The total forest area in the State as in 2002-03 was 20230 sq kms. which forms over 19 per cent of the total geographical area falling this side of the line of control (see Table 2.9 showing forest area by composition in the state). The area under forests is more in Kashmir province and least in Ladakh division. Of the three provinces, Kashmir is richer in forest wealth. State forests which are famous for scenic beauty and for many health resorts also constitute an important source of revenue to the state exchequer and source of raw-material to wood based industries in the state. The main raw-materials that can be

Table 2.9: Specie-wise Provisional Forest Area by Composition (Sq. Kms)

Classification wise	1996-97	1998-99	1999-00	2000-01	2001-02	2002-03
Coniferous (soft wood)						
• Deodar	1277	1075	1075	1075	1075	1075
• Chir	1825	1825	1825	1825	1825	1825
• Kail	1991	1969	1969	1969	1969	1969
• Fir	3534	3401	3401	3401	3401	3401
• Others	9698	10075	10075	10075	10075	10075
Total Coniferous	18325	18345	18345	18345	18345	18345
Non-coniferous(soft & hard wood)						
• Noncommercial reserves	1905	1885	1885	1885	1885	1885
• Rakhs and Wild life reserves	1962.90	1962.90	1962.90	1962.90	1962.90	1962.90
Grand Total	22192.9	22192.9	22192.9	22192.9	22192.9	22192.9

Source: *Digest of Statistics*, Directorate of Economics and Statistics, Planning and Development Department, J&K Government, 2002-03

extracted from state forests for any meaningful industrial activity includes, timber for joinery mills, plywood industry, willow for sports good industry, herbs for drug industry, soft wood for rayon grade pulp unit and Rosin and turpentine. Such forest based industries in the state would not be falling short of raw materials and will be able to explore the demand for their end products in other parts of the country.

Plywood/Board Industry: The demand for veneer sheets, plywood etc. in the construction industry is rapidly increasing due to increase in construction activities and partly due to shortage of certain construction materials, such as, iron, steel etc. The increasing standard of living of the people in the country is going to supplement the demand on continuous basis. The veneer sheets, plywood and other plywood products are extensively used in the ceilings, in making of cupboards, doors and various furniture items. The demand for wooden products is more in cold temperate regions. The veneer sheets, plywood etc. can be made both from soft and hard wood. The state of Jammu and Kashmir is well endowed with different species of soft and hard wood like, Kail, Chir, Chinar, Popular etc. Thus raw-material would be no problem to the plywood industry in the state particularly in Kashmir province. To utilize the large resources of both soft wood and hard wood, a unit in the Joint sector, namely Plywood Industries Ltd., with M/S Shaujain as partners was established in 1962 with an authorized capital of Rs one crore to manufacture plywood, hard board and chip board. The unit, however, did not run well for various reasons and finally taken over by JKI in 1976 after a prolonged closure. At present, the unit remains closed for manufacturing operations as was being marred by number of inefficiencies like other public sector enterprises. Although, long back JKI has drawn a plan to restructure the whole unit with the installation of modern technologies and other facilities yet, the same could not be done due to unknown reasons.

In the recent past, many units were set up to manufacture veneer sheet in Kashmir division, but most of these units were closed subsequently. At present there are just a few units manufacturing veneer sheets, plywood etc. in the state. In fact, the potential in plywood industry remains grossly under-utilized, in spite of having rich forest base. The demand for plywood, veneer sheets etc. in the state is largely fulfilled from the imports from other states. This industry has a much in stock to offer to the industrial economy of the state. The units to be located in the state would be enjoying cost competitiveness in the local markets as compared to the manufactures from outside the state. Marketing of plywood, veneer sheets etc. is not a difficult task in the absence of any branding in the industry. The future of this industry is full of promises in this growing economy.

Joinery: Joinery items which include, doors, window frames, shutters, ceiling, and paneling are much in demand in spite of new developments that have taken place in the shape of angle iron frames etc. The angle iron frames are not readily acceptable to the customers as these do not give a desired look and also due to many other inherent defects. In fact, a number of alternatives have been developed to replace wooden joinery items, which met with a very little success, particularly in cold temperate zones. Different joinery items made out of impregnated wood give definitely a far better look as compared to angle iron and are preferred by the customers of all classes. In the sub-provinces of Jammu and Kashmir occur valuable coniferous forests where are home to Deodar, Kail, Chir and Fir, which are famous for fine texture, durability and strength. Deodar is the only available coniferous timber in the country which is next to teak in all its physical, mechanical and other properties. Further, the joinery items made out of deodar wood behave very well in tropical climate and are also famous for its look when sprayed with clear glass varnish. People have a tremendous desire for the items made out of deodar and Kail. As on 2002-03, the total forest area in the state under *'Deodar'* is 1,075 sq kms, under *'Kail'* 1,969 sq kms, 3,401 sq kms is under *'Fur'* plantation and under *'Chir'* trees is 1,825 sq kms. (see table 2.9 showing specie-wise provisional forest area in the state) The total output from the state forests is around 162.46 thousand cubic meters in the year 2002-03.

Realizing the tremendous industrial potential that the state enjoys in joinery, the state government had established two joinery mills in the public sector, one in Srinagar and the other at Jammu to manufacture different joinery items with the total plant capacity of 85,000 shutters and frames per annum on two shift basis. The product range of the two mills comprise of doors, windows, shutters and frames, common and sophisticated articles of furniture, tongued and grooved ceiling and paneling, profiled decorative timber and prefabricated timber hutments.

The products are marketed within the state to different government departments and outside the state to different agencies, like Delhi Development Authority, Haryana Housing Board, Utter Pradesh Housing Board and National Building Corporation Ltd. Delhi. However, both of these mills were gutted in a mysterious fire destroying number of valuable machines. At present the two mills are operating, but at a very low scale, leaving enough of opportunity to the competitors to encroach upon their market share. In 1988, JKI has drawn investment plant to install new plant and machinery in these two mills, but so far no headway has been made in its implementation. In addition to these two public sector units, there are many more private units operating in small scale sector which are spread all over the state catering to the requirements of local market. However, some of these units at present stand closed either due to raw-material problems or due to personal failures. Further, these units are lacking organized sales agencies as such have failed to penetrate deep into the market.

Joinery industry in the state is full of promises and has still much more to offer. Although, the joinery industry in the state has entered into the national market but still most of the market segments remains untapped. This industry of the state can benefit much more both within and outside the state, but there is a need to organize and develop the industry on the modern lines. There is also a need to develop new designs, achieve cost efficiency, evolve regressive publicity in the national market and evolve effective marketing strategies.

Willow and Mulberry: Sports have become an integral part of modern generations and are taking its roots in all societies irrespective of geographical location, race, religion, colour etc. In this modern world, sports have become a mark of identity for different nations. A sport has become a lucrative profession and every youth irrespective of class play games either out of love or to make a future out of it. Hockey is the national game of our country, however, cricket is more famous followed by football in the country. On account of an improvement in the standard of living, the youth in the country are now playing with the equipments made in modern factories. But the practice of playing with better equipments in the state or else where in the country is in its early stage.

Willow trees are the only species which are best suited for cricket bats and mulberry trees for hockey sticks and stumps. Cricket bats made out of willow is known for desired stroke play and durability. The state of Jammu and Kashmir is fortunate enough to grow willow and mulberry trees. As a matter of fact, Kashmir valley is the only place in the country suitable for growing willow trees. The willow in Kashmir valley is grown in plains and can be found almost at all the road sides, river banks etc. There are huge plantations of willow. Mulberry trees are also grown in abundance in the valley, however, used mainly for getting leaves for cocoon rearing. The total annual yield of willow in the state has been estimated at around1.5 lakh cubic meters.

As early as in 1938, the state government established a factory namely 'Kashmir Willow Works' at Miran Sahib, Jammu to manufacture cricket bats, stumps and hockey sticks, which was later on taken over by JKI. At present, there are many private concerns which are actively engaged in the industry both in Jammu and Kashmir provinces. However, the concentration of these units is around Bijbehara, as one can find huge temporary stalls of semi-finished bats along the national highway around Bijbehara. Although sufficient production capacity has been created in the industry, however, most of these units are ill-equipped both in terms of technology and resources.

As a result, these have failed to make the best use of this potential resource. In fact, the initiative by real entrepreneurs is missing in this industry. The people who are in this industry are because their forefathers have passed on this skill to them. As a result these have failed to organize their units on modern lines to derive maximum dividends from this potential industry. At present raw form bats in cleft form are surreptitiously exported. There is immense potential for developing cricket bat industry in the state not only to meet the country's requirements but also to tap the export potential. To make the best use of this natural economic advantage, there is a need to develop this industry on scientific lines, and the government has a definite role to play in the development of this potential industry. The market for this industry lies beyond national boarders, therefore, it is suggested that the JKI unit at Miran sahib should explore export markets. The government has taken steps to develop separate industrial estate at Bijbehara for cricket bat manufacturers and this step is expected to go a long way in promoting this potential industry provided the government bans export of clefts outside the state and at the same time encourage investment in this industry.

Rosin and Turpentine: The forests of J&K state are also rich enough in resin, the important industrial raw-material which is being collected from pine trees which are grown in abundance in the state forests. The resin so collected is then distilled into Rosin and Turpentine. From resin easter gum and phenolic modified resin is manufactured and turpentine oil can be fractionally distilled into Aloha pinene, Beta pinene, Delta careen and Longifolene. Easter gum and phenolic modified resin are required in the manufacture of glossy varnishes and paints, chewing gums, paper and plastic products. Turpentine oil with its derivatives finds its use in paint industry and in many other industries. At present, there are three public sector units in the state working under the banner of JKI which are actively engaged in the extraction of rosin and turpentine oil and their derivatives. The Modern Rosin and Turpentine Factory, Miran Sahib Jammu which is equipped with modern technology, further processes

Rosin and Turpentine for derivatives through fractional distillation. These units are operating almost at 100 percent capacity and are. There is sufficient demand pull for Rosin and Turpentine oil in the country that is why sales do not pose any problem to these units. In fact, these are only units of JKI which are earning profits and provide funds for meeting the overhead expenses of other units of the corporation.

The sufficient and growing market avenues and the availability of fresh oleo-resin in abundance, provide scope for the expansion of this industry in the state. For the purpose, there is a need to encourage more and more local people in the collection of oleo-resin by rill method and also widen the area of collection. The forest department may be engaged in the collection of oleo-resin particularly in the areas not accessible by the common people. Further, the Rosin and Turpentine oil output should first be processed in to different derivatives then be exported outside the state, which will provide scope for fractional distillation units in the state.

In spite of having definite comparative advantage in this natural resource like Rosin and Turpentine oil, the basic ingredients for varnish and paint industry, the state could not make any worthwhile progress in paint industry. Number of units both in Kashmir and Jammu provinces of the state were established to produce paints and varnishes, however, today almost all of them stand closed thus posing a question what causes their failure? Some paint units have stopped their operations reportedly due to the failure to maintain good quality and others due to raw-material problems. In varnish production some progress has been made in the state, however, there is still a long way to go. Seemingly there is no such impediment that can hinder the development of paint industry in the state into one of the prominent industries. In fact, state enjoys definite comparative advantage in basic raw-material for paint industry, thus provide some leverage to the units located in the state to compete. There is a need to think seriously that how this industry can be developed into a viable and potential industry in the state.

Pulp-Paper-Viscose Production: Wood particularly soft wood forms the basic raw-material for pulping unit for the manufacture of rayon grade pulp, paper and viscose fiber. Jammu and Kashmir forests are well endowed with soft wood like fur and spruce and it is estimated that these species yield on a average 52 lakh cubic meters per annum. The pilot studies conducted by the National Chemical Laboratory, Pune for producing the rayon grade pulp from fur and spruce available in the state forests have revealed that rayon grade pulp of the specifications conforming to international standards could be produced from the soft wood found in the state (Industrial Potential Survey, 1972). Earlier, the establishment of two pulping projects in the state was under active consideration, one each at Jammu province and Kashmir province. One such unit in the public sector with a planned capacity 100 tonnes per day in Kashmir province and the other in private sector by house of Modi's at Jammu. There was also a plan to establish chemical plant in the state to meet the requirements of the two pulping projects. For unknown reasons, both the projects could not come up in the state.

The pulping unit in the state is found to be a viable activity and which would provide direct and indirect employment to thousands of people and may also give birth to many other industrial units in the state. The study team for industrial potential in the state (1972) was surprised to see that despite the availability of rich forest resources no pulping unit has been set-up in the state and suggested that the reserves are quite adequate to sustain a good size pulping project. Establishment of a multi-grade pulp-cum-paper-cum viscose fiber project in the state would be a welcome step provided it does not pose any problem to our forests which have commitments towards other age-old wood based industries and also did not cause any ecological imbalance. There is also a need to explore the possibilities of using popular, willow etc. in the manufacture of rayon grade pulp and paper which are grown in abundance in the plains of the state. To make best use of soft wood available in the state in abundance, setting up of two pulping units one each at Jammu and Kashmir provinces would be a viable proposition.

Medicinal Herbs

State forests are also the home for many valuable medicinal herbs which grow wild. Some herbs are also cultivated in the plains of the state. The medicinal herbs that are found in the forests and cultivated include, Belladona, Artemesia, Dioscorea, Pyretherum, Acontitum, Digitalis, Hyoseyamus, Kuth, Colchium, Luteum etc. These herbs have been found to be very suitable for the manufacturing of drugs and other pharmaceutical agents, like Sentonin, Diosgenine, Belladonna flio, Colchicine, Sapogenin, Prethru-oleo-resin etc. It is being reported that the different herbs found in the state forests are in abundance. Kuth which is being found extensively in Kishan Ganga forests is presently exported without any value addition. Thus the availability of valuable medicinal herbs in sufficient quantities and active demand for their medicinal extractions provided scope for intensive commercial exploitation of these herbs. However, at present this potential resource remains grossly under-utilized.

At present pharmaceutical unit at Baramullah, Kashmir which was established in the year 1928, is utilizing some herbs in the production of Sentonin. The two drug research laboratories, one each at Srinagar and Jammu are also using some of the herbs on pilot plant at semi-commercial scale. It is stated that the condition of both of these laboratories is not satisfactory. "The Sentonin, which was enjoying monopoly and brisk demand till 1978 when synthetic products like peperzin derivatives were introduced in the market (Status paper on JKI). In fact there is still a demand for Sentonin produced at Baramullah both in national and international markets, only the monopoly that it was enjoying till 1978, has been lost after the introduction of peperzine derivatives. The demand for Diosgenine, Belladona folio, Sapogenin, Pyrethrum-oleo-resin, Colchine etc. that can be produced from the herbs found in the state enjoys very good market. In fact this natural economic advantage of the state provides scope for some industrial activities based on these herbs. Prospects of setting-up some units with a wide product range preferably by science graduates are bright. To realize the maximum dividends from these natural resources, among other things the following few steps are needed to be taken:

- The Kuth Act which prohibits the private cultivation of medicinal plants be repealed so that the cultivation of medicinal plants is undertaken on commercial basis at a large scale by the people.
- Although the state has established two regional Drug Research Laboratories One each at Jammu and Srinagar. However, there are clear indications that these Laboratories have done little with regard to the commercial exploitation of medicinal herbs found in the state. To make a best use of these natural resources, an equal need is to intensify research on medicinal plants. For this purpose, the responsibility lies with the universities of the state, however, the two Drug Research Laboratories have catalytic role to play in this regard.
- Awareness among the masses in general and rural people in particular about the identification, collection, conservation and cultivation need to be intensified.

Summary

The state of Jammu and Kashmir, located on the extreme of northern India is famous for its scenic beauty and landscape all over the world. Agriculture is the main sector of the state's economy. Due to the limited cultivable land and serve agro-climatic conditions, the development of agriculture at large scale is ruled out in the state. Large scale industrialization is the only way out to take the state out from age old stagnation and economic backwardness. However, the peculiar physical conditioning of the state, like extreme location, difficult mountainous terrain, transportation bottlenecks, and extreme climatic conditions which cannot be improved upon except transportation to some extent, limits the scope for industrialization. Where state does not enjoy the comparative advantage in natural resources, industries in such areas can be taken-up at a small scale to cater the local demand.

On the positive side, the state is well endowed with some proven large mineral resources, like limestone, gypsum, quartzite, coal and lignite. The state is fortunate enough to be rich in forest wealth and some agricultural and horticultural products. Due to temperate climatic conditions, the state is the only place in the country highly suitable for rearing Uni-voltine and Bi-voltine silk worm races which are famous for high quality silk. The definite comparative advantage which the state enjoys in these natural resources provides sufficient scope for industrialization in the lines based on these resource endowments. Cement industry, Gypsum based industry, joinery mills, ply-board industries, turpentine and rosin extraction units, paints and varnishes manufacturing units, apple juice plants, asparagus and mushroom canning industry, leather tanneries, Glass Industry, woolen textiles, silk industry etc. have a lot to offer to the states industrial economy. The market for such industries falls beyond the state boarders as well. State is also gifted with scenic beauty, world famous health resorts, fascinating landscape and historical legacies in craftsmanship skills, thus enjoying a distinct and important place in the hotel industry and handicrafts. The state has not been able to develop these industries to their full potential so far.

References

Bamzai, P. K. (1979), 'A History of Jammu and Kashmir', Metropolitan Book Company Ltd., Delhi.

Digest of Statistics, (2002-03), Planning & Development Department, Govt. of Jammu & Kashmir.

Gain A. (1991), 'Labour–Management Relations: A Study of Textile Industry in Jammu and Kashmir', Concept Publishing Company, New Delhi.

Industrial Potential Survey of Jammu and Kashmir, 'Report of a Study Team sponsored by the IDBI, RBI, ICICI & IFCI, (1972).

Industrial Potential Survey of District Srinagar, 'Directorate of Industries and Commerce and Small Industries Services Institute (SISI), Srinagar, (1973).

Kesar U. (1980), "Wonders of Sericulture", Kashmir Today, IV (9-10), PP. 14-15.

Khan A. R. (1981), "Sericulture and Kashmir", Kashmir Today, Volume 12, PP. 14-16.

Khursheed A. (1982), "Silk Originated in Kashmir and not in China", Kashmir Today, Volume 12, PP. 22

Nisar A. (1987), 'Problems and Management of Small Scale and Cottage Industries', Deep and Deep Publications, New Delhi.

Sadhu A. N. and Singh A. (1984), 'Jammu and Kashmir Economy', Trikuta Publishing House, Jammu.

Shah A. M. (1989), "Production Problems of Silk Industry of Kashmir", Unpublished M.Phil Thesis, Submitted to the Department of Commerce, University of Kashmir, Srinagar

Status Report of JKI, Jammu and Kashmir Industries Ltd. Srinagar, J & K State.

Status Report of JKML, Jammu and Kashmir Minerals Ltd. Srinagar, J & K State.

3

Industrial Economy: Structural Analysis

Introduction

At the time of independence there was no worthwhile industrial base in the state. The industrial sector was consisting of some cottage industries and a few factories. However, handicraft was the main industrial industry in the state and it continues to occupy a place of pride in the state's economy. It was Sultan Zain-ul-Abdin who introduced handicraft skills in the state during his reign from 1420-1470 AD and made all out efforts to develop this industry. The later rulers of the state also contributed to the development of handicrafts in the state. "However, during the reign of Maharaja Hari Singh, the last Dogra ruler of the state, this industry got some set-back as his policy was to replace hand made articles by machine-made goods" (Nisar, 1987). In fact he was aiming to introduce modern means of production and replace hand-made goods by the machine-made products. This prestigious industry of the state has many ups and downs right from the beginning. Over and above the handicraft industry, there were also some factories in the state, which included Silk filatures at Srinagar and Jammu, Karan Singh Woolen Mills, Silk weaving factory Rajbagh, Kashmir Pharmaceutical works, Baramullah, Rosin and Turpentine factory, Miran Sahib and Kashmir Willows, Miran Sahib. According to Bamzai (1979) "Silk weaving, Smithy, Casting and Molding of metals, Pottery, Glass manufacturing and Bangles were developed in ancient Kashmir".

The industrial census of 1911 indicates the existence of 57 factories in which 12,128 males and 266 females were employed (see Table 3.1 for the number of units in different industries along with employment). A textile was the major industry constituting 24.56 percent of the total industrial units with an employment of 4,930 persons. This industry was mainly consisting of silk spinning, shawl making, carpet weaving and manufacture of woolen blankets. Silk industry is the age old industry of the state and Kashmir silk is famous for its texture and beauty throughout the world.

Table 3.1: Number of Industrial Units Along with Employment in Different Industries in J&K State (Census 1911)

Industry	No. of Units	% of Total	Employment	% of Total
Textile	14	26.66	1930	39.78
Wood	9	15.79	1445	11.66
Industries of Dress	8	14.04	224	1.81
Building	7	12.28	588	4.75
Production & Transformation of Physical Forces	6	10.53	172	1.72
Construction of Means of Transport	5	8.77	4528	36.53
Industries of Luxuries	4	7.02	287	2.31
Metal	4	7.02	126	1.02
Furniture	1	1.75	26	0.21
Growing of Special Products	1	1.75	26	0.21
Total	57	100.00	12,394	100.00

Source: Census of India (1911), Kashmir, Part I, P No. 231.

Prior to 1947, agriculture was the main stay of the people in the state employing near about 90 percent of the total work force. However, this sector of the state's economy was suffering from many inhibiting factors like severe-agro climatic conditions, single cropping, low yielding seeds; crude and conservative methods, lack of proper irrigation and in egalitarian agrarian social structure characterized by feudal and semi–feudalism. The area under cultivation was 4.9 lakh hectares only viz. 4.25 percent of the total reported area. In fact, there was over–dependence on agriculture. People were finding it difficult to find a work. *'Beggary'* was common in the state during the reign of *Dogra* rule. In fact, the whole of the state was entangled in the chains of poverty and underdevelopment.

Post-1947 Industrial Scenario

Till 1947, the state of Jammu and Kashmir was a sovereign state throughout its life. But after the dawn of British rule in India, a part of the Kashmir was annexed by Pakistan and the other part by India through a much talked about instrument of accession signed by the then Maharaja of Kashmir. At the time of accession to India, the state was having a very little industrial base with very poor industrial infrastructure. In 1948-49 the installed capacity for electric power was merely to the tune of 6.5 MWs and the total road length was to the order of just 3460.45 kms (Directorate of Information). The means of communication were very little. At the time of independence, there were a few industrial units worth mentioning owned by the government. The silk industry was the major industry of the state providing direct and indirect employment to thousands of people. Large number of people were also engaged in handicraft industry which was mainly concentrated in Kashmir valley. The share of J&K in the industrial production of the country was only 1.26 percent in 1960-61. Immediately after 1947, the war between India and Pakistan in Kashmir gave a heavy setback to the little industrial base particularly export oriented units in the state as can be observed from the following figures. Of the 99 registered factories in 1946, the number of factories declined to 60 in 1947, 54 in 1948 and to only 33 in 1950. The annual production of 11 cottage crafts and art industries declined from Rs. 1.63 crore in 1947 to Rs. 23.10 lakh in 1950 (Nisar, 1987).

Soon after independence, there was confusion in the minds of industrialists in the country about the pattern of industrialization the country will follow. Some industrialists were apprehending that all the industries will be nationalized. To remove all such doubts of nationalization and to provide industrial peace for private investment, the government of India immediately after independence in 1948 announced its first industrial policy, which had classified the industries into four categories, viz; State Monopolies, the industries for exclusive investment of government, the industries where private investment is allowed, however, subject to the approval of the government and the industries where ownership and control is left in the hands of private entrepreneurs. The role of cottage and small scale industries was duly recognized and the government's role and responsibility in the development of this sector was also emphasized. In the same year, the Industrial Finance Corporation was set–up to meet the long term financial needs of the industry. In 1951, the Industrial Development and Regulation Act was also passed to regulate the process of industrialization in the country. The Act was extended to the state of Jammu and Kashmir also to bring it within the ambit of the Industrial Policy Resolution of the centre.

On account of certain developments witnessed by the country, like, enactment of constitution, acceptance of socialistic pattern of society by the parliament etc. the government under the stewardship of then Prime Minister Jawaharlal Nehru in April 1956 replaced 1948 policy resolution by new industrial policy. The industrial policy of 1956 has given new classifications of industries. Seventeen industries were listed in 'Schedule A' for exclusive investment by the government. Another 12 industries were grouped in 'Schedule B' which will be progressively owned by the state and the private entrepreneurs also allowed to supplement the efforts of the state. The rest of the industries were left for private participation. Realizing the employment potential of cottage and small scale industries, the 1956 policy resolution emphasized to promote and develop this sector and for the same purpose came up with the package of incentives and measures to protect them from large scale industries like, subsidies, preference in the allocation of raw materials, reservation of lines of production for small sector etc. The policy also provided for the establishment of industrial estates and the rural community workshops to overcome their deficiencies. Achieving balanced regional development, providing better place to labour in the industries and coordinated development of public and private sectors were the other directions of the 1956 policy resolution.

Industrial policy 1956 was considered as the landmark in the history of Indian Industrial Economy. It was regarded as the economic constitution of the country. The policy had put more emphasis on state enterprises and simultaneously limited the role of private sector. Bureaucrats were left with the powers to decide about the fortunes of industrial units. The serious lapses were found by Hazari Committee and Dutt Committee in the grant of licenses. In the light of the recommendations by the planning commission, the administrative reforms commission and the industrial licensing inquiry committees, the government announced its new Industrial licensing policy in 1970, which was further amended in 1973 to stimulate growth in the priority sector by allowing the large business houses and also foreign concerns and their subsidiaries to enter into core sectors. The new licensing policy was further modified in 1976 to regularize the unauthorized expansion by large industrial houses.

In 1976 Janata government came in power at the centre and announced its new Industrial policy in 1977 with the rationale that the industrial policy of 1956 has resulted in widespread unemployment, rural-urban disparities etc. The new policy carried many elements of the 1956 policy and to generate more employment and to achieve balanced regional development, more thrust was placed on the development of cottage and small scale industries. The new policy has categorized small sector into three categories viz: cottage and household industries, tiny sector and small scale industries and came-up with the package of assistance for the promotion of each category of this sector. The items reserved for the sector has been increased from 108 items to 800 items and number of monetary and fiscal incentives were provided in the new policy. The policy also envisaged to set-up 'District Industries Centres at each district to provide all services to the entrepreneurs under one roof and directed to create separate wing in Industrial Development Bank of India to meet the credit needs of the small scale sector. Special incentives were announced for the industries located in backward areas. The new policy resolution has expanded the role of public sector, encouraged participation of labour in equity, prescribed areas for large industries and intended to control the disproportionate growth of big industrial houses. The Janata government also declared that the control should lay in the Indian hands, however, in case of hundred percent export oriented industries, the government may allow foreign control. Although, this new policy had emphasised on the development of small scale and cottage industries yet, the government allocated only 2 per cent of sixth plan outlay as against 4 per cent in the last plan towards this sector.

In the bye-elections of 1980, the Janata government was defeated and Congress under the stewardship of Mrs. Indira Gandhi came into power with a thumping majority. The new government immediately in 1980 announced new industrial policy based on the industrial policy resolutions of 1956. The new policy aimed at achieving optimum utilization of installed capacities, achieving higher employment generation, promotion of export oriented industries, promoting economic federalism etc. Major concessions were announced for the small, medium and large scale industries and the emphasis was laid on the balanced development of all sectors. The government through the new industrial policy aimed to develop economic viability of the villages and achieve economic federalism by setting- up some nucleus plants in ancillaries. Such policy initiatives were also enunciated to achieve the efficiency in public sector enterprises, to regularize the excess capacity, for the modernization of industries, technology transfer and research and development. The policy statement also noted the growing Industrial sickness and recognized the need to devise an early warning system to detect sickness at an incipient stage. The mergers and take-overs of sick units were encouraged through different incentives and schemes by the new policy.

Of the different policy statements enunciated from time to time to govern the industrial functioning since 1948, the one announced in 1956 was the major policy statement which held ground all through these years and the subsequent statements made were by and large in the nature of minor changes to 1956 policy. In spite of having sufficient reservoir of different resources, these policy initiatives did not help the country to experience industrial take-off. Realizing that there are some serious lapses in the old policy and the changing global realities, the government of India in 1991 announced new industrial policy which marked a big departure from the old policy. The new policy resolution has transformed the Indian economy into a market economy from socialistic economy. In real the new policy aimed at globalizing the Indian markets through the process of Liberalisation, Privatisation and Globalisation. This new policy statement has redefined the role of public sector; only six lines of activity which are of strategic importance have been left for public sector, the industrial licensing has been abolished except for just 15 specified groups, direct investment allowed up to 51 percent or more, automatic approval to technology transfer in high priority industries.

In fact, new policy statement was directed at getting more foreign investment and achieves more market-orientation of industrial economy. Policy makers regard new policy a step towards 'growing Indian economy as part of the world economy and not in isolation'. Most of the people are highly optimistic about the outcome of new policy however, there are also some people who have some apprehensions about the new economic system that the country adopted since 1991. But the outcome of the new economic system over the last decade or so has proved the critics wrong. In real, the then Finance Minister Dr.

Manmohan Singh in 1991 did nothing of his own; he had just fallen in line with the universal trend.

As in other parts of the Indian union, the different industrial policy statements announced at the centre have set the tone for industrialization in Jammu and Kashmir as well. These policy initiatives have given some flip to the industrial scene in the state particularly in the small scale sector for which the state is more suitable. The state government at its own also came-up with certain policy initiatives and packages of incentives for the promotion and development of industries in the state. Industrial Advisory Board and Industrial Development Board represented by prominent industrialists of the country was set-up to suggest viable industrial projects to be taken in the state. After thorough deliberations, the boards have recommended certain industrial projects viz: cotton spinning mills, worsted yarn spinning mill, manufacture of spun silk from silk waste, manufacture of paper, manufacture of bricks, manufacture of ceramics and sanitary ware at Kathua, renovation of existing rosin and turpentine factory at Miran Sahib, manufacture of decorative veneers, plywood and chip-boards, manufacture of camphor and other allied products and Expansion of medicinal herb cultivation, however, most of these proposed projects could not come-up till today.

In the beginning of seventies, the state government announced a comprehensive set of incentives for the industries located in the state and following the passing of new industrial policy in 1977 at the centre which envisages the setting-up of District Industries Centres, the state government immediately in 1978 followed the direction and has set-up such centres in all districts of the state which have generated some rapid industrialization in almost all districts particularly in the small scale sector. A single window scheme was also introduced in the state where-in all the sanctions like power, water etc. were being granted at one place. In seventies the state government also constituted a 'Development Review Committee' to study the problems and prospects of industrial developments. Industrial potential surveys in the state were also conducted by the team of experts from the central organizations, to look into the industrial potential lying in different sectors in the state.

However, it is surprising to see that most of their recommendations went unheard in the state. The state government also formulated a package of incentives for attracting investments from large business houses of the country, however, the state has failed to get any favourable response from them. Recently in 2004, the state government came-out with the new industrial policy which among other things includes a package of incentives for improving the competitiveness of the industries located in the state. However, the best deal is being offered to the small scale sector. These and other efforts initiated by the state government from time to time have given some push to the industrialization in the state. However, the state needs to go a long way to achieve a meaningful industrial development.

Industrial Development under Five Year Plans

After independence, the Indian union had chosen a socialistic pattern of society, the term was commented in the second Five Year Plan as "essentially this means that the basic criterion for determining the lines of advance must not be private profit but social gain, and that the pattern of development and the structure of socio-economic relations should be so planned that they result not only in appreciable increases in national income and employment but also in greater equality in income and wealth. The benefits of economic development must accrue more and more to the relatively less privileged classes of society and there should be a progressive reduction in the concentration of incomes and wealth.

Like other states in the country, the process of industrialization in the state was started on a planned basis, aiming at achieving economic development mostly on socialistic pattern. So far nine plans have been completed and the tenth plan is in operation. Tables 3.2 and 3.3 which contain data about plan allocations by sectoral break-up under different plans reveal that

Table 3.2: Sector-wise Plan Allocation in the State of J&K (Rs. lakh)

Sectors	1st Plan	2nd Plan	3rd Plan	4th Plan	5th Plan	6th Plan	7th Plan	8th Plan	9th Plan
Agriculture	52.00 (4.51)	267.11 (10.29)	506.66 (8.19)	2260.05 (13.87)	3034.10 (10.89)	16901.03 (18.41)	34245.16 (20.92)	56026.89 (12.39)	108943.50 (14.44)
CD & Co-operatives	36.98 (3.21)	360.02 (13.87)	417.31 (6.74)	266.69 (1.63)	215.97 (0.82)	1345.87 (1.46)	1787.86 (1.09)	5174.36 (1.14)	14635.85 (1.94)
Irrigation & Power	488.14 (42.38)	451.73 (17.41)	1612.63 (26.07)	6670.21 (40.95)	12067.63 (43.32)	21178.59 (23.07)	52221.73 (31.91)	143945.02 (31.84)	161290.49 (21.38)
Industries & Mining	66.49 (5.77)	114.99 (4.443)	175.71 (2.84)	748.15 (4.59)	1945.30 (6.98)	5983.30 (6.52)	9957.24 (6.08)	20575.54 (4.55)	22668.15 (3.00)
Transport & Communication	305.90 (26.56)	516.05 (19.88)	1028.67 (16.63)	2905.03 (17.83)	3084.14 (11.75)	10790.67 (11.75)	25288.48 (15.45)	53884.97 (11.20)	40211.39 (5.33)
Services	178.05 (15.45)	613.46 (23.64)	1480.37 (23.93)	2602.80 (15.98)	5370.16 (19.28)	27658.01 (30.12)	60883.98 (37.20)	124695.06 (27.58)	232186.45 (30.78)
Miscellaneous	24.15 (2.09)	167.60 (6.46)	279.27 (4.51)	730.87 (4.48)	2128.41 (7.64)	15957.30 (17.38)	16238.19 (9.92)	47705.87 (10.55)	174351.86 (23.11)
Total	1151.71 (100.00)	2594.75 (100.00)	6185.09 (100.00)	16284.80 (100.00)	27854.71 (100.00)	91814.83 (100.00)	163662.17 (100.00)	452077.71 (100.00)	754287.75 (100.00)

Note: Figures in Parenthesis Indicate Percentage Plan Allocation to the Total Plan Size.

Source: *Digest of Statistics*, Directorate of Economics and Statistics, Planning and Development Department, J & K Government, 2002-03.

Table 3.3: Growth in Total Plan Expenditure and Sub-Sectors of Industry and Power and Irrigation (Rs. lakh)

Plan	Total Plan Expenditure			Industry & Mining			Power & Irrigation		
	Total Expenditure	Absolute Growth	%age Growth	Total Expenditure	Absolute Growth	%age Growth	Total Expenditure	Absolute Growth	%age Growth
1st	1151.71	-		66.49	-		488.14		
2nd	2594.75	1443.04	125.29	114.99	48.5	72.94	451.73	-36.41	-7.46
3rd	6185.09	3590.34	138.36	175.71	60.72	52.86	1612.63	1160.9	256.98
4th	16284.80	10099.71	163.29	748.15	572.44	325.78	6670.21	5057.58	313.62
5th	27854.71	11569.91	71.04	1945.30	1197.15	160.01	12067.63	5397.42	80.91
6th	91814.83	63960.12	229.62	5983.30	4038.00	207.57	21178.59	9110.96	166.65
7th	163662.17	71847.34	78.25	9957.24	3973.94	66.42	52221.73	31043.14	146.57
8th	452077.71	288415.54	176.22	20575.54	10618.30	106.63	143945.02	91723.3	175.64
9th	754287.75	302210.04	66.84	22668.15	2092.61	10.17	161290.49	17345.47	12.50
Total	1515913.52			62,234.87			399926.17		
Cg		**72.65**			**51.77**			**39.12**	

Note: Cg Stands for Compound Growth.

Source: *Digest of Statistics*, Directorate of Economics and Statistics, Planning and Development Department, J&K Government, 2002-03.

industry and mining has received very low share as compared to other sectors of the economy. Power development and social sector got the most of the investible funds in all the plans. The plan expenditures towards industry and mining was 5.77, 4.43, 2.84, 4.59, 6.98, 6.52, 6.08, 4.55 and 3.00 percent of the total plan outlay respectively right through first plan to ninth plan. It becomes clear from the above figures that the plan outlays towards industry and mining were quite less and were no match to the plan expenditures in the industrially developed states of the country. Right through the first plan to the ninth plan, it was the irrigation and power and social services which have shared the major chunk of plan funds. These two sectors together have shared on an average near about 50 per cent of the total plan funds. However, it is surprising to see that in spite of placing major thrust on these two important sectors right from the beginning that the state still suffers from the lack of adequate social capital and more importantly from power shortages. This prompts one to ask for a detailed scrutiny of the accounts

During the First and the Second five year plans, the state could not witness any industrial progress largely due to weak infrastructural facilities and political chaos and uncertainties prevailing in the state. As a matter of fact, the emphasis in the first two plans was not on industrial development but on power generation and on the development of roads. The meager allocations towards industries which remained underutilized were mostly spent on the establishment of few public sector enterprises and re-organization and expansion of some existing public sector enterprises. In the private sector, the quinquennium did not witness any worthwhile industrial activity.

Up to the third plan period most of the industrial activity in the state was confined to, handicrafts, Sericulture, woolen and some wood based industries. However, the first initiative to industrialize the state was taken in the last years of the second plan by starting work on the development of three industrial estates in the state. However, these three estates remained under-utilized for a long time. In addition to this, Small Industries

Services Institute (SISI) and two Handloom Co-operative societies were established during the second plan to promote and develop small scale industries and handicrafts. Creation of more employment opportunities was the main goal of the third plan and the industries were considered the potential employers by the planners.

Accordingly many proposals were included in the third draft plan for large scale development of industries, in particular, cottage and small scale industries. However, much could not be done towards the industrialization in the state during the third plan due to the freezing of proposed schemes on account of the economy drive that followed the Chinese attack in 1962. During the above plan period some beginning was made in the private sector, particularly in the small scale sector by providing financial assistance to 650 parties (Third Five Year Plan Document). Development and exploration of mineral resources was also included for the first time in the third plan. The percentage plan allocation towards industries and mining was on decline in the first three plans, however in the fourth plan percentage share of industries and mining had gone up. The development and exploration of mineral resources was badly affected in the fourth plan as the allocation to mining has been significantly cut down. It was during the fifth plan the initiative to industrialize the state got some momentum. During the said plan focus was on the development of such industries which are based on locally available raw-materials and suited to our conditions. Many new projects in public sector like Wool Combing Plant, Joinery Mill, Rosin Factories and Scooter Factory were established and some existing public sector enterprises were renovated and expanded. These two plans also laid emphasis on board basing the level of production in handicraft industry and also to disperse it to rural areas. For the purpose, massive training programmes were launched throughout the state.

During seventies the Janata government formulated new industrial policy which laid more emphasis on the development of small scale industries. In falling in line with the central policy, the state government formulated a comprehensive set of incentives for the development of industries in the state particularly small scale industries. As part of the national policy, the scheme of District Industries Centres was launched throughout the state. As a result industrial estates were established in all the districts of the state which in turn has given flip to the process of industrialization particularly in the small scale sector. Due to different policy initiatives taken during the fifth plan, sixth plan and subsequent plans significant progress was made in the industrial development. The number of small scale units went-up to 42,808 in 2000-01 from 2,203 units in 1973-74. The contribution of manufacturing sector which was just about 6 percent in 1987 as against 16 per cent at the all India level, has gone-up to 14.11 percent in 2001-02. The value of industrial production went-up from Rs. 99 crore in 1971 to Rs. 963.67 crore in 2001-02 (Digest of Statistics, 2002-03). The areas of activity that recorded significant growth are rosin, woolen industry, services, cement industry and food production. In the latter stages of the planning era, the unregistered sector which consists of small scale sector, Khadi and village industries witnessed some considerable progress in the state.

Industrial development which was emphasized in the successive economic plans of the state could not witness take-off as yet. However, handicrafts and some small scale industries witnessed some rapid progress. The plan allocations for the industrial sector have revolved round 4-5 per cent of the total outlays only. The plan outlays for the industrial sector were primarily been towards meeting the costs on account of loans, subsidies, acquisition of land for development into industrial estates, publicity and promotional measures and towards increasing the equity capital of state public sector undertakings. In fact, plan priorities were accorded to the development of infrastructure, like power, roads and transport. However, in spite of spending major chunk of plan outlays on power, roads and transport, the state still lacks in desired infrastructure in particular electric power for meaningful industrial activity. Most of the allocations towards power sector were spent on rural electrification than on power generation. This was the major flaw with the policies towards infrastructure development in the state. The whole economy continues to be a victim of this policy flaw. In fact, the policy of big push strategy was needed to be followed towards this sector of crucial importance. The state continues to suffer from acute shortage of electric power and rail link connecting the state with the rest of the country. It is worth mentioning here that industrial estates were established in almost all the districts of the state and number of supporting institutions was created to promote and develop different types of industries in the state. These and other steps taken so far have certainly helped to industrialise the state to some extent.

Industrial Structure

At the time of independence, the industrial activities in the state were mainly concentrated in handicrafts. However, on account of different measures taken by the state since independence, the industrial structure in the state has gone a sea change. The industrial structure of the state is now made of all the three sectors viz; large scale, medium scale and small scale. However, perusal of Table 3.4 reveals that the industrial structure leans quite heavily towards small scale sector. Product-wise in small scale industries, the maximum growth has been reported in hosiery and garments. The uptrend has also been found in food products and miscellaneous

Large industries are almost absent in the state. As on 2001-02, there are only two large scale industrial units, one each in the private sector and in the central public sector and 28 medium scale units. Out of these, 5 units are in the private sector while remaining are in the state public sector. The data contained in table 3.4 makes it clear that the number of units in the public sector have declined over a period of time. The product profile of the state public sector mainly include, textiles, joineries, cement, silk, woolens, rosin and turpentine, sports goods and apple juice concentrates. It is displeasing to note here that all these corporations except J&K Cements Ltd. continue to incur losses, thus turning as parasites for the state.

Table 3.4: Composition of the Industrial Economy of J&K State

Sector	1980-81	1990-91	2000-01	2001-02
Large Scale Industries	3	2	2	2
• State Public Sector	NIL	NIL	NIL	NIL
• Central Public Sector	1	1	1	1
• Private Sector	2	1	1	1
Medium scale Industries	34	32	29	28
• State Public Sector	31	28	25	25
• Central Public Center	1	1	1	1
• Private Sector	2	3	3	2
Small Scale Sector	11,606	50,927	71,172	43,689
• Small Scale Industries	8,428	29,963	42,808	43,689
• Khadi & Village Industries	3,178	20,964	28,364	NA
• Registered Factories	574	833	964	NA

Source: Compiled on the basis of the Data Provided in *Digest of Statistics*, Directorate of Economics and Statistics, Planning and Development Department, J & K Government, 2002-03.

Public Sector Enterprises

In 1944, the policy document commonly known as 'Naya Kashmir' was adopted which emphasized on the importance of the development of public sector enterprises in pushing the economic growth in the state. This document envisaged that the sectors which are important for achieving meaningful development in the state would be kept for the public sector and the private investment shall be promoted in the small scale sector. As a matter of fact, this policy statement was in tune with the industrial policy resolution 1951 of the government of India which set the tone for socialistic pattern of economy. Consequent to this policy resolution which found its place in the constitution of the state, the state government assigned public sector a place of pride and went in a big way in establishing public sector enterprises in the state. At present there are 19 public sector corporations in the state, out of which 9 relate to industrial sector and five of these corporations are manufacturing enterprises while the remaining are industrial promotional corporations

Soon after independence, the Indian Union followed a mixed economic system, however, with more emphasis on Public Sector Enterprises to act as important economic institutions to accelerate economic growth. As such, to quickly build the productive capacity of the economy, wide variety of heavy industries to manufacture basic and capital goods were set-up in the country to provide strong base for the future growth of the economy. The Public Sector was aimed at attaining other purposes including those relevant for the industries. Accordingly, the Public Sector has ventured into the manufacturing of several intermediate and consumer goods. Over the time, the different public sector undertakings have grown rapidly in many fields of economic activity with massive investment and have contributed a lot to the progress of the Indian economy (Aggarwal, 1999). The contribution of Public Sector in the economic development of the country cannot be under-emphasized. There is no doubt that the public sector in the economic development of the country has contributed immensely towards strengthening industrial structure, modernizing technological base in achieving development of different regions and promoting social interest but their working has been faulty too in several respects. These enterprises are condemned for their poor performance on profitability front by all.

Although the public sector at the national level has contributed a lot in setting the pace for accelerated economic growth, though at huge economic cost yet, in the state of J&K the public sector enterprises have failed miserably on the economic front. Their dismal performance has been despite the fact that most of these enterprises have been promoted in those areas where state enjoys definite comparative advantage in resource endowments. Almost all the Public Sector Enterprises in the state have been incurring losses for a long period of time. As a result of continued losses, most of the enterprises have turned red thus causing a big drain on the state exchequer. Their borrowings have piled-up to alarming proportion and even the net worth in most of the cases got totally eroded due to galloping rise in their accumulated losses. The different enterprises in the state live on budgetary support from the state Government, however, at the cost of other developmental programmes. By now their social role has got too thin to hide their commercial nudity. As a mater of fact, promoting social interest was not at all thought to eclipse their economic viability which in itself is an important social obligation (Khan, 2003).

Given the precarious financial health of the state, the state can no more afford to continue to support these economic parasites. As a result, there is a great urgency to take some radical measures with regard to these ailing Public Enterprises. The fast changing economic milieu also necessitates to reform the public sector enterprises. The different Governments in the state have made some modest attempts to reform the state public sector enterprises. In the past, it tried the mechanism of signing the MOU's with these enterprises which, however, did not prove to be useful mechanism due to the fact that the Government has failed to fulfill its commitments as spelled-out in the agreement. The fact of the matter is that the Govt. as yet has not gone whole heartedly to reform the Public Sector. As a matter of fact, the much needed political-will to go ahead with radical measures to reform the state public sector in the state is lacking for that matter in the whole of the country.

A brief description of the various state and central public sector enterprises in the state is given in the following paras:

J&K Industries Ltd.: This corporation was incorporated in 1963. Most of the units that now form a part of Jammu and Kashmir Industries Limited (JKI Ltd.) were being run departmentally by Jammu and Kashmir Industries Department. At the time of take-over by JKI, most of these units were either closed or running on losses. In total 15 units were transferred to JKI at the time of its incorporation and four more units were taken over later on. JKI Ltd. at its own established two rosin factories at Rajouri and Sunderbani, another joinery mill at Jammu and Bemina Woolen Mills at Srinagar. Further number of units were expanded and modernized. However, in 1980 four units namely Brick and Tile factory, Leather Tannery, Match Factory and Handloom Silk Weaving factory were divested from JKI. Further Watch Case Factory, Shodey Factory at Srinagar, Pharmaceutical unit at Baramulla stands closed now and waiting for final disposal.

At present there are 19 units working under the banner of JKI Ltd. out of these 12 units are in Kashmir division and 7 units in Jammu division. The production range of JKI includes Drugs, Silk and silk yarn, Woolen Blankets, Tweed, Worsted, Rosin and Turpentine, Joinery products, Sports Goods, Knitwear and Sole Leather. The value of production and sales has shown an uptrend for the last ten years, however if the prices are taken at constant prices, then there will be down ward trend in both of these variables. (Digest of Statistics, 2002-03). The number of persons employed in JKI Ltd. has declined from 3022 to 2865 persons in 2003. Since 1980 no new unit has been established by the corporation. The corporation has drawn an ambitious corporate plan in 1986, for improving the performance of different units, however, even after the elapse of nearly 17 years no worthwhile headway has been made in this direction. In fact, there is enough scope to improve upon the present poor performance of different units of JKI ltd.

The corporation has been incurring losses since 1986-87 and it reported cumulative cash losses of Rs. 197.32 crore as on 2002-03 (Official Records). It is surprising to see that in most of the units working under the banner of JKI even the cost raw-materials is not being recovered through sales. While as, the units operating in the private sector in the same areas are being found making sufficient profits. As a result of mounting cash losses, the corporation has to depend on the budgetary support from the government to meet various operating expenses. The main reasons reported to be responsible for the poor performance of this corporation are; overstaffing, underutilization of installed capacity due to lack of raw-materials and working capital and old and obsolete plant and machinery. Large scale corruption, lack of professional management and political interference are equally responsible of the dismal performance of this and other public sector enterprises in the state. Godbole Committee on economic reforms has recommended the closure or privatization of various units of JKI except silk units on the rationale that the units have lost their relevance due to the coming-up of the private sector in the related lines

J&K Minerals Limited: Jammu and Kashmir is well endowed with some proven mineral resources which are quite useful for industrial development like, gypsum, limestone, quartzite, lignite, sulphur and borax, coal etc. To make the best of these natural advantages by establishing mineral based industries in the state, a public corporation namely "J&K Minerals Ltd (JKML)" was floated in the state in 1960 with an authorized capital of Rs. 8 crore which stands fully subscribed and paid-up by the state government. The corporation has established 10 mineral based production and mining units in the state namely, 60 TPD cement plant at Wuyan, Kashmir; two pre-caste concrete factories one each at Kashmir and Jammu; coal mining unit at Kalakote; 22.5 MW thermal power plant at Kalakote; gypsum mining at Assar-kanga and Buniyar; lignite mining unit at Nichhahome; marble extraction/cutting/polishing unit at Kupwara; borax extraction plant at Pugga Valley, Ladakh; and Sapphire mining at Paddar, Kishtwar. However, of these 10 units, at present only five units are in operation viz. two precaste concrete factories, coal mining, gypsum mining unit at Assar and Wuyan cement factory. The Wuyan cement factory also remained closed for some time and it was only when the plant was renovated and converted to vertical shaft kiln, it became operational again.

A review of performance of individual units working under the banner of JKML reveals that the different units are running at losses. One of the dominating causes for the losses is that these units are operating much below their installed capacities. This is in spite the fact that the products of these units expect pre-caste concrete plants have ready market. The pre-caste concrete units were established with the purpose to become captive suppliers of Power Development Department. However, with the coming-up of private sector units in this field, these two units have witnessed slump in demand for their products due to their very poor cost competitiveness, which in turn has affected their operating performance very dearly. As a result of under-utilization of installed capacities, the production cost of their products is much higher than the average selling price. For example, for Wuyan cement factory, the cost PMT comes out to be Rs. 14,589.27 while as, the selling price PMT during the same period is Rs. 3,857.64 thus resulting into a loss of Rs. 10,731.63 PMT (Godbole Committee, 1997). At one point of time this sad state of affairs about this corporation is attributed to power shortages and disproportionately more overheads. But even though the corporation has started getting regular power supply after the commissioning of 33 KV line and the installation of transformer, there has been no improvement in the utilization of plant capacities, thus hinting out at some important causes for poor performance.

J&K Cements Limited: The state is well endowed with huge reserves of high grade lime stone and gypsum which offer huge potential in cement industry. To make the best use of these natural advantages, among other things, the state government floated a company namely J&K Cements Ltd in 1974 under the Indian Companies' Act of 1956 to make a commercial exploitation of lime stone and gypsum with which the state is well endowed by establishing a large cement plant. The corporation has established a cement plant at Khrew, Pulwama district with an installed capacity of 600 TPD and has been in commercial production since 1982-83. The company has seen many ups and down during the last 18 years of its life. However during the last few years the company has achieved a significant progress in capacity utilization as can be seen from the data presented in Table. 3.5. The capacity utilization which was a mere 20.10 percent in 1996-97 has gone to 60 percent in 2003-04. The company earned a profit of Rs. 243.73 lakh during the year 2001-02 which is the highest achieved since its inception and the company expects to surpass 2001-02 profits.

Table 3.5: Year-wise Production and Capacity Utilisation in J&K Cements Ltd.

Year	Clinker	Cement (MT)	%age Capacity Utilisation
1996-97	64,755	40,350	20.10
1997-98	81,285	75,830	37.91
1998-99	90,845	11,2075	56.03
1999-00	91,786	96,136	48.06
2000-01	98,149	1,08,802	54.40
2001-02	11,2095	1,35,856	67.93
2002-03	10,6002,	1,13,832	57.50
2003-04	11,9384	1,19,166	60.00

Source: Official Records of J&K Cements Ltd., Srinagar, Kashmir.

As a result of improved profitability over the past few years, the company has repaid all loans and has also paid dividend to the shareholders for three successive years. The company is supplying most of its production to the different state and central government departments and is selling very little of its output in the open market thus enjoying some sort of protection from open market competition. Its cost of production is reported to be more than its competitors. Therefore, its profitability will be under tremendous strain if the comparative advantage of captive supplier to the government departments is removed. To improve its cost competitiveness, the company has started manufacturing blended cement using *'Fly Ash'* after getting authorization from Bureau of Indian Standards (BIS). Further, it has made some major improvements in the plant. However, to improve cost competitiveness to the required level, the company would be required to do much more than this. More importantly, it would need to achieve cent percent utilization of its installed capacity. This would go in a long way in reducing cost of production because the company is operating at 60 percent capacity only. The company is planning to expand its production capacity by 600 TPD at a cost of 64.16 crore. The board of directors and the state government has already conveyed their concurrence for the proposed expansion project. The proposed expansion rises following two pertinent issues:

- The proposed expansion seems to be unwarranted as the company is currently operating only at 60 percent installed capacity.
- Given the new economic realities that have changed the industrial landscape in the country, more appropriate for the JKLM would have been to seek private participation in the proposed expansion plan with some leading national or international player rather than with the government. In the changed economic system the role of the government has changed from that of an entrepreneur and regulator to that of promoter and facilitator. The partnership with the private entity would benefit the company by way of an access to improved technology, sufficient financial support, support of professional management and country-wide dealer network. The private-public partnership trend is picking-up fast in the country in the industrial sector.

J&K Horticulture Produce, Marketing and Processing Corporation: The state of Jammu and Kashmir is also known for different varieties of temperate fruits grown in the state. Apple constitutes a major and important fruit of the state which is grown in larger quantities and exported to different states of the country.

In 2003, the production of apples in the state was 3.05 lakh tonnes. The state government floated a company namely 'J&K Horticulture Produce, Marketing and Processing Corporation' under the Indian companies act of 1956 in 1978 as an International Development Association (IDA) assisted project in horticulture sector with share participation of government of Jammu and Kashmir, government of India and growers with IDA assistance of one percent of service charges per annum. But instead of treating IDA assistance as grant, the IDA contribution was treated as loan at normal bank lending rates. The corporation was aimed at improving the position of marginal fruit growers by streamlining and modernizing the marketing mechanism of horticulture products in the state. For the purpose, the corporation has endeavored to create various infrastructural facilities for the upliftment of fruit industry in the state. However, most of these facilities remains incomplete due to non-availability of funds as can not be operationalised for the benefit of growers. Whatever facility was completed, the same were either gutted in fire or damaged during the period of insurgency or remains occupied by the paramilitary forces, thus depriving fruit growers from their use.

The corporation operates Apple Juice Concentrate Plant which was initially set-up by M/S HCPL Bombay at Doabgah, Sopore. The plant was purchased by the state government at a cost of Rs. 2 crore after the HPCL has closed it due to some technical problems. The plant is running quite successfully, providing market for the culls and off-grade apples to the fruit growers thus helping them in generating additional income from the sale of culls. The successful running of this juice concentrate plant has proved the economic viability of apple juice industry in the state, thereby setting a trend for private entrepreneurs to venture into this potential industry IN the state. The turnover of the plant has registered an increasing trend right from the beginning though with wide fluctuations. It has marketing tie-up with prestigious multinational firms which purchase apple juice concentrate in bulk from JKHPMC. The corporation is also endeavoring to popularize in the local market. To position its product in the local market, however, it needs to do product innovations, introduce tetra pack and more importantly promote its brands aggressively. The other pleasing aspect about the corporation is that it is helping the cherry growers in marketing their products under refrigerated conditions. It is being reported that this has proved very helpful in maintaining quality and in fetching good returns to the growers. For providing refrigeration facilities, the corporation has purchased two refrigerated vans for carrying cherries.

Like other public corporations the corporation is incurring losses. As on 2002, the cumulative losses of the corporation are Rs. 12,255.08 lakh which are more than its net worth (Status Paper of JKHPMC). For this sad state of financial health, the management of the corporation attributes continuing operating losses to host of factors like, depreciation on non-operational assets, cost and time over-runs, implementation of crop loan scheme, lack of provisions for meeting establishment costs and non-operation of various infrastructural facilities which remained incomplete due to the lack of funds and frequent changes in the top management. The other commonly known factors like corruption, management incompetence etc. in the poor financial performance of the corporation can not be discounted.

Promotional Corporations: Number of promotional organizations was created in the state to regulate and promote various types of industries by the state and central governments. Such corporations are engaged in providing different services and facilities to different types of industrial enterprises like, marketing and raw-material support, help in the preparation of project/feasibility reports, providing financial assistance etc. The performance of these promotional agencies is far fetched. As such these organisations have largely failed in making any worthwhile impact on the industrial map of the state even after decades of efforts. The state could not witness an industrial take-off as yet. The important promotional institutions in the state are, State Industrial Development Corporation (SIDCO), Small Scale

Industries Development Corporation (SICOP) and State Financial Corporation (SFC).

State Industrial Development Corporation: For the promotion of large and medium scale industries, the state government in 1969 established State Industrial Development Corporation (SIDCO) as a promotional-cum-financial institution. The corporation was specifically charged with the responsibility of:

- Developing of industrial estates.
- Providing financial assistance to medium and large scale industries in the private and joint sector by way of equity participation or term loans.
- Preparing project profiles/ reports of the projects well suited to the state and to mobalise investments.
- To work for the development of electronic and IT Industry in the state by creating necessary infrastructural facilities

The corporation has so far developed two food parks, one industrial estate for electronic and Information Technology (IT) industry and 6 general purpose industrial estates in the state. Except industrial growth centers at Lassipora, Pulwama and Samba, Jammu which were recently thrown open. All other industrial estates remain fully allotted. There is a proposal with the corporation to develop leather park at Lassipora. The industrial estate at Rangreth which was specifically developed for electronic and IT industry has been turned into general purpose estate. Today industrial enterprises other than electronics and IT are also operating in this estate. This is due to the fact that the corporation has failed miserably in promoting electronic and IT industries in the state. This despite the fact that the valley of Kashmir is ideally suited for IT industries. Contrary to our state, the other states in the country have been very successful in the promotion and development of this sunrise industry.

Initially the corporation was also charged with the responsibility of providing term loans and seed capital to medium and large scale industrial enterprises in the state under the refinancing scheme of IDBI and SIDBI. Now it no more provides finances to industrial enterprises for the reason that the refinance from IDBI and SIDBI is no more available. IDBI and SIDBI could not continue with the refinance facility to the SIDCO as it had failed to repay loans to them. The corporation attributes failure to pay dues to IDBI and SIDBI to the more default rate caused partly due to the disturbed law and order situation in the state since 1989. Careless lending practices by the corporation can not be underemphasized in the poor performance of the corporation.

One of the important activities of the corporation was to prepare project profiles so that the same are marketed to promote investment in the state. To promote investment in the industrial sector in the state, the corporation has promoted some manufacturing units in the joint sector. However, all such units have failed to run successfully resulting in huge losses to the corporation. Such a disturbing feature about the working of this important developmental corporation prompts one to suggest to make a critical analysis of its performance in particular in this regard so that the responsibility for the same is fixed.

Small Scale Industrial Development Corporation (SICOP): On account of extreme location in the national setting, poor resource base, lack of entrepreneurial class, smallness of the markets, infrastructural bottlenecks, etc. the state has witnessed very little industrial activity in the medium and large scale sector. It is believed that the state is more suited to the small scale sector and consequently the state has taken number of policy initiatives from time to time, formulated a comprehensive set of incentives and developed supporting institutions for the development of small scale industries in the state in a big way. One such agency is Small Scale Industries Development Corporation (SICOP) which was floated under the Indian companies' act of 1956 in 1975 as a public corporation with an authorized capital of Rs. 5 crore to promote the development of small scale industries. The role profile of the corporation includes the development of industrial estates, providing raw-material support, providing marketing support by getting supply orders from the government departments, common testing facilities and help in quality control. So far the corporation has developed six industrial estates viz, Gangyal, Birpur and Kathua, Jammu; Zainakote (Srinagar) and Zakura (Srinagar) and sports goods complex at Bijibehara. In Gangyal and Zainakote estates, common testing facilities are available to the industrial units. These estates are reasonably well laid with regard to roads, electric transmission lines, water and drainage. The total strength of these estates is 371 industrial plots which stand fully occupied as on 2003. Apart from these estates, one IID Centre under a centrally sponsored programme, spread over an area of 524 Kanals is nearing completion at Battal Ballian, Udhampur.

The corporation is also supplying selected raw-materials to small scale industries in the state such as, wax, steel, wire for nails etc. A review of the performance of the corporation in this regard has revealed that it has failed in meeting the requirements of raw-materials of small industrial units fully. The units that are being supplied with the raw-materials are provided quite less than the actual requirement, "On an average, a unit holder is provided with the raw-materials only up to the extent of 25 percent of his actual requirement". (Bakal, 1989). Raw-material problem is reported to be one of the factors responsible for sagging performance of this prime sector of the state. So far the corporation did nothing to overcome this problem of the unit holders. As against this, it is indulging in such trading activities that in no way contributes to the achievement the of basic objective for which this corporation was created like sale of coal, RCC pipes, cement, corrugated sheets etc. The role profile of SICOP also includes providing marketing support to the small scale units. The state government has ordered reservation of 15 items for exclusive purchase by the government departments from small scale industries through SICOP. Although the annual marketing turnover which was Rs. 65 lakh in 1975-76 has recorded a substantial growth and has increased to Rs. 2,476.25 lakh in the year 1999-2000 (Official Records) yet, it is far from desirable.

More disquieting feature in this regard is that the corporation has failed in securing the scrupulous observance of the instructions issued by the sate government in this direction by all the government departments. It is amazing to see that the corporation did nothing to explore other markets in this era of globalisation. There has been no effort by the corporation to explore export market for export oriented units. In fact it has misconstrued its role of a marketer to the extent of seeking orders from government departments only. More importantly it did nothing to diversify its role pattern with the changing business realities. Further the development of estates should not have been assigned to this agency as it has a more crucial role to play in providing marketing and raw-material support. As a matter of fact, if it has to play any concrete role in the development of small scale industries in the state there is an immense need to restructure and redefine the role profile this corporation.

J&K State Financial Corporation: Finance occupies a pivotal position in the process of industrialization. Finance is assumed to be the "life blood" of business. To meet financial needs of industries, the state government under State Financial Corporation Act, 1951 (Lx 111 of 1951) has incorporated J&K State Financial Corporation on 2nd of December 1959. The corporation is providing term loans to small scale industries, artisans, hoteliers, houseboat owners and transporters. The corporation has played a key role over the last three decades by providing assistance to various sectors of industry. The total amount of loans sanctioned and disbursed by the corporation since inception amounted to Rs. 42,351.38 lakh and Rs. 35,588 lakh respectively. However, the recovery of loans has been far from satisfactory. The total amount of loans outstanding including interest liability as on 2002-03 stood at Rs. 68,801.21 lakh. Out this, Rs. 65,917 lakh are overdue, accounting for a little over 95 percent of the total amount of loans outstanding (Table 3.6). This sad state of affairs is being attributed mainly to the liberal lending policy followed by the corporation right from the beginning.

Table 3.6: Sector-wise Loans Outstanding to J&K State Financial Corporation (Rs. lakh)

Sector	2000-01	2001-02	2002-03
Industries	34,152.44 (64.22)	40,092.66 (66.26)	49,786.82 (72.36)
Tourism	5,557.13 (10.45)	5,786.86 (9.56)	5,571.03 (8.10)
Transport	13,469.84 (25.33)	14,631.45 (24.18)	13,443.36 (19.54)
Total	53,179.41 (100.00)	60,501.97 (100.00)	68,801.21 (100.00)

Source: 43rd Annual Report (2002-03), J&K State Financial Corporation, Srinagar, Kashmir.

According to Godbole Committee Report, the lack of appraisal of the viability of the projects and credit worthiness of applicants has resulted in careless lending practices. The out break of violence since 1990-91 has further compounded the problem of defaults by various categories of borrowers. As a result of more defaults, the corporation has failed to fulfill its commitments with SIDBI and IDBI resulting into the loss of refinancing facility from SIDBI. This in turn has reduced its loaning capacity to a great extent. The total sanctions which were Rs. 42.43 crore in 1991-92 declined to Rs. 2.91 crore in 1996-97 (Annual Report, 2002-03). However, during the last few years, the corporation has been able to provide more financial assistance (Table 3.7).

The corporation has launched a well geared and purposeful recovery campaign as a result, it has achieved some improvement in the recoveries. In 2003, the corporation recovered all time high of Rs. 2399.99 lakh. To put the corporation on the track of performance, there is a need to revise its loaning procedures and check the inordinate delays in the processing of loan applications which is causing much trouble in the way of achieving meaningful industrial development in the state. It should give-up a policy of 'Touch Stone Theory' to project evaluation so that only viable units are allowed to come into existence.

Table 3.7: Sector-cum-Region-wise Over Due Loans to J& K State Financial Corporation as on 2002-03 (Rs. lakh)

Sector	Jammu Region	Kashmir Region	Total State
Industries	17920.45 (68.75)	31364.50 (78.71)	49284.95 (74.77)
Transport	7153.01 (27.44)	5292.84 (13.28)	12445.85 (18.88)
Hotels	993.44 (3.81)	3167.21 (7.95)	4160.65 (6.31)
Artisams	-	25.67 (0.06)	25.67 (0.04)
Total	26.66.90 (100.00)	39850.22 (100.00)	65917.21 (100.00)

Source: 43rd Annual Report (2002-03), J&K State Financial Corporation, Srinagar, Kashmir.

Central Public Enterprises: The central investment in the state is negligible compared to the other states. There are only two central public sector undertakings namely HMT Watch Factory at Zainakote (Srinagar) and Indian Telephone Industries, Srinagar. HMT Watch Factory is a large scale industrial unit with an investment of Rs. 300 crore, providing employment to nearly 1040 persons. The unit is producing watches of different qualities which are being sold in different parts of the country. The unit has performed very well till 1989, thereafter; it has witnessed a downward trend in production, sales and employment. The production of watches in the factory has grown at the rate of 9.22 percent from 1973-74 to 1989-90 and thereafter it has declined on an average rate of 6.10 percent per annum (Digest of Statistics, 2002-03).

The decline from 90 onwards is due to the disturbed conditions in the valley. There is a little impact on the average daily employment in these enterprises which has declined from 1278 persons in 1990-91 to 1040 persons in 2002 - 03. Indian telephone industries another central public enterprise in the state, manufacturing telephone apparatus and other related parts has also been adversely affected by the ongoing disturbances in the valley. The value of production which was going up at the rate of 7 percent per annum started declining from 1989-90 at the rate of 5.25 per cent per year. The total employment as on 2001-02 in the factory was 180 persons (Digest of Statistics, 2002-03). Both of these units have continued to operate in spite of many odds and are trying very hard to recapture lost glory. The onus of putting them in right order lies on the central government.

Small-scale Industries

Jammu and Kashmir has witnessed very little industrial activity in the large and medium scale sectors, particularly in the private sector. In the state there is just one large scale industry namely Chinar Textiles (Kathua) and a few other medium scale units in the private sector. The development of large scale industries in the state is ruled out except in few selected lines on account of some unfavorable factors like, extreme location, deficiency of natural resources, lack of sufficient capital and entrepreneur class, infrastructural bottlenecks etc. In view of these and other facts, the government focused more on the development of small scale industries in the state. Most of the industrial activity in the state, thus has taken place in the small scale sector. The small scale sector in the state consists of small scale industrial units, Handicrafts, Handlooms and Khadi and Village industries. The major thrust of the different policy initiatives and incentive packages formulated by the government from time to time was on the promotion and development of modern small scale industries in the state as these are assumed to dovetail well with economic imperatives of the state.

State registered sufficient growth in small scale industries since 1970s when the state government when the real initiative to industrialise the state was taken by offering a comprehensive set of incentives for the development of industries particularly small scale industries. There has been marked growth in the number of units formally registered. The number of units have grown from just 2,203 units in 1973-74 to 4,44,707 units in 2002-03 (Digest of Statistics, 2002-03). This sector of crucial importance to the state's economy has employed 1 98,338 persons as on 2002-03. The small scale sector in the state is widely diversified and the product profile of this sector mainly consist of; paints, biscuits, confectionary, wax candles, joinery, furniture, steel wire, barbed wire, channel fencing, textile, pharmaceuticals, plastic products, chemicals, fruit juices, sanitary wares, paper products, printing, and electrical. The major product lines are; metallic (18.21 percent), food products (17.1 percent), wood products (12.9 percent), paper products and printing (16.27 percent) and repairs and services (12 percent). The fact of the matter is that the state has made its place on the industrial map of the country, however still needs to go a long way to achieve industrialization of the size and magnitude required to take the state out of economic backwardness. There is an immense need to remove the different bottlenecks that are coming in the way of sustained industrial development in the state. Time has come to take bold steps to improve the industrial environment for large scale investment which calls for a pragmatic and long term result oriented policy initiatives on the part of the government.

Handicrafts and Handlooms

Jammu and Kashmir has a long tradition in handicrafts and has won the national and international acclimation in traditional arts and crafts. Kashmiri handicrafts are famous for its artistic beauty and are one of the major export earners to the state. The handicraft industry is agglomerated around Kashmir valley. The state government under the successive five year plans tried to broad base handicraft industry in the state and to make it more competitive to reclaim the glorious past but without much success. Important handicrafts of the state include Carpets, Namdas and Gabba making, Chain Stitching, Paper Machie,

Shawls, Embroidery and Willow Wicker. The value of handicraft production in 2003 was 240.00 crore and the number of persons employed in the industry were 2.59 lakh persons. As per handicraft census 1978-79, there were 25,806 handicraft units in Kashmir valley. Of the different handicrafts, carpet is the main item contributing 45.58 percent of the total production and 29.34 percent of the total employment in the handicraft industry. The production of handicraft goods has increased from Rs. 20 crore 1974-75 to Rs. 63.74 crore in 1978-79. (Digest of Statistics, 2002-03). However, if these figures are taken at constant prices in that case there will be either very negligible or no increase in the production during the period. The handicraft industry in the state is confronted with number of challenges and problems, like growing competition, lack of competitiveness, ineffective market promotion, dishonest manufacturers and traders, poor quality and design, conventional methods of production, raw-material problems and less takers to the art.

Under the fifth and sixth plan, government tried to broad base handicraft industry and established training centres in different parts of the state in which nearly 50,000 boys and girls were trained, however, only few of them have taken-up this as their profession. The solution to most of the above problems would lie in developing this industry on scientific lines and provide financial assistance and certain incentives to the artisans to systematize their production and marketing. The potential lying in the industry remains underutilized, as such, need to be developed by using the modern market concepts and strategies.

Handloom sector in the state is also worth mentioning in view of its size and contribution. As per handicrafts census of 1978-79, there are 10853 units providing employment to 17569 persons (Digest of Statistics, 2002-03). The product profile of the handloom sector of the state includes, tweeds, woolens, Pashmina, cotton, silk etc. Pashmina which is famous for its texture, blend etc has been banned by the government. The state government under successive five year plans has taken number of initiatives to develop this sector. Handloom Development Corporation was set up to meet the raw-material requirements of the weavers and to help them in marketing the handloom products. Further a cotton process house at Jammu and woolen process house at Srinagar were established to provide dyeing and bleaching facilities to the weavers in the state. During sixth, seventh and eighth five year plans, number of schemes were also formulated and implemented to modernize looms. As on 2002, 15,000 looms were modernized.

In spite of these and other measures taken, this sector in the state is not yet fully developed. The sector has not yet been fully diversified and penetrated in the Indian market. "Almost 70 percent of the cloth used for embroidery, chain stitch etc. is exported from outside the state" (Sadhu & Singh, 1984). The designs and quality of some handloom products does not satisfy the competitive standards. To capitalize on the vast potential in the handloom sector, the state government needs to give it a new direction by putting it on modern lines. There is a need to guide the weavers for better quality and range, upgrade their skills and help them to overcome the different problems that the handloom sector is facing. Setting-up of separate industrial complex for handloom units, may be on district-wise, where different facilities under one roof are provided, will be a step in the right direction.

Cocoon rearing and silk reeling and weaving have been the age old activities of many Kashmiri's and the state has a glorious past in this industry. For decades it continued to be the major industry in the state. Kashmir silk was known for its beauty, texture and blend and was famous throughout the world. At the time of independence, India was almost at the bottom in the world in raw silk production and in the country, J&K was next to Karnataka in silk production. Today in 2002, the Indian country is next to China in silk production. While as, J&K in the country has slipped almost to the bottom. Instead of recording any growth in the industry, it has witnessed a declining trend. The production of cocoons and raw-silk has declined from 9.62 thousand quintals of cocoon and 59.684 kgs of raw-silk in 1947-48 to 8.48 thousand quintals and 30.41 thousand kgs in 2002-03 respectively. The actual utilization of cocoons has gone down from 8.69 thousand quintals in 1947-48 to a mere 8.32 thousand quintals in 2002-03 (Digest of Statistics, 2002-03).

The actual consumption of cocoons produced in the state during the last few years was about 30 percent only. However, the industry still employs a large number of people. In 2002-03, nearly 5000 workers were directly involved in manufacturing activity in the silk industry and 23. 13 thousand households were engaged in rearing of silkworms (Table 3.8). This age old industry of the state attracted the attention of the government right from the date of drafting the fifth plan, during which the problems confronting the industry have been identified and consequently various schemes were launched in the said and successive plans to win back the lost glory in the industry.

To boost the sagging performance, the silk industry in the state was demonopolised in 1986. As a result of this structural change, many private silk reeling and weaving units were setup in the state and open cocoon markets are being held to enable the rearers to get the remunerative price for their crops. A World Bank funded project was also launched in the state to develop the silk industry. However, in spite of decades of efforts and huge expenditures made to revive silk industry in the state, nothing satisfactory has surfaced so far. Even we could not control decline in production cocoons etc. As such, there is a need to investigate how not the different endeavors made so far have not materialized in the growth of the industry? However, the opportunity to put this industry on the track of growth and prosperity has not been lost. Kashmir still enjoys market credibility and is fortunate to have conducive environment for rearing Uni-voltine and Bi-voltine worms which are famous for producing quality silk. But the need is to investigate with an open mind to reveal where the wrong has gone and now what needs to be done to win back the lost glory in the industry.

Relative Position of Various Industrial Sectors

This section of the chapter is devoted to highlight the relative position of different industrial sectors in the state's industrial

Table 3.8: Sericulture Development in the State of J&K

Year	No. of Sericulture Villages (000s)	No. of Sericulture House holds (000s)	Production of Cocoons (000 qts)	Utilisation of Cocoons for Rearing (000 qts)	Production of Raw silk	
					Quantity (000 kg)	Value (000 lakh)
1980-81	2.70	38.50	10.36	7.70	75.85	234.98
1985-86	2.26	32.50	6.42	4.51	33.70	291.28
1990-91	2.59	29.19	7.00	2.39	20.74	55.35
1995-96	2.36	23.53	6.66	0.51	9.50	140.16
1996-97	2.24	25.52	7.67	7.33	85.10	1076.00
1997-98	NA	NA	NA	NA	NA	NA
1998-99	2.307	22.737	8.29	8.10	92.10	1288.00
1999-00	2.15	25.28	8.25	8.04	80.00	960.00
2000-01	2.166	26.052	8.90	8.68	21.00	---
2001-02	2,164	20.249	7.07	6.92	37.00	---
2002-03	2.179	23.138	8.489	8.329	30.41	---

Source: *Digest of Statistics*, Directorate of Economics and Statistics, Planning and Development Department, J & K Government, 2002-03.

economy. The very purpose of the analysis of relative position of various industrial sectors in the state's industrial economy is to capture the growth movement in different sectors and more specifically to identify that which one is the major sector of the state's industrial economy. To highlight the relative position of various industrial sectors in the state's economy, industries have been classified into Public Sector and Private Sector Enterprises. In the private sector, the position of small scale industries, Khadi and Village Industries and handicrafts has been analysed. Large and medium sectors have been omitted from the private sector for two reasons; one, there are just a few large and medium scale industrial units in the private sector; second, the data about different dimension of large and medium scale enterprises is not available in various Govt. publications in the state. A relative position of different industrial sectors has been analyzed on the basis of number of units, employment and industrial output. However, the relative position of different sectors could not be analysed on the basis of their contribution to State Domestic Product as the data about the distribution of State Domestic Product is not given by Industry-wise.

Number of Industrial Units: As on 2001-02, there were 43,689 small small-scale units, 28,364 Khadi and Village Industries, 25 State Public Sector Enterprises and two Central Public Sector undertakings respectively. The Small-scale industries and Khadi and Village industries have registered significant growth in the number of units since 1980-81. On the other hand, State Public Sector Enterprises witnessed fluctuating fortunes during the same period. Of all the above-mentioned industrial sectors, it is only small-scale industries and Khadi and Village Industries which have registered sufficient growth in the state over a period of time. Due to obvious reasons there has been zero growth in Public Sector Enterprises. The most intriguing aspect of investment in Public Sector enterprises is that the investment in central public undertakings eludes the state. This is despite the fact that the state was more deserving candidate for central investment for being one of the industrially and economically backwards states of the country. The state Govt. did make investment in Public Sector undertakings but failed to guide these enterprises to grow as commercially viable entities. As a result most of these enterprises are suffering from various operating inefficiencies and have become recurring parasites for the state exchequer.

Industrial Output: Among other things, the industrial sector has an important role to play in the economic development by expanding the productive capacity of the economy. The industrial output in the state has registered some definite growth both in terms of volume and variety of products. The aggregate industrial output of the state as on 2001-02 was of the order of Rs. 2,343.3 crore which has grown from Rs. 188.74 crore in 1980-81. Major contributor's to the industrial output in the state are registered factories which have contributed nearly 59 per cent to the industrial output in 2001-02, followed by handicrafts which account for 32 per cent of the total industrial output (Digest of Statistics, 2002-03). Compared to these two major sectors, Khadi and Village Industries account for a mere 3.8 percent of the total output. Public Sector Enterprises are also minor contributors to the Industrial output, accounting for a little over 4 per cent.

Although the number of Khadi and Village Industries has swallowed into 28,364 units in 2001-02 from a mere 3,178 units in 1980-81 yet, their contribution to the industrial output is paltry. This is because of the fact that these enterprises produce tradition products at a very small-scale to meet the demands of the local market only. However, a small contribution of the public sector enterprises to the industrial output is indicative of the fact that one; that the sufficient investments have not gone into the manufacturing Public Sector Enterprises and second these enterprises are being marred by various operating inefficiencies resulting into lower utilization of their installed capacities.

Employment: Industrial sector in the country has generated a lot of employment over the last few decades in particular. However, the same is not true about the industrial sector in the state of Jammu and Kashmir. The state did make a beginning in the industrial sector but still it has to go a long way in achieving sustainable industrial development to the magnitude needed to absorb under-employed and unemployed people to a considerable extent. The total number of persons employed in different industrial sectors have gone to 6,82,973 persons as on 2001-02 from 2,14,076 persons in 1980-81, thus recorded a little over three fold growth in 20 years period (Digest of Statistics, 2002-03). Of all the sectors, handicraft sector turned out to be the major employer in the state which alone accounted for more than 56 percent of the total persons employed in different sectors of the industrial economy.

Next to handicraft sector are small-scale industries which accounts for more than 28 percent of the total employment generated in the industrial sector in the state. The public sector enterprises are employing less than one percent of the total number of persons employed in the Industrial Sector. In fact, the number of persons employed in the Public Sector Undertakings has declined from 6588 persons in 1980-81 to 4843 persons in 2002-03 (Digest of Statistics, 2002-03). This is due to the fact that the Govt. is not making any new appointment in the public sector enterprises. The small-scale industries have witnessed some marked growth, though not satisfactory. The contribution of small-scale industries in employment generation once again reinforces the importance of this sector for solving the various problems with which the states economy is confronted with. The handicraft sector though important on account of many reasons yet, cannot solve the problem of large-scale unemployment particularly among the educated youth. The future hope of the state with regard to the generation of meaningful employment avenues for the educated youth lies in the development of modern small-scale industries.

Although small-scale industries if developed properly have the potential to generate sufficient employment yet, alone it cannot free the state from the clutches of backwardness and poverty. To achieve these cherished goals, it is equally important to emphasise on the development of other sectors though with more emphasis on the development of modern small scale industries, the essential features of modern industries are modern technology and entrepreneurial class adaptive to changing market realities with outward looking approach. The state does enjoy some scope to promote modern large manufacturing enterprises in the areas where it enjoys some comparative advantage in resource endowments.

From the analysis of relative position of different industrial sectors in the state's economy brings to fore that the small-scale industrial sector is the major sector in the state. This sector which is considered as the future hope of the state's economy has witnessed sufficient growth during the last two decades or so. A handicraft is the other major sector in the state contributing to the states economy in many respects to a considerable extent. Handicraft though enjoys a place of pride both in the national and international market yet, among other things it is confronted with the problem of declining trend in exports due to increasing competition etc. The medium and large-scale sectors mainly consist of Public Sector enterprises. Private initiative in these two sectors is missing in the state. There was a time when various Public Enterprises in the state were established to achieve commanding heights as important economic institutions but today due to their dismal financial performance and changing economic milieu, these enterprises have lost their prominence and relevance as institutions for accelerating the economic growth.

Intra-State Dispersion of Industries

One of the important objectives of the economic system that the country adopted soon after independence was to achieve balanced development of different regions. The Govt. of India has shown considerable interest in achieving balanced development of different regions right from the beginning. Towards this direction, the Govt. of India appointed number of working groups to recommend mechanism for selecting backward areas and to suggest fiscal and non-fiscal measures necessary for the upliftment of backward regions. On account of different measures taken towards the balanced development of different regions in the country, some achievement in this regard has been made in the country. However, a great disparity still exists between different states with regard to economic growth and development.

Being a welfare state, different governments in the state have aimed to achieve balanced development of different regions of the state through the dispersion of industries. An attempt is being made in the subsequent pages to analyse how far the state has succeeded in achieving wide dispersion of industries to achieve balanced development of different regions. To analyse this aspect of planned economic system which the state followed right from the beginning, the data about the distribution of number of small-scale industries, handicraft units and handloom units has been used. The data about the distribution of number of medium scale industries, large-scale industries and registered factories could not be used as the division cum district-wise data about these important sectors of the industrial economy is not available.

Geographically the state is divided into three distinct regions –Kashmir, Jammu and Ladakh. There are large variations in climatic conditions, geo-physical and demographic features between these regions. Kashmir is more populated while as, Ladakh Division is sparsely populated. Kashmir and Ladakh regions of the state are mostly mountainous as such difficult to reach in and out. In Jammu Division some parts are mountainous and some namely Kathua and Jammu districts have a strip of plains which connect the state with the rest of the country. Jammu & Kashmir provinces have six districts each while Ladakh has two districts–Leh and Kargil.

Distribution of Small Scale Industries: Small-scale industries dovetail well with the economic imperatives of the state. It is in view of this fact that the developmental priorities set by the state have focused more on the development of small-scale industries in particular modern small-scale industries. As a result of various policy measures taken from time to time, there has been marked growth in the proliferation of number of small-scale industrial units in the state. The number of small scale industrial units has gone to 42,808 units in 2000-01 from 8,428 units in 1980-81. Table 3.9 which contains data about region-cum-district-wise distribution of small scale industries and registered factories reveals that the small scale industrial units in the state are fairly distributed between Jammu and Kashmir provinces. Surprisingly there has been more than sufficient growth in the number of SSI units in Ladakh region as well. Number of Small Scale Units in Ladakh region has grown from 122 units in 1980-81 to 1373 units in 2001-02. However, most of the industrial activity is concentrated in Kashmir and Jammu regions. Together the two regions account for more than 96 percent of the total industrial activity in the small-scale sector as on 2001-02. There is nothing surprising about this concentration as these two regions are well endowed with the various resources considered essential for imparting necessary impulse towards industrial growth as compared to Ladakh region.

In Kashmir region, small-scale industries are concentrated in the metropolis of Srinagar and Budgam districts which together account for more than 51 percent of the total units as on 2001-02, followed by Anantnag and Pulwama districts. Similarly in Jammu division, Small Scale Industrial units are concentrated more in Jammu and Kathua districts, the two districts together accounts for 63 percent of the total Small Scale Industrial units as on 2001-02. Sufficient growth has also taken place in the industrial activity in Udhampur district. The other districts have witnessed little industrial activity in Small Scale Industries due to their unique geographical features. What becomes clear from the data contained in Table 3.9 is that although most of the industrial activity is concentrated around metropolis of Jammu and Srinagar cities yet, the state has achieved significant success in achieving the dispersion of industries towards other districts. This is despite the fact that most of these districts are constrained with serious impediments.

Dispersion of industries is important but more important is their survival and growth in rural areas. However, nothing can be said about the survival and growth of industries established in backward districts and elsewhere as data about the failures in Small Scale Industries is not available in the state. But there are vivid indications that the industrial sickness in Small Scale Industries is widespread in the state and more so in the backward districts of the state.

Table 3.9: Region-cum-District-wise Distribution of SSI Units & Registered Factories in J&K State

Region /District	1980-81	1990-91	2000-01
Kashmir Region			
• Anantnag }	1005	2536	3312
• Pulwama }		1608	2017
• Srinagar }	2313	5231	7701
• Budgam }		1820	2941
• Baramulla }	782	2750	3391
• Kupwara }		1047	1321
Total Kashmir Region	**4100**	**14992**	**20683**
Jammu Region			
• Jammu	1838	5849	8730
• Udhampur	692	2408	3444
• Kathua	706	2883	4404
• Doda	361	1115	1549
• Rajouri	352	832	1236
• Poonch	257	974	1389
Total Jammu Region	**4206**	**14061**	**20752**
Ladakh Region			
• Leh }	122	610	870
• Kargil }		300	503
Total Ladakh Region	**122**	**910**	**1373**
Grand Total	8428	29963	42808

Source: *Digest of Statistics*, Directorate of Economics and Statistics, Planning and Development Department, J&K Government, 2002-03

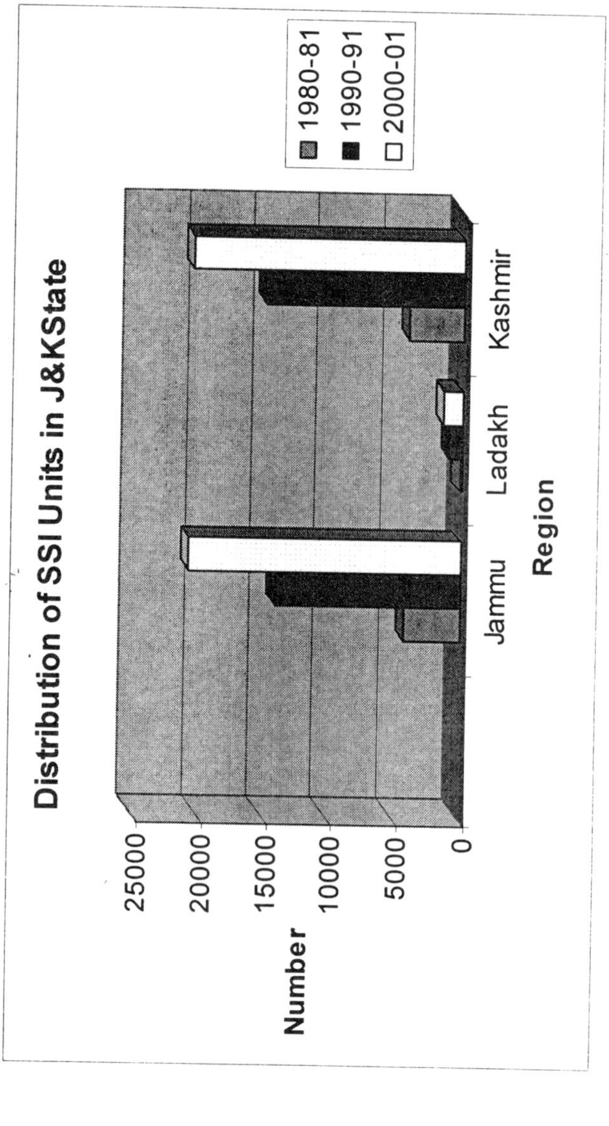
Distribution of SSI Units in J&KState
Number
25000
20000
15000
10000
5000
0
Jammu
Ladakh
Kashmir
Region
1980-81
1990-91
2000-01

Distribution of Handicraft Units: Large number of handicrafts is being practiced in different parts of the state. The important handicrafts of the state include Carpets, Crewel and Sozni Embroidery, Chain Stitch, Wood Carving, Papier Machie, Willow Wicker, Gabba and Namda making and Zari embroidery. All these handicrafts of the state are enjoying name and fame both in the national as well as in the international markets. However, these crafts are practiced in the valley of Kashmir only. As can be seen from Table 3.10 that the number of units manufacturing these important crafts in Kashmir Valley are somewhat fairly distributed between different districts. However, the units practicing *Sozni* embroidery and *Papier Machie* are more concentrated in Srinagar district while as chain stitch and crewel embroidery units are largely located in Anantnag district. The willow wicker is largely concentrated in Baramulla and Kupwara districts of Kashmir Valley. Compared to other districts, Kupwara is the only district in Kashmir Valley which is not fortunate enough to have sufficient concentration of different handicraft units.

Kani Shawl, the most important craft, which was practiced right from the beginning in Kashmir Valley has almost disappeared. There were 166 units involved in the making of Kani Shawls in 1978 which were located in Srinagar district have declined to zero in 1988-89. The Govt. of J&K though lately has made efforts in regaining this precious craft. Although such efforts have helped to a great extent to regain this lost treasure yet, there is a long way to go to redeem the glorious past of this craft. The other age-old crafts that are not being practiced now in the valley include costume jewellery, Turquise, silverware, metalware, tapestry, precious jewellery, copperware and knitting. All these crafts were mainly practiced in Srinagar district.

The craft tradition is less pronounced towards Jammu and Ladakh regions of the state. The handicrafts that are generally practiced in these two regions of the state hardly enjoy place both in the national and international markets. The products of different crafts practiced in Jammu and Ladakh regions are

Table 3.10: District-wise Distribution of Handicraft Units in Kashmir Region

Activity	Srinargar/Budgam			Anantnag/Pulwama			Baramulla/Kupwara			Leh/Kargil			Total	
	1978-79	1988-89		1978-79	1988-89		1978-79	1988-89		1978-79	1988-89		1978-79	1988-89
Carpet	4735	3751	6341	823	4960	5171	1653	5173	214	-	-	-	7211	25610
Namda	235	181	69	46	17	35	112	70	58	-	-	-	393	430
Kani Shawl	166	-	-	-	-	-	-	-	-	-	-	-	168	-
Crewel Emb.	1466	926	618	558	2322	275	192	159	38	-	-	-	2216	4338
Sozni Emb.	9332	8997	1237	119	186	334	617	445	185	-	-	-	10068	11384
Chain Stitch	91	62	40	-	3202	22	-	25	1	-	-	-	91	3352
Wood Carving	320	208	128	27	-	37	-	13	7	29	-	-	358	393
Paper Machie	710	555	180	-	10	2	-	72	-	-	-	-	710	819
Leather Emb.	70	52	24	-	-	-	-	-	-	31	-	-	101	76
Costume Jewellery	10	-	-	-	-	-	-	-	-	-	-	-	10	-
Turquise	3	-	-	-	-	-	-	-	-	-	-	-	3	-
Willow Wicker	562	403	193	528	277	400	2055	1097	1086	-	-	-	3145	3456
Gabba	30	38	20	137	105	47	-	44	42	-	-	-	244	296
Zari Emb.	144	132	44	65	25	304	105	71	44	-	-	-	314	620
Silver Ware	4	-	-	-	-	-	-	-	-	-	-	-	15	-
Metal Ware	12	-	-	-	-	-	-	-	-	11	-	-	12	-
Pottery	4	-	-	4	-	-	159	-	-	-	-	-	167	-
Knitting	-	-	-	50	-	-	-	-	-	-	-	-	97	-
Tapestery	64	-	-	7	-	-	-	-	-	47	-	-	71	-
Precious Jewellery	5	-	-	-	-	-	-	-	-	-	-	-	5	-
Copper ware	7	-	-	-	-	-	-	-	-	-	-	-	7	-

Emb. Stands for Embroidery.

Source: *Digest of Statistics*, Directorate of Economics and Statistics, Planning and Development Department, J&K Government, 2002-03.

generally sold in the local markets only. The important handicrafts of Jammu region are Bamboo craft, Leather embroidery, Wicker craft and Palm leaf. The data about the distribution of handicraft units by craft-wise in Jammu and Ladakh regions is presented in table 3.11. It can be seen from the above table that the bamboo craft and leather embroidery units are somewhat evenly dispersed in different parts of the region except Rajouri and Poonch, while as units practicing palm leaf, chickery wood, glazed pottery and sozni crafts are concentrated in Kathua district only. Compared to other districts this district is rich in traditional crafts practiced in Jammu region. Rajouri and Poonch, the two most backward districts of Jammu Province, are not fortunate enough to enjoy historical legacies in different handicraft skills. The major craft of these two districts is Sozni only.

The thing that emerges from the above is that the crafts that are acclaimed both in the national and international markets are concentrated in Kashmir region only. Considering the importance of this sector in the states economy, the efforts were made to broad base the handicraft sector. Accordingly the Directorate of handicrafts has launched training programmes to train boys and girls in important crafts of the state like carpet weaving, shawl making and embroidery. No of training centres have been established in different parts of the state and so far thousands of boys and girls were trained in different age old crafts. For detailed information see Table 3.12. As a result of this, carpet weaving and embroidery which were practiced only in Kashmir Valley are now practiced in Jammu region as well though to a very little extent only. As per 1988-89 handicraft census, there are 12 crewel embroidery and three carpet weaving units in Jammu and Kathua. On the other hand, some age-old crafts in the Jammu region like knitting, straw work, spinning and weaving and wood carving have been given-up by the artisans. This is partly due to the declining demand for these crafts and partly due to other reasons.

Table 3.11: District-wise Distribution of Handicraft Units in Jammu Region

Activity	Jammu		Udhampur		Kathua		Doda		Poonch		Rajouri	
	1978-79	1988-89	1978-79	1988-89	1978-79	1988-89	1978-79	1988-89	1978-79	1988-89	1978-79	1988-89
Knitting	237	-	20	-	35	-	96	-	45	-	-	-
Bamboo Craft	333	351	455	471	359	363	40	44	-	-	-	-
Straw Work	67	-	5	-	69	-	34	-	-	-	-	-
Leather Emb.	20	35	97	107	198	10	51	54	-	-	9	-
Spinning & Weaving	50	-	-	-	23	-	46	-	52	-	83	88
Wicker Craft	45	224	9	139	5	315	37	39	-	-	37	-
Palm Leaf	12	-	24	-	12	92	22	-	9	11	-	-
Wood Carving	-	-	22	-	-	-	-	-	-	-	-	-
Sozni	-	-	-	-	-	8	-	1	55	29	25	27
Chikery Wood	-	-	-	-	200	206	-	-	-	-	-	28
Glazed Pottery	-	-	-	-	92	-	-	-	-	-	-	-
Carpet Weaving	-	1	-	-	-	251	-	-	-	-	-	-
Crewel Emb		12	-	-	-	2	-	-	-	-	-	-
Other Crafts	56	-	21	86	20	2	32	231	-	130-	-	49
Total	**820**	**1033**	**653**	**803**	**1031**	**1247**	**358**	**369**	**161**	**170**	**154**	**192**

Emb. Stands for Embroidery

Source: *Digest of Statistics*, Directorate of Economics and Statistics, Planning and Development Department, J&K Government, 2002-03.

Table 3.12: Number of Craft Training Centres and Number of Persons Trained in Different Crafts in Jammu and Kashmir

Year	Number of centres	% age growth	Persons trained	% age growth
1980-81	451	-	4500	
1985-86	459	1.77	7949	76.64
1990-91	513	11.76	7932	-0.21
1995-96	535	4.28	8262	4.16
1996-97	535	0	8729	5.65
1997-98	540*	0.934	8505	-2.56
1998-99	552	2.22	7450	-12.40
1999-00	562	1.81	8918	19.70
2000-01	554	-1.43	8251	-7.48
2001-02	553	-0.18	8307	0.67
2002-03	553	0	8640	4.01
Cg		**1.12**		**13.98**

Cg Stands for Compound Growth.
Source: *Digest of Statistics*, Directorate of Economics and Statistics, Planning and Development Department, J&K Government, 2002-03.

Distribution of Handlooms: As per 1978-79 census of handicrafts and handloom products, there were 10,835 handloom units in the state manufacturing wide variety of products. About 60 percent of the units were located in Kashmir Province and the remaining units in different parts of Jammu region. The data about district-wise distribution of handloom units in Kashmir province presented in Table 3.13 reveals that most of the units are concentrated in the twin districts of Anantnag/Pulwama and Baramulla/Kupwara. As far as the Jammu region is concerned, most of the units were located in Kathua and Doda districts, the two districts together account for more than 55 percent of the total units in Jammu region. Thus it becomes quite evident from the distribution of handloom units that the units are not fairly distributed between different districts in both the regions of the state.

Table 3.13: Region-cum-District-wise Number of Handloom Units as per Handloom Census 1978-79 (Activity-wise)

Region/District	Loies	Puttos	Tweeds	Blankets	Raffal	Pashmina	Silk	Dusote	Khadi
Kashmir Region									
Sgr/Budgam	623	10	43	165	30	146	58	39	-
Anantnag/Pulwama	2745	-	147	67	-	-	-	-	-
Baramulla/Kupwara	2555	-	45	49	-	-	-	-	-
Leh/Kargil	-	318	-	-	-	-	-	-	-
Total Kashmir Region	**5923**	**328**	**235**	**281**	**30**	**146**	**58**	**39**	-
Jammu Region									
Jammu	153	-	-	10	-	-	-	-	154
Poonch	358	-	-	3	-	-	-	-	-
Rajouri	120	54	-	97	-	-	-	-	-
Doda	792	-	-	52	-	-	-	-	200
Udhampur	540	-	32	185	-	-	-	-	1
Kathua	601	141	-	320	-	-	-	-	-
Total Jammu Region	**2564**	**195**	**32**	**667**	-	-	-	-	**354**
Total State	8487	523	267	948	30	146	58	39	355

Source: *Digest of Statistics*, Directorate of Economics and Statistics, Planning and Development Department, J & K Government, 2002-03

The different products manufactured in the handloom sector in the state include Loies Puttos, Tweeds, Blankets, Raffal, Pashmina, Silk, Dusote and Khadi. Of these the major products are Loies, Blankets in both the regions, Tweeds in Kashmir province and Khadi in Jammu region. These four products account for about 93 per cent of the total handloom units in the state. The manufacturing of Putto is the only activity undertaken in the handloom sector in the Ladakh region. The manufacturing of Raffal, Pashmina, silk and Dusote is undertaken in Kashmir Division only while as manufacturing of Khadi is concentrated in Jammu region only. In Kashmir region, it is only the Srinagar and Budgam districts which are home to all the products manufactured in the handloom sector in the region while as, in other districts only Loies, Tweeds and blanket manufacturing is taking place. In Jammu region manufacturing of Loies and blankets is undertaken in all the districts whereas Khadi manufacturing is concentrated in Jammu, Kathua and Udhampur districts only.

One important fact that becomes evident from the distribution of handloom products in the state is that it is the local needs only rather than the external demand that gave birth to different handloom products in different regions of the state. For example Khadi is concentrated in Jammu and Kathua only because Khadi is highly suitable for the areas having tropical heat. Similarly Putto which is an ideal cloth to protect from biting arctic cold, that is why Putto manufacturing is widespread in Ladakh region. The same is true about the various handloom products manufactured in Kashmir Division.

Summary

The analysis of dispersion of small-scale industries, handloom and handicraft units in the state reveals that the small-scale industries are equally concentrated in the two regions of Jammu & Kashmir, with somewhat more concentration in the metropolis of Srinagar and Jammu cities. But the handicrafts which enjoy a place of pride both in the national and international markets are concentrated in Kashmir region only. The Jammu region has its own age-old crafts, however, these are not enjoying any place of pride neither in the local market nor in the national market. It is also that due to the expansion of modern industries, the artisans in Jammu region have given-up some age old crafts. Although handloom sector is well-dispersed yet, the dispersion is more pronounced towards the Kashmir province which account for about 65 percent of the total units in this sector. The major product of this sector is Loies which account for more than 78 percent of the handloom units in the state.

References

43rd Annual Report (2002-03), J&K State Financial Corporation, Srinagar, Kashmir

Aggarwal A. N. (1994), 'Indian Economy: Problems of Development and Planning', Wishwa Prakashan, A division of Wiley Eastern Ltd., New Delhi.

Bakal, G.M. (1989), "Role of DICs in the Industrial Development", Unpublished Ph. D. Thesis, Submitted to the Department of Commerce, University of Kashmir.

Bamzai, P.K. (1979), 'A History of Jammu and Kashmir', Metropolitan Book Company Ltd., Delhi.

Digest of Statistics, (2002-03), Directorate of Economics and Statistics, Planning & Development Department, Govt. of Jammu & Kashmir.

Jammu and Kashmir Economic Development in Figures, Directorate of Information, Government of Jammu and Kashmir, (1956).

Khan M.A. (2003), "Seminar Report on the Problems and Remedies of J & K Public Sector Undertakings", J&K Institute of Management, Public Administration & Rural Development, Srinagar, Kashmir.

Nisar A. (1987), 'Problems and Management of Small Scale and Cottage Industries', Deep and Deep Publications, New Delhi.

Official Records of Jammu and Kashmir Small Scale Industries Development Corporation, Srinagar, Kashmir.

Physical Achievements of Third Five Year Plan, (1962-67), Jammu and Kashmir, Department of Planning, Government Jammu and Kashmir.

Sadhu A.N. and Singh A. (1984), Jammu and Kashmir Economy, Trikuta Publishing House, Jammu.

Status Paper on JKHPMC (2001-02), Directorate of JK Horticulture Produce and Marketing Corporation, Srinagar, Kashmir.

Status Paper on JKI Ltd. (2000-01), Directorate of Jammu and Kashmir Industries Ltd. Srinagar, Kashmir, J & K State.

Status Paper on JKML. (1997), Directorate of Jammu and Kashmir Minerals Ltd. Srinagar, Kashmir, J & K State.

4

Industrial Growth and Development: An Analysis

Introduction

For a predominantly agrarian economy like ours, development of industries is highly essential in view of the fact that the primary sector in the state which is constrained with low man-land ratio and other structural limitations can not take the state to high growth path. The industrial sector which processors relatively high marginal propensity to save and invest, contributes significantly to the eventual achievement of a self-sustaining economy with continued high levels of investments and a rapid rate of increase in income and industrial employment. Industrialization is inseparable from substantial and sustained economic advance, because it is both in *'Consequence'* of higher incomes and a *'Means'* to higher productivity (Stately, 1963). It acts as an instrument both for creating productive capacity to absorb excessive labour force and of creating for the diversification of the market required at higher stages of economic development. In any scheme of development, however, development of primary sector should receive due attention because of its complementary relationship with the industry. However, a change in balance between agriculture and industry is evident in predominantly agrarian economies like ours with somewhat more emphasis on industrial development so as to attain desired structural diversification.

The peculiar physical conditioning of the state like, extreme location in the national setting, difficult mountainous terrain, and extreme climatic conditions limits the scope for industrialisation in the areas where the state does not enjoy the advantage of natural resources. Industries in such areas can be taken-up somewhat at a small scale to cater the local demand only.

However, on the positive side, the state is well endowed with some proven natural resources like, lime-stone, gypsum, coal, lignite, quartzite, while clay, Borax etc. The state is also rich in forest wealth and in some industrially important agriculture and horticulture products. Due to temperate climatic conditions, Kashmir is the only place in the Indian union highly suitable for rearing Uni-voltive and Bio-voltive silkworm races, which are famous for high quality silk. The definite comparative advantage in these and other natural resource endowments, certainly provide sufficient scope for industrialization in the lines based on these resources. The state is also gifted with scenic beauty, world famous health resorts, fascinating landscape and historical legacies in craftsmanship skills, thus enjoying a distinct end an important place in handicrafts and tourism industry.

At the time of independence, the industrial activities were mainly concentrated in handicrafts. On account of different developmental interventions initiated by different governments from time to time, the industrial structure has gone a sea change. The industrial structure now leans quite heavily towards small scale sector. Large scale industries are almost absent in the state. There has been a marked growth in the number of industrial units in particular in small scale sector since 1970 when the real initiative to industrialise the state was taken. However, quantitative advancements in the process of industrialization are important but more important is the survival and growth of industrial enterprises established. An industrial enterprise established should run efficiently and demonstrate constant growth otherwise, the very purpose of its establishment is lost. An enterprise which does not work efficiently continues to be a recurring parasite for the economy as a whole rather than a useful productive asset. So to Judge the industrial progress achieved so far, it becomes imperative to analyse both the qualitative and quantitative indicators of industrial development with the help of some tested tools. An attempt has been made in this chapter to critically analyse the achievements made in the industrial sector in the state of Jammu and Kashmir so far.

Industrialization in predominantly agrarian economies is very much needed to expand production capacity of the economy, to generate employment to absorb ever increasing workforce, reduce pressure of more workforce on agricultural sector, increase in the share of non-agricultural sector in the State Domestic Product (SDP), overcoming disparities in export-import elasticity's, raising per capita income contribute significantly in foreign exchange earnings, and provide security. Therefore, given the purpose and role of industrialization, growth in number of units, industrial production, export earnings, employment and per capita income; contribution to SDP and Import- Export elasticities are the various indicators that can guide in concluding about the industrial progress achieved over a period of time in a given economy. Unfortunately the database about the industrial sector in particular about the unorganized sector is weak in the state. As such it is not possible to analyse the industrial development using all the performance indicators. But every effort has been made to collect data on important indicators from all possible sources. The industrial progress achieved in the state so far has been measured by comparing the different performance indicators with the national averages and with other states of the Indian union. Absolute numbers, percentages, growth rates; ratio's etc. have been used to reflect the true picture of industrialization that has taken place in the state to observe the trends over the period in various indicators of industrial development, 'Exponential Growth' has been calculated by solving equation of the form:

$$Y = ab^x$$

To get the value of b, the above equation has been put in logarithmatic form of:

$$\text{Logy} = \text{loga} + X\ \text{logb}$$

To obtain the values of the constants a and b, the ıwo normal equations solved are:

$$\sum \text{Log } y = \text{Nloga} + \text{logb}\sum x$$

$$\sum(\text{xlogy}) = \text{loga}\sum X + \text{logb}\sum X^2$$

An effort has also been made in this chapter to analyse the impact of militancy on the economic development in general and on the industrial development in particular. For this purpose, the time period of two decades (1980-81 to 2001-02) has been divided into three time intervals viz, pre-militancy period (1980-81 to 1990-91); militancy period (1991-92 to 1998-99); and post militancy period (1999-00 to 2001-02). However, it may be mentioned here that the peace has not yet returned to the state. But there is a marked improvement in the overall condition.

It is pertinent to mention here that the small scale industries account for more than 70 per cent of the total industrial units, therefore, any achievement made in industrialization will be attributed to this sector of crucial importance to the state's economy. It is in view of this fact that wherever consolidated information is not available about all the industrial sectors, the data pertaining to small scale sector has been used to analyse industrial performance.

Growth in Number of Industrial Units

As a result of various policy measures initiated from time to time by the state and central Governments, not only there has been sufficient growth in the number of industrial units but structurally also the industrial economy in the state has witnessed some noticeable change. At one point of time, the industrial activities in the state were mainly concentrated in cottage industries. Today industrial economy is indeed well diversified, consisting of all the three sectors producing traditional as well as modern products. However, industrial growth in the state is pronounced more towards small scale sector than other sectors. Sector-wise, Small Scale Industries (SSI) sector has achieved phenomenal growth and diversification over the time. The number of SSI units in the state have gone to 43,689 units in 2001-02 from 8,428 units in 1981-82. On an average the number of units in this sector of great importance to the state's economy have grown at the rate of 7.1 per cent annually which does not compare favourably with the figures at the national level. Compared to small scale industries, the factory sector has not grown much during the said period. The number of registered factories which were 574 in 1981-82 have grown to 964 in 2001-02, thus have grown at a meager rate of 2.7 percent. Of all the sectors, Khadi and Village industries have registered maximum growth. It has grown at the rate of 8.6 percent during 1981-82 to 2001-02 as can be seen from the data contained in Tables 4.1 and 4.1a.

Small scale industries have registered maximum growth during the decade of 80's and thereafter the number of units have grown but at a decreasing rate of 4.85 percent. The same is true about Khadi and Village industries and registered factories. The declining fortunes of different industrial sectors in the state during the decade of 90's to a great extent is attributed to the onset of militancy in the state which has given a crippling blow to the industrial sector in particular

The state has witnessed very little industrial activity in the medium and large scale industrial sectors. Whatever industrial activity exists in these two sectors mainly consist of State Public Sector and Central Public Sector Enterprises. There are nineteen state public sector corporations, out of which nine relate to industries. Of these, five are manufacturing corporations and the remaining four are for the promotion of industries. As becomes clear from the above table that there has been steady growth in the number of State Public Sector Enterprises till 1985-86. The number manufacturing units in the state PSUs which were just nine in 1960-61 have grown to 31 in 1985-86. Thereafter a declining trend has been witnessed both in the number of units and investments in the state public sector. As far the present state of affairs of state PSUs goes, number of manufacturing units have been closed and many more are suffering from serious operating inefficiencies. It is surprising as well as disheartening to note here that the central government has done very little to push industrial activity in the state by investing in central public sector enterprises. There are only two Central Public Sector Units in the state viz. Hindustan Machine Tools (HMT) and Indian Telephone Industries (ITI). Although the state was a fit case to have more central investment in central public sector undertakings yet, it is the state of J&K only that received very little investment in

Table 4.1: No of SSI Units, Khadi & Village Industries, Registered Factories, State PSUs & Central PSUs

Year	SSI	Ab. Growth	%age Growth	Cg	K & V Ind.	Ab. Growth	%age Growth	Cg	Reg. Factories	Ab. Growth	%age Growth	Cg
1980-81	8428				3178				574			
1985-85	18520	10092	119.74	23.55	11553	8375	263.53	23.96	720	146	25.4	4.5
1990-91	29963	11443	61.78		20964	9411	81.45		833	113	15.7	
1995-96	36821	6858	22.88		25989	5025	23.96		876	43	5.16	
1996-97	38029	1208	3.28		27100	1111	4.27		899	23	2.62	0.82
1997-98	39805	1776	4.67	1.28	27127	27	0.09	1.02	899	0	0	
1998-99	40620	815	2.04		27537	410	1.51		934	35	3.89	
1999-00	41950	1330	3.27		28306	769	**2.79**		938	4	0.43	
2000-01	42808	858	2.04		28312	6	0.02	1.00	955	17	1.81	1.07
2001-02	43689	881	2.05	1.92	28364	52	0.18		964	9	0.94	
2002-03	44707	1018	2.33									
Cg			**7.1**				**8.6**				**2.7**	

Note: K&V Stands for Khadi & Village Industries; Cg Stands for Compound Growth; Ab Growth Stands for Absolute Growth; SSI Stands for Small Scale Industries

Source: *Digest of Statistics*, Directorate of Economics and Statistics, Planning and Development Department, J & K Government, 2002-03.

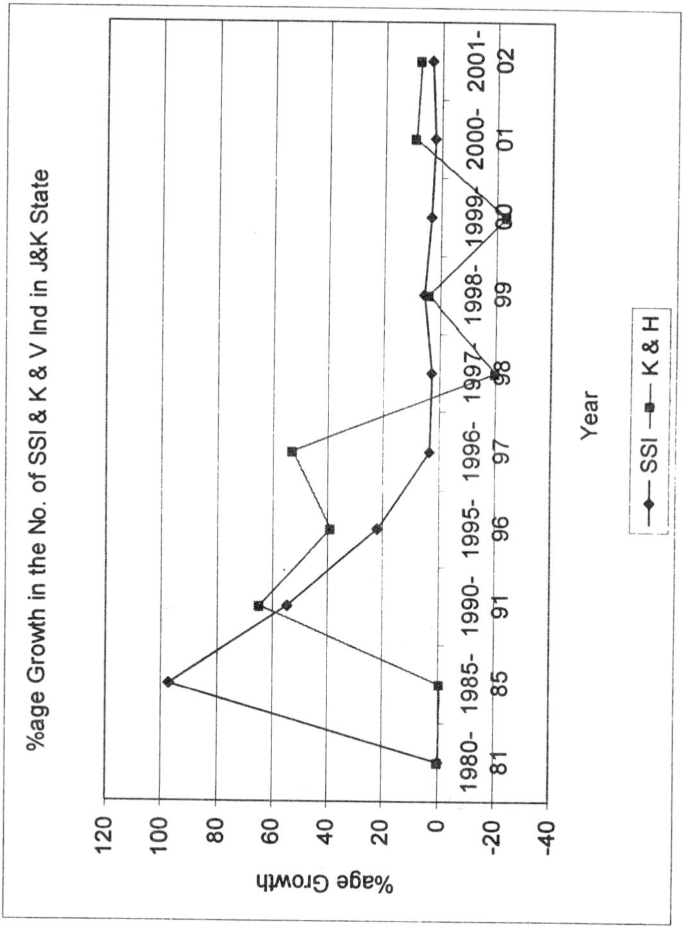
%age Growth in the No. of SSI & K & V Ind in J&K State
%age Growth
120
100
80
60
40
20
0
-20
-40
1980-81
1985-85
1990-91
1995-96
1996-97
1997-98
1998-99
1999-00
2000-01
2001-02
Year
SSI
K & H

Table 4.1a: State PSUs & Central PSUs

Year	State PSUs	Ab. Growth	%age Growth	Cg	Central PSUs	Ab. Growth	%age Growth	Cg
1980-81	25				2			
1985-85	31	6	24.00	1.2	2	0	0	0
1990-91	28	-3	-9.67		2	0	0	
1995-96	30	2	7.14		2	0	0	
1996-97	31	1	3.33		2	0	0	
1997-98	26	-5	-16.12	-4.35	2	0	0	0
1998-99	16	-10	-38.46		2	0	0	
1999-00	27	11	68.75		2	0	0	
2000-01	25	-2	-7.40		2	0	0	
2001-02	26	1	4.00	2.91	2	0	0	0
2002-03	24	-2	-7.69		2	0	0	
Cg			-1.14				zero	

Source: *Digest of Statistics*, Directorate of Economics and Statistics, Planning and Development Department, J&K Government, 2002-03.

central public sector enterprises reportedly due to the lack of political stability with which the state is suffering right from the beginning. Investment in central public sector enterprises in the state is less than 0.01 per cent of the total investment in the country. This sad state of affairs on the part of Central Govt. is beyond one's imagination thus has given raise to the number of questions.

Group-wise, the proliferation of small scale industries has been more in hosiery and readymade garments; wood products; food products; metal and allied products and repairing and servicing industries as can be seen from Table 4.2.

Table 4.2: Group-wise Number of SSI Units Formally Registered as on 2001-02

Industries	Number of SSI units	Number of factories
Food Products	2,815	165
Beverages	204	12
Hosiery and RMG	1,002	1
Wood Products	4,281	97
Paper Products	3,467	25
Leather Products	2,262	6
Rubber and Plastics Products	2,167	13
Textiles	1,620	107
Chemical Products	1,282	45
Non-Metallic Mineral Products	2,611	96
Metal and Allied Products	4,192	60
Basic Metal	2,910	80
Transport Equipment	734	9
Machine Parts Except Electricals	882	34
Electrical Machinery & Apparatus	1,209	44
Repairing and Servicing	3,492	60
Miscellaneous industries	4,767	61
Total	**43,689**	**964**

Source: *Handbook of Industrial Statistics*, Directorate of Industries & Commerce, Jammu and Kashmir Government, (2001).

These industries together account for more than 69.5 per cent of the total units that are registered with the Directorate of Industries and Commerce as on 2001-02. The factory sector mainly consist of food products, wood products, textiles, non-metallic mineral products, basic metal products and repairs and services. The important products manufactured in the state public sector include: textiles, joineries, cement, chemicals, wool and silk. Since 1980's there has been an upsurge in the proliferation of Modern Small Scale Industrial Units producing modern products and these are largely located around the metropolis of Kashmir and Jammu cities.

Industrial Employment

The role of industries is even more pervasive in the state of J&K given its rapidly growing population and the excessive workforce. The growth in the number of industrial units though not unsatisfactory, is not sufficient enough to make any worth while change in the product-employment multiplier in the state. The growth in industrial employment has not been sufficient to absorb the growing workforce. As per the available data, the total number of persons employed in the industrial sector have gown to 2,70,981 persons in 2001-02 from 70,076 persons in 1980-81, thus registered a growth rate of 5.01 per cent while as, industrial employment at all-India level has grown at 12.52 per cent during the same period. The total workforce in the state from 1981 to 2001 has grown at the rate 22.02 per cent, while as employment generated by the industrial sector has grown only at the rate of 5.01 percent. Thus it becomes clear from these figures that the industrial sector in the state has failed to keep pace with the growing work force. It is because of this, the state suffers from large scale unemployment and under-employment.

Sector-wise, small scale industries which dovetail well with the economic imperatives of the state account for most of the employment generated in the industrial sector. It accounts for more than 71 percent of the total industrial employment as on 2001-02 (Table 4.3). The small-scale industries in the state

Table 4.3: Employment generated by the SSI, Khadi & Villege Industries, State PSUs & Central PSUs

Year	SSI	Ab. Growth	%age Growth	Cg	K&V Ind.	Ab. Growth	%age Growth	Cg	State PSUs	Ab. Growth	%age Growth	Cg
1980-81	42992				28396				5249			
1985-85	84821	41829	97.29	20.5	28110	-286	-1.00	6.28	6932	1683	32.06	1.49
1990-91	131164	46343	54.63		46241	18131	64.50		5994	-938	-13.53	
1995-96	159671	28507	21.73		64074	17833	38.56		6001	7	0.11	
1996-97	165064	5393	3.37		98019	33945	52.97		5673	-328	-5.46	
1997-98	169050	3986	2.41	2.87	78019	-20000	-20.40	9.38	5554	-119	-2.09	4.99
1998-99	178004	8954	5.29		80965	2946	3.77		3597	-1957	-35.23	
1999-00	183698	5694	3.19		61998	-18967	-23.42		5148	1551	43.11	
2000-01	187399	3701	2.01		67433	5435	8.76	3.56	4427	-721	-14.00	
2001-02	193285	5886	3.14	2.84	72309	4876	7.23		4919	492	11.11	1.90
2002-03	198238	4953	2.56						3803	-1116	-22.68	
Cg			**6.6**				**5.11**				**-0.79**	

Note: K&V Stands for Khadi & Village Industries; Cg Stands for Compound Growth; Ab Growth Stands for Absolute Growth; SSI Stands for Small Scale Industries.

Source: *Digest of Statistics*, Directorate of Economics and Statistics, Planning and Development Department, J&K Government, 2002-03.

recorded a growth rate of 6.47 percent in the number of persons employed during 1980-81 to 2001-02 period while as, at all India level the growth has been 8.42 percent during the same period. It can also be seen from Table 4.3 that the maximum growth has been achieved during the decade of 80's. During this decade, the number of persons employed in small scale industries grew at an annual rate of 9.34 per cent.

Next to small-scale industries with regard to employment are Khadi and Village industries. It accounts for nearly 27 per cent of the total industrial employment as on 2001-02. Khadi and Village industries have recorded less growth than the small scale industries. It has grown at a rate of 5.11 per cent only during 1981-82 to 2001-02. Public Sector Enterprises, both state and central together, account for 2 per cent of the total employment generated by the industries in the state as on 2001-02. It can also be seen from the Table 4.3a that the public sector enterprises have witnessed a declining trend in the employment. The employment in state public sector enterprises and central public sector undertakings has declined by 0.79 percent and 1.1 per cent respectively during 1981-82 to 2001-02.

Table 4.3a: Employment Generated by the Central PSUs

Year	Central PSUs	Ab. Growth	%age Growth	Cg
1980-81	1339			
1985-85	1431	92	6.87	-0.46
1990-91	1278	-153	-10.69	
1995-96	1286	8	0.62	
1996-97	1277	-9	-0.69	
1997-98	904	-373	-29.20	-3.37
1998-99	933	29	3.20	
1999-00	933	0	0.00	
2000-01	993	60	6.43	
2001-02	960	-33	-3.32	3.82
2002-03	1040	80	8.33	
Cg			**-1.10**	

The industrial growth though has been somewhat satisfactory yet, it has failed to generate employment to any significant extent as becomes clear from the data detailed out in Table 4.4.

Table 4.4: Occupational Classification of Workforce in J&K State

Sector	Census 1971	Census 1981	Census 2001
Primary Sector	982372 (71.50)	1161736 (63.65)	1848233 (50.10)
Secondary Sector	125993 (9.17)	259190 (12.60)	581255 (19.82)
Tertiary sector	265536 (19.32)	397648 (23.51)	1109385 (30.70)
Total	**1373901** **(100. 00)**	**1818574** **(100. 00)**	**3688875** **(100. 00)**

Source: Census of India.

As a result, the primary sector continues to employ major chunk of workforce in the state. Out of the total workforce of 36.88 lakh main workers as per census 2001, 50.10 percent are engaged in agriculture. Manufacturing together with household industries employs 15.75 percent of the total workforce. This is in contrast to the occupational structure in developed economies. For example in USA, Japan, U.K., France 60 to 70 percent workers are engaged in tertiary sector and the industry in these countries employs between 20 to 30 percent of the total workforce. However, during the last two decades (1981-2001), the secondary sector has recorded sufficient growth in employment while as, the number of persons employed in the primary sector have declined from 63.88 per cent to 50.10 per cent during the same decade as can also be seen from the table.

An increase in the number of persons employed in the secondary sector and a corresponding decrease in the workforce engaged in agricultural sector is indicative of the desired structural adjustment in the states economy. But the occupational structure in the state is still like that of an under-developed economy with agriculture as the main stay of the major portion of the population. It is because of the under-development of industrial economy that a major chunk of workforce is engaged in agriculture. Further in the absence of requisite industrial base, the state suffers from large-scale unemployment. Although the problem of unemployment is a country-wide phenomenon yet, it is less prevalent in industrially developed states in the country and more serious in less developed states like ours. Such a gloomy picture of the states economy calls for large scale change in occupational structure which, however, can be attained through the process of industrialization.

Employment in Government Sector

In industrially developed economies, industries together with services employs large proportion of workforce while as government sector employs less number of people. Contrary to it, here in the state, the government is the main employer. The latest data about the number of persons employed in the state is not available. A cursory look into the Table 4.5 reveals that as on 1991, the state sector provided employment to 2,15,002 persons while as industries provided employment to 1,84,677 persons only. The table also reveals that the employment in the state sector has grown at 10.92 percent during 1973 to 1980.

Table 4.5: Employment in State Sector

Year	Number of persons	Absolute growth	%age growth	Cumulative. growth
1973-74	112262			
1981-82	168010	55748	49.65	6.20
1984-85	190366	22356	13.30	
1990-91	215002	24636	12.94	3.10
Cumulative growth		**0.478**		

Source: *Digest of Statistics*, Directorate of Economics and Statistics, Planning and Development Department, J&K Government, 2002-03.

On the other hand the employment generated by the industrial sector during 1982 to 2002 has grown only at 5.01 per cent. What can be concluded from this is that the industrial sector has miserably failed to generate sufficient jobs. As a result, the state government was constrained to provide more jobs to the citizens in the state. The latest data about the employment in Govt. sector is not available, however, it is reported that the state and central governments together currently employ nearly 70 per cent of the total number of persons employed in the state. This is indicative of the fact that the state suffers from low level of industrial base. The pressure on the government to provide more jobs has serious economic consequences. The increasing pressure on the state sector of employing more and more is resulting in a strain on the budgetary resources to an unbearable extent thus, has reduced its capacity considerably to make much needed investment in infrastructure development. The lack of sufficient and quality infrastructure capital in the state is reported to have significantly halted the pace of economic development.

Industrial Output

Establishing an industrial enterprise serves the purpose only when it continues to operate efficiently. As such, the growth in the number of industrial units cannot be taken as a real indicator of industrial progress. An analysis of the trends in industrial production provides a more candid picture of the advancements made on the industrial front. The growth rate in industrial output has been satisfactory but not commensurate with the investment that has gone into the industrial sector over a period of time as becomes clear from the data detailed out in Table 4.6. A cursory look into the above table brings to fore that the industrial production in the state has grown at the rate of 11.25 per cent during 1980-81 to 2001-02, however, it does not compare well with the growth in industrial output at the national level. If handicraft and Khadi and Village industries are excluded, then the growth rate in industrial production will be less than 11.25 per cent. What emerges from the above is that when the country as

Table 4.6: Annual Production of Registered Factories, Handicrafts, Khadi & Villege Industries, State PSUs & Central PSUs (Rs in Lakhs)

Year	Reg. factories	Ab. Growth	%age Growth	Cg	Handi-crafts	Ab. Growth	%age Growth	Cg	K&V Ind.	Ab. Growth	%age Growth	Cg
1980-81	9904				5782				426.72			
1985-85	28594	18690	188.71	25.7	10500	4718	81.59	14.5	1601.46	1174.75	275.29	61.4
1990-91	35420	6826	23.87		20000	9500	90.47		4331.13	2729.66	170.44	
1995-96	104448	69028	194.88		25000	5000	25.00		4639.67	2108.54	48.68	
1996-97	114320*	9872	9.45	29.5	26000	1000	4.00		7137.39	697.72	10.83	
1997-98	129080*	14760	12.91		27210*	1210	4.65	1.5	7137.39	00.00	00.00	2.6
1998-99	141735	12655	9.80		28000	790	2.90		7819.68	682.29	9.55	
1999-00	164584	22849	16.12		63303	35303	126.08		7852.04	32.36	0.41	
2000-01	134272	-30312	-18.41	-0.8	69633	6330	9.99	4.4	8016.20	164.16	2.09	4.8
2001-02	138201	3929	2.92		76594	6961	9.99		9000	983.80	12.27	
2002-03					77500	906	1.18					
Cg			**20.30**				**11.79**				**13.66**	

Contd...

Year	State PSUs	Ab. Growth	%age Growth	Cg	Central PSUs	Ab. Growth	%age Growth	Cg
1980-81	2899.9				661.40			
1985-85	3486.92	587.02	20.24	1.90	1637.51	976.11	147.58	3.59
1990-91	3450.77	-36.15	-1.03		898.90	-738.61	-45.10	
1995-96	4148.10	697.33	20.20		939.61	40.71	4.52	
1996-97	4785.73	637.63	15.37		1350.88	411.27	43.77	
1997-98	5102.07	316.34	6.61	8.71	1842.42	491.54	36.38	6.72
1998-99	5856.90	754.83	14.79		1445.16	-397.26	-21.56	
1999-00	6725.04	868.14	14.82		1445.16	00.00	00.00	
2000-01	6408.16	-316.88	-4.71	10.61	1511.09	65.93	4.56	2.22
2001-02	8987.84	2579.68	40.25		1550.46	39.37	2.60	
2002-03	8763.55	-224.29	-2.49		1196.22	-354.24	-22.84	
Cg			**8.9**				**3.39**	

Note: K&V Stands for Khadi & Village Industries; Cg Stands for Compound Growth; Ab Growth Stands for Absolute Growth; SSI Stands for Small Scale Industries.

Source: *Digest of Statistics*, Directorate of Economics and Statistics, Planning and Development Department, J&K Government, 2002-03

a whole is moving on high growth path, the state is moving on low growth path in the industrial sector. Low growth in industrial output is reported partly due to low investments in the industrial sector and partly due to the various inefficiency that are plaguing state's industrial economy. A growth rate of 11.25 per cent in industrial output as compared to 7.02 per cent in the number of industrial units during the same period brings to fore the other important fact that whatever little investment has gone into the different industrial sectors that too is not in good state of health. The state suffers from widespread industrial sickness and the number of sick units that have gone sick have reached to dizzy figures.

The profile of industries in the state has undergone a radical change from one of old (handicraft industries) to one of new modern small scale industries. This is evident from the fact that till 1960, the industrial landscape of the state was dominated by handicraft and Khadi and village industries. Since 1980's there has been considerable growth in the production curve of registered factories as can be seen from Table 4. 6. The output of the factory sector which was just Rs. 9,904 lakh in 1980-81 has grown to Rs. 1,38,208 lakh in 2001-02, thus has grown at the rate of 20.30 per cent during the period. As on 2001-02, factory output account for 57 percent of the total industrial output. The handicrafts and Khadi and village industries together account for 36 percent of the total output as on 2001-02.

Though the handicraft sector where state enjoys some definite comparative advantage yet, it has grown at a meager rate compared to registered factories and Khadi and Village industries. The handicraft sector has grown only at the rate of 13.79 per cent which is less given the potential of this age old industry of the state. The output of Khadi and village industries has grown at 13.66 per cent which compares well with the figures at the national level. More contribution of factory sector is a healthy sign in the sense that some modernisation in the state's economy has taken place, though there is still a long road to tread in this regard. To raise the industrial output it is imperative that we need to reshape our industrial structure in a manner that it becomes compatible with our resources with greater emphasis on the growth and development of modern industries which are capable of solving most of our economic problems.

Public sector enterprises, both state and central account for a mere 5 per cent of the total industrial output in the state as on 2001-02. The output of state public sector enterprises has grown at a rate of 8.9 per cent while as, the central public enterprises have recorded a paltry growth of 3.39 per cent. There is nothing surprising about the insufficient growth in the output of public sector undertakings in the state as it is a national phenomenon. There is no denying the fact that the public sector in the country has to its credit some notable achievements but all is not well with its workings. Due to the large scale failures, the very purpose of the existence of the public sector is being questioned. Today many of the public sector enterprises have become awesome burden on the state exchequer. By now the social development role of these enterprises has got too thin to hide their commercial nudity (Khan, 2003). As a matter of fact, the social role of these enterprises was not at all thought to eclipse their economic viability which in itself is an important social purpose. Given the gloomy picture of public sector, the Government at the centre has initiated various measures like disinvestment, privatization, giving greater autonomy etc. to reform these enterprises. Given the precarious financial health of the state and the fast changing economic milieu in the country, there is a fervent need to evolve some radical measures to reform state public sector enterprises.

Composition of Net Domestic Product

Industrial progress is more candidly reflected in the distribution of Net Domestic Product by industry of origin. The composition of net domestic product in advanced countries is tilted heavily towards non-agricultural sector. For example in USA, Canada, Germany,

Japan etc. the percentage share of non-agricultural sector is nearly 96 per cent. A pleasing aspect of the Indian Economy is that it is falling in line with the economies of advanced countries in structural composition, though it has still to go a long way to achieve the desired diversification. The contribution of agricultural sector is on steady decline and that of non-agricultural sector is on rise. All this is symbolic of a movement towards development. A structural transformation has also taken place in the state's economy over a period of time. Like that of whole nation, the state economy is dictated by declining share of agricultural sector in the states domestic product with the corresponding increase in non-agricultural sector.

Perusal of Table 4.7, which contains data about the percentage distribution of State Domestic Product (SDP) by industry of origin reveals that the state which was predominantly an agrarian economy is now drawing only to the extent of 36.34 percent from the primary sector in 2001-02 as against to 47.40 percent in 1980-81. However, the growth in the contribution from non-agricultural sector is pronounced more towards tertiary sector than the secondary sector. As can be seen from the above table that the secondary sector contributed only 14.11 per cent to the SDP in 2001-02, which has grown from 12.9 per cent in 1980-81. The manufacturing sector excluding construction, gas, electricity and water contributes a mere 6.43 per cent to the SDP.

This is in contrast to the composition of Net Domestic Product at the national level, where agriculture contributes only 26.72 per cent and the secondary sector account for more than 21 per cent in 2001-02, which is symbolic of underdevelopment of secondary sector in the state. The other discerning aspect of the secondary sector in the state is that it has witnessed fluctuating trends in its growth during 1980-81 to 2001-02. The contribution from the secondary sector which was 12.90 per cent in 1980-81 has grown to 16.81 per cent in 1990-91 and then declined 14.11 per cent in 2001-02. Such a fluctuating behavior of the share of manufacturing sector to SDP is indicative of the fact that the states industrial economy lacks stability and resilience. However, the decline during the decade of 90's can also be attributed to the disturbed conditions in the state which has given a crippling blow

Table 4.7: Percentage Distribution of State Domestic Product by Sectoral Breakup at Constant Prices (1980-81)

Year	Primary Sector	Ab. Growth	%age Growth	Cg	Secondary Sector	Ab. Growth	%age Growth	Cg	Tertiary Sector	Ab. Growth	%age Growth	Cg
1980-81	47.40				12.90		16.27		39.70			
1985-85	44.84	-2.56	-5.40	0.04	15.00	2.1	12.06	0.46	40.16	0.46	1.15	0.03
1990-91	38.49	-6.35	-14.16		16.81	1.81	-10.41		44.70	4.54	11.30	
1995-96	39.58	1.09	2.83		15.06	-1.75	-11.35		45.36	0.66	1.47	
1996-97	40.31	0.73	1.84		13.35	-1.71	10.03		46.34	0.98	2.16	
1997-98	36.74	-3.57	-8.85	8.08	14.69	1.34	1.36	0.05	48.57	2.23	4.81	6.67
1998-99	36.52	-0.22	-0.59		14.89	0.20	-20.88		48.59	0.02	0.04	
1999-00	38.12	1.6	4.38		11.78	-3.11	1.69		50.10	1.51	3.10	
2000-01	36.99	-1.13	-2.96	-8.7	11.98	0.20	17.77	0.05	51.03	0.93	1.85	0.09
2001-02	36.34	-0.65	-1.75		14.11	2.13	8.57		49.51	-1.52	-2.97	
Cg			**-1.12**				**-0.75**				**1.37**	

Note: Cg Stands for Compound Growth; Ab Growth Stands for Absolute Growth

Source: *Digest of Statistics*, Directorate of Economics and Statistics, Planning and Development Department, J&K Government, 2002-03.

to the economy in general and the industrial economy in particular.

The data exhibited in table 4.8 makes it amply clear that the state's economy is moving on a low growth path. The SDP in the state has grown at a rate of 9.35 per cent during 1981-82 to 2001-02 which does not compare well with the national averages. It can be seen from the above table that the primary sector has grown at the rate of 9.4 per cent during 1980-81 to 2001-02 and the secondary sector at the rate of 8.92 per cent. Compared to these sectors, tertiary sector has grown somewhat at a satisfactory rate of 11.43 per cent during the same period. Within the secondary sector, mining has registered more growth than manufacturing, electricity and construction. Mining has registered growth of 5.02 per cent whereas manufacturing and electricity has grown at a rate of 2.37 per cent and 3.85 per cent respectively during the same period. Low growth in these sub-sectors of the secondary sector indicates that a little development has taken place in the process of industrialization and infrastructure development in particular power generation. Among other things, the lack of sufficient and quality power to a great extent has constrained the development of the states economy.

Some diversification has taken place in the state's economy over a period of time but a trend which is somewhat disturbing is about the slow and halting growth in the commodity sector (Primary and Secondary) and more growth in the tertiary sector. The share of tertiary sector in the State Domestic Product has grown to 49.51 per cent in 2001-02 from 39.70 per cent in 1980-81, whereas at the national level it accounts for 41.87 per cent in 2001-02. In underdeveloped economies like that of ours, till commodity sector grows sufficiently, a faster growth in the tertiary sector is not a healthy sign. Since tourism is the most important industry in the state, therefore, more than normal growth in services sector is justified to meet the growing demand for services by the tourism industry and the commodity sector. But the contribution of services sector to SDP in the state still seems to be more than normal. A high growth in services sector is

Table 4.8: Net State Domestic Product by Sectoral Breakup at Constant Prices (1980-81) (Rs. lakh)

Year	Primary sector	Ab. growth	%age growth	Secondary sector	Ab. growth	%age growth	Tertiary Sector	Ab. growth	%age growth	Total State	Ab. growth	%age growth
1980-81	497.44			135.40			416.66			1049.5		
1985-85	551.48	54.0	10.8	184.48	49.08	36.24	493.88	77.2	18.53	1229.8	180.3	17.1
1990-91	523.48	-28.0	-5.0	228.59	44.11	23.91	607.82	113.9	23.07	1359.8	130.0	10.5
1995-96	2387.08	1863.6	356.0	908.25	697.66	297.32	2736.15	2128.3	350.15	6031.4	4671.5	343.5
1996-97	2547.55	160.4	6.7	843.87	-64.38	-7.08	2929.23	193.0	7.05	6320.6	289.1	4.7
1997-98	2343.83	-203.7	-7.9	977.10	133.23	15.78	3231.31	302.0	10.31	6552.2	231.5	3.6
1998-99	2558.12	214.2	9.1	1043.09	65.99	6.75	3404.12	172.8	5.34	7005.3	453.0	6.9
1999-00	2771.62	213.5	8.3	856.20	-186.89	-17.91	3642.33	238.2	6.99	7270.1	264.8	3.7
2000-01	2736.96	-34.6	-1.2	886.59	30.39	3.54	3775.35	133.0	3.65	7398.9	128.7	1.7
2001-02	2930.29	193.3	7.0	1137.98	251.39	28.35	3994.54	219.1	5.80	8062.8	663.9	8.9
Cg			**9.4**			**8.92**			**11.43**			**11.0**

Note: Cg Stands for Compound Growth; Ab Growth Stands for Absolute Growth.
Source: *Digest of Statistics*, Directorate of Economics and Statistics, Planning and Development Department, J&K Government, 2002-03.

not purely due to large scale expansion and diversification of commodity sector or due to the dominance of tourism in the states economy. The state has been witnessed political turmoil since 1991 which has significantly reduced the tourist flow into the state, therefore, tourism industry cannot be accounted for the expansion of services sector to such an extent. However, it is an open fact that lot of unaccounted money has flown into the state from different quarters to defeat the political aspirations of the masses. This has resulted into higher level of incomes of some portion of population otherwise by all standards J&K state is one of the poor states of the country. It is also the government services account for loins share in tertiary sector in the state. More than 3.5 lakh families directly depend upon employment from the government sector (Godbole, 1997).

Per Capita Income

The per capita income of the state has remained almost stagnant from 1980-81 to 1990-91, thereafter, it has grown steadily at the rate of 16.02 per cent while at the national level, the per capita income grew at 18.29 percent during the same period (Table 4.9).

Table 4.9: Per Capita Income in J&K State (Constant Prices)

Year	Per capita income (Rs.)	Absolute growth	%age growth	Cumulative growth
1980-81	1776	-	-	
1985-86	1832	56	3.15	0.00045
1990-91	1784	-48	-2.62	
1995-96	6732	4968	2.77	
1996-97	6978	246	3.65	
1997-98	7128	150	2.14	0.162
1998-99	7296	168	2.35	
1999-00	7384	88	1.20	
2000-01	7385	01	0.00013	0.018
2001-02	7841	456	6.17	
Cg		**15.92**		

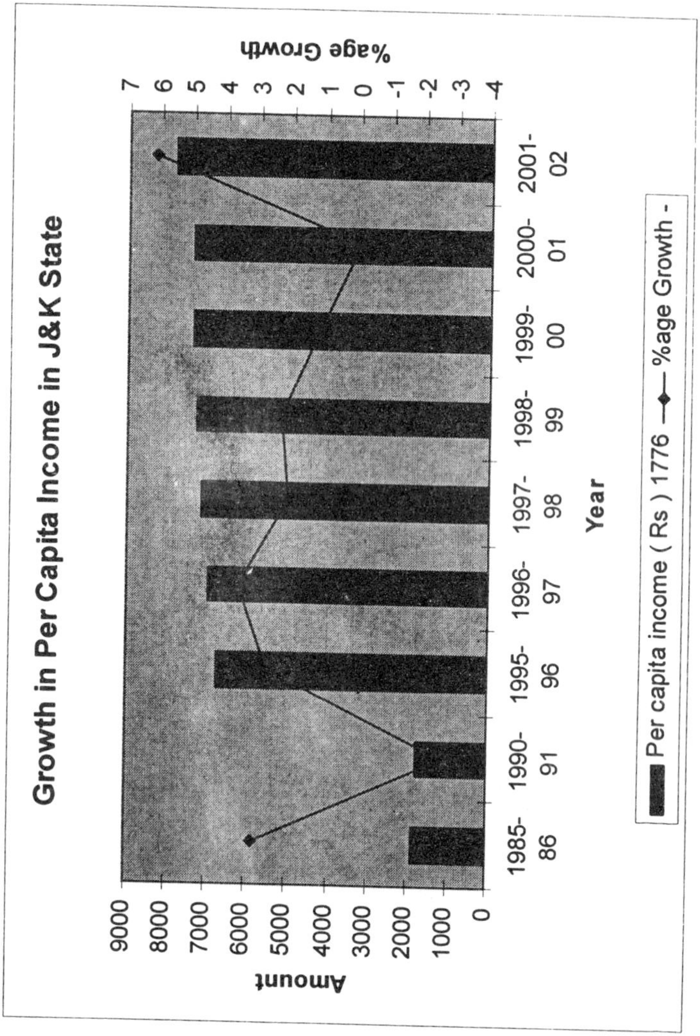
Growth in Per Capita Income in J&K State
Amount
9000
8000
7000
6000
5000
4000
3000
2000
1000
0
%age Growth
7
6
5
4
3
2
1
0
-1
-2
-3
-4
1985-86
1990-91
1995-96
1996-97
1997-98
1998-99
1999-00
2000-01
2001-02
Year
Per capita income (Rs) 1776
%age Growth -

Growth in per capita income has a close correspondence with the growth in different sectors of an economy. As the production curve of agricultural and industrial goods did not rise enough, the growth in per capita income in the state could not be satisfactory.

The per capita income of the state as on 2001-02 was Rs. 7,841 (at constant prices: 1980-81) which is by far less than the national per capita income of Rs. 10,254. As per the per capita income, the state of Jammu & Kashmir ranks 18th of the 23 states in the country (Table 4.10).

The Himachal Pradesh with similar geo-physical and other features is ranking ahead of J&K state. It ranks 9th with a per capita income of Rs. 10,942 (at constant prices) which is more than the All-India average of 10,254. The per capita income (at constant prices) of the state is quite less than that of industrially developed states like Maharashtra (Rs. 15,172); Karnataka (Rs. 11,910); Tamil Nadu (Rs. 12,779); Andhra Pradesh (Rs. 10,059); Punjab (Rs. 15,390); Gujarat (Rs. 12,976); West Bengal (Rs. 9,778).

The low per capita income is another aspect symbolic of under-development of secondary as well as primary sectors in the state. Given the above state of affairs, the state needs to improve upon its income capacity which can be attained by improving upon its capital-output ratio, creating more productive capacity and reducing the population growth. However, all this among other things would require to improve infrastructural index in the state.

Import-Export Elasticity

Another aspect, symbolic of underdevelopment of the state's economy is the over-dependence on imports to meet the growing needs of the population. The state of J&K is suffering from very high import-export ratio implying that the state is suffering from very large trade deficit. The Import-Export Ratio, which was 2.73:1 in 1983-84, has gone to 5.28:1 in 2002-03.

Table 4.10: State-wise Per Capita Income in India (Constant Prices)

State	Per Capita Income (Rs)	Rank
Andhra Pradesh	10,059	11
Arunachal Pradesh	9,013	14
Assam	5,867	20
Bihar	3,345	23
Delhi	24,450	2
Goa	26,106	1
Gujarat	12,976	6
Haryana	14,331	5
Himachal Pradesh	10,942	9
Jaharkhand	N.A.	-
Jammu & Kashmir	7,383	18
Karnataka	11,910	8
Kerala	10,712	10
Madhya Pradesh	7,198	19
Maharashtra	15,172	4
Manipur	N.A.	-
Meghalaya	8,118	16
Mizoram	N.A.	-
Nagaland	8,726	15
Orissa	5,187	22
Punjab	15,390	3
Rajasthan	7,932	17
Sikkim	N.A.	-
Tamil Nadu	12,779	7
Tripura	9,072	13
Uttranchal	N.A.	-
Uttar Pradesh	5,770	21
West Bengal	9,778	12
All India	**10,254**	

Source: *Digest of Statistics*, Directorate of Economics and Statistics, Planning and Development Department, J&K Government, 2002-03.

In absolute terms the trade deficit of the state has went-up from Rs. 188.67 crore in 1983-84 to a whopping figure of Rs. 4,171.11 crore in 2002-03. The imports into the state have grown at the rate of 8.75 per cent while as exports from the state have grown only at a rate of 5.83 per cent (Table 4.11). The exports from the state mostly include handicraft products, horticulture products, skins and hides, rosine and turpentine and wood products. Further, the export of most of the commodities is made in raw form only in the absence of necessary industrial base. The fact that becomes evident from the above is that the state has failed to expand its productive capacity in particular in the secondary sector.

Although, given the unique geo-physical and socio-political features of the state, the state has to have a trade deficit but not to the extent it is having at present. In fact, the state has turned into a consumption economy. Given the resource base of the state, there is enough scope to reduce the trade deficit. This would require re-shaping and expanding the production base in a manner that it becomes compatible with our resources. This involves two things – one assessment of our resources and the second to evolve effective strategies to develop economic strength based on the resource endowments. Though the state is not fortunate enough to have wide variety of resources yet, it has certainly some proven natural and other advantages which definitely promise great industrial potential. But unfortunately most of these resources remained underutilized.

Summary

Taking together the shortcomings and the achievements made so far, the picture of industrial development in the state appears gloomy. The Industrial growth has been relatively late, slow and halting. The state still remains one of the industrially backward states of the country. Its backwardness can be judged from its sect oral break-up of SDP; Import-export ratio etc. The secondary sector contributes only to the extent of 12.37 percent in 2001-02 which is symbolic of less developed nature of the states industrial

Table 4.11: Import-Export Elasticity in the State of J&K

Year	Value of Imports (Taxable)	Ab. Growth	%age Growth	Cg	Value of Exports (Taxable)	Ab. Growth	%age Growth	Cg	Import-Export Ratio
1983-84	29756				10889				2.73:1
1984-85	33451	3695	12.41		20785	9896	90.88		1.61:1
1985-86	41877	8426	25.19		18444	-2340	11.25		2.27:1
1986-87	42126	248	0.59	0.217	23205	4760	25.80	0.087	1.81:1
1987-88	56791	14665	34.81		18670	-4534	-19.53		2.72:1
1988-89	77069	20277	35.70		20169	1499	8.02		3.82:1
1989-90	115733	38664	50.16		27848	7678	38.06		4.16:1
1990-91	125375	9641	8.33		50740	22892	82.20		2.47:1
1991-92	177041	51666	41.20		58362	7621	15.02		3.03:1
1992-93	181659	4618	2.60		59123	761	1.30		3.07:1
1993-94	204071	22412	12.33		62303	3179	5.37		3.28:1
1994-95	253653	49582	24.29	0.036	56084	-6219	-9.98	0.269	4.52:1
1995-96	309183	55529	21.89		67214	11130	19.84		4.60:1
1996-97	296617	-12566	-4.06		69848	2634	3.91		4.24:1
1997-98	326514*	29897	10.07		72125	2276	3.25		4.52:1
1998-99	341484	14969	4.58		76128	4002	5.54		4.48:1
1999-00	377205	27721	15.32		88858	12730	16.72		4.43:1
2000-01	393824	16619	11.50	**0.023**	93980	5121	5.76	**0.0007**	4.67:1
2001-02	439146	45322	8.66		94964	983	1.04		5.02:1
2002-03	477209	38063	7.83		97477	2513	2.64		5.28:1
Cg			**8.75**				**5.83**		**5.28:1**

Note: Cg Stands for Compound Growth; Ab Growth Stands for Absolute Growth.

Source: *Digest of Statistics*, Directorate of Economics and Statistics, Planning and Development Department, J&K Government, 2002-03

economy. Due to low growth in production capacity in the secondary sector, the state is suffering from very large trade deficit, which is widening on an average at the rate of 5.34 percent.

Another disquieting feature is that the industrial growth though somewhat satisfactory, has failed to generate employment to any significant extent. As a result, the primary sector continues to employ a major chunk of work force. As per census 2001, out of the total work force of 20.01 lakh workers, 62.97 percent are engaged in agriculture. The manufacturing sector employs only 11.24 percent of the total work force as on 2001. This is in total contrast to the occupational structure of developed economies where secondary sector employs large proportion of work force. As the agricultural sector itself is backward and constrained with low land-man ratio, all the workers are not needed their either thus, resulting in large scale underemployment and underemployment in rural Kashmir. This explains why the overall picture of the states economy looks gloomy. In the absence of sufficient industrial base, the state suffers from large scale unemployment among the educated youth. The under-development of industrial sector has forced the state government to create more employment avenues for its citizens. The increasing pressure on the state government to employ more and more has reduced its capacity to make much needed investment in the development of infrastructure and other facilities.

An important development in the states economy has been an increase in the share of non-agricultural sector and a steady decline in the share of agricultural sector in the States Domestic Product, thus falling in line with the desired economic transformation. But the shift has been more pronounced towards territory sector. The fast growth in territory sector is not a healthy sign. This is because that before the commodity sector grows sufficiently, high growth in services is not considered a healthy trend. A low growth in primary and secondary sectors is being reflected in a low growth in per capita income of the state. The state ranks 21st on the basis of per capita income in the country.

The state today is suffering from low industrial output; high import-export ratio; more unemployment among the educated youth; lower capital productivity, high fiscal imbalance with excessive reliance on the union. All these are symbolic of underdevelopment of the economy. This is being mainly attributed to the small and shrinking production base in particular in the industrial sector. The Industrial sector is beset with number of problems which among other things have resulted into wide spread sickness in small-scale industries. There is no statistics about the incidence of sickness in SSI, however, there are indications that large number of units have gone sick. In fact, industrial scenario in the state is in the state of paralysis rather than sickness, which had the most dampening effect on the industrial development. Therefore, to usher in a healthy and self-sustaining industrial economy, there is an immense need to rationalize our thinking about the issues that inhibit growth and prosperity of industrial sector and what needs to be done to improve-upon the weaknesses that are coming in the way of quick and expansive industrial transformation of the state.

References

Khan M. A. (2003), "Seminar Report on the Problems and Remedies of J & K Public Sector Undertakings", J & K Institute of Management, Public Administration & Rural Development, Srinagar, Kashmir.

Staley, E. (1963), "The Future of Underdeveloped Countries",

5

Issues Concerning Industrial Development

Introduction

The canvas of industrial development drawn in the previous chapter depicts that the industrial growth in the state is marked by some success and some failures, with the net outcome far from desirable. In spite of decades of efforts to industrialise, the state still continues to be one of the industrially under-developed states in the country. The state today is suffering from low industrial output; high import-export ratio; large scale unemployment; low capital productivity, high fiscal imbalance with excessive reliance on the union. All these are symbolic of underdevelopment of the state's economy. This is being mainly attributed to the small and shrinking production base in particular in the industrial sector. The less developed nature of the state's industrial economy can be judged from the fact that it draws only to the extent of 12 per cent from the secondary sector which does not compare well with the national figures. Though the relative share of tertiary sector has increased considerably over the years yet, it is the government sector which accounts for major part of the tertiary sector's contribution to the SDP.

As a matter of fact, the state though not fortunate enough to have a potential for wide variety of industries, but certainly it enjoys definite potential in some selected lines of activity. Unfortunately the same remains largely under-utilised as becomes clear from the fact that the state is dependent on outside markets even for those products where state enjoys definite comparative advantage in resource endowments. It is not that the successive governments have done nothing to accelerate the industrial tempo in the state. But the fact of the matter is that the different state governments right from the beginning have taken number of initiatives to take-off the state to the higher growth path through the process of industrialization. For this purpose, a network of promotional institutions was created and have offered very attractive package of incentives to different types of industries. Against a background such as this, to usher in a healthy and self sustaining industrial economy, there is an immense need to rationalize our thinking about the various issues that inhibit growth and prosperity of industrial sector and what needs to be done to improve upon the weaknesses that are coming in the way of quick and expansive industrial transformation of the state's economy (Table 5.1).

Table 5.1: Balance Sheet of Industrial Development in the J&K State (1980-81 to 2001-02)

Indicators of Development	J&K State 1980-81	J&K State 2001-02	Cg %age
Number of Industrial units:			
• Small scale industries	8,428	43,689	7.1
• Khadi & Village industries	3,178	28,364	8.6
• Registered Factories	720	964	2.7
• Medium Scale Industries	25	25	0
• Large Scale Industries	2	2	0
Industrial Output (Rs. lakh)			
• Registered Factories	9,904	1,38,201	20.30
• Khadi & Village industries	426.72	9,000.00	13.66
• Handicrafts	5,782	76,594	11.79
• State Public Sector Enterprises	2,099	8,987.84	8.9
• Central Public Sector Enterprises	661.40	1196.22	3.39

Contd...

Industrial Employment			
• Small Scale industries	42,992	1,93,285	6.60
• Khadi & Village industries	20,396	72,309	5.11
• State Public Sector Enterprises	5,249	4,427	-0.79
• State Public Sector Enterprises	1,339	1,040	-1.10
Distribution of Work force			
• Agriculture	63.65%	50.10 %	-
• Secondary Sector	12.60%	19.82 %	-
• Tertiary Sector	23.51%	30.70 %	-
Sectoral Break-up of SDP			
• Primary	47.40 %	36.34 %	9.40
• Secondary	12.90 %	14.11 %	8.92
• Tertiary	39.70 %	49.51 %	11.43
Total	-	-	11.38
Per Capita Income			
• At constant prices	Rs. 1,776	Rs. 7,841	15..92
• At current prices			
Import-Export Elasticities (Rs. lakh) (1983-84–2001-02)			
• Imports	29,756	4,77,209	8.75
• Exports	10,889	94,964	5.85
• Import-Export Ratio	2.73 : 1	5.20 : 1	

Note: Cg Stands for Exponential Growth.
Source: Summary of Data Presented in the Previous Chapter.

Visibles and Invisibles

Most of the issues that are generally being talked about to have resulted in unimpressive development of different industrial sectors in the state are what may be called as apparent causes which are seemingly responsible for the lack of development but there are some fundamental (invisible) forces working behind these apparent forces. It is in view of this fact that this chapter focuses more on the invisible issues that have impeded the growth and development of the industrial sector with the purpose to chalk out future policy for sustainable industrial development. To get a candid picture of the different issues concerning meaningful industrial development, more particularly the invisible issues research evidences drawn from different sources have been used. The various factors that are reported to be responsible for poor industrial growth are discussed as under:

Infrastructural Bottlenecks

Adequate infrastructure of good quality is an essential pre-requisite for industrial growth and development. Economy progresses only when infrastructural facilities are adequate and of good quality, but breaks the wheels of an economy if in bad shape. The infrastructural index of the state is poor by all means, as a result of which the industrial growth has been very low. The data on relative Infrastructure Development Index (1998-2003) with all India index being 100, shows that in respect of J&K State, the index witnessed a marginal increase while as other states for example Himachal Pradesh registered a significant growth in infrastructure index (CMIE, 2003).

Industries in the state and more so in the Kashmir Division have suffered significantly for want of adequate and quality electric power. Although industrial estates are being given some priority in the supply of electric power yet, the problem of shortages of electric power continues to be one of the serious problems confronting industries in the state. In terms of per capita consumption of electricity in 2003, J & K State ranks 18th in the country (See Table 5.2 for further details). The industries in the state are not constrained only by power shortages but also by the poor quality of power. For example instead of providing 400-440 volts for which the power development is committed, the voltage ranges between 200–240 volts only (Nazim, 1999).

Table 5.2: Power Generated and Per Capital Power Consumption in Different States in India as on 1998-99

State	Power Generated (crore kwhs)	Per Capita Consumption (kwhs)	Rank as per Per Capita Consumption (kwhs)
Andhra Pradesh	3,080.50	404	8
Arunachal Pradesh	6.60	87	24
Assam	106.60	123	21
Bihar	422.50	152	19
Chattisgarh	N.E	NE	-
Delhi	189.40	689	4
Goa	N.A	740	2
Gujarat	3,435.70	724	3
Haryana	830.20	503	6
Himachal Pradesh	148.50	334	11
Jaharkhand	NE	NE	-
Jammu & Kashmir	71.30	292	15
Karnataka	1,718.20	349	10
Kerala	760.20	305	14
Madhya Pradesh	2,056.30	398	9
Maharashtra	5,663.90	594	5
Manipur	0.10	75	26
Meghalaya	55.50	150	20
Mizoram	1.70	114	22
Nagaland	0.20	81	25
Orissa	635.80	313	13
Punjab	2,088.00	861	1

Contd...

Rajasthan	1,196.40	329	12
Sikkim	5.40	185	18
Tamil Nadu	2,327.90	498	7
Tripura	39.30	110	23
Uttranchal	NE	NE	-
Utter Pradesh	2,493.80	196	17
West Bengal	1,588.30	211	16
All India	**44,854.40**	**360**	

Source: *Digest of Statistics*, Directorate of Economics and Statistics, Planning and Development Department, J&K Government, 2002-03

The root cause of this problem basically lies in the fact that the successive governments have miserably failed in setting the developmental priorities towards the development of industrially important infrastructure in the state, in particular electric power. As a matter of fact, the state has miserably failed in the generation of hydel power even though the state enjoys potential of a magnitude which no other state in the country can match. There is only 205 MWs installed capacity in the state sector whereas the peak demand in the state is reported to be around 1030 MWs. During the period of two decades (1978-97) no new hydel project has been commissioned in the state sector. More disquieting feature of hydel power development in the state is the glaring mismatch between power generation projects and Transmission and Distribution System (Godbole, 1998). At present only 340 MWs can be evacuated to the valley through Kishenpur–Pampore and the Udhampur–Bemina transmission lines. The state is also constrained with a limited transmission capacity from the Northern Grid.

The NHPC which is responsible for hydel power development in the Central Sector has also failed in the development of hydel power development in the state. It dismal performance in the state has also contributed its bit in the lack of electric power. It has so far executed only two projects in the state – Salal (690 MW) and Uri (480 MW) and has failed to commission Dulhasti (390 MW),

Baghlihar (450 MW), Kishenganga (330 MW) and Savalkote (600 MW). The Baghlihar and Savalkote projects have been taken by the state govt. though with financial assistance from the centre. If such projects would have been commissioned by the NHPC, the state would have surplus power not to talk of meeting its requirements internally in full. One fails to understand why NHPC has failed to commission these projects when it has executed so many projects in other parts of the country.

Although, power sector was allocated sufficient funds all through the first plan yet, that was spent mostly on rural electrification rather than on power generation. Thus this has been used more as a social service rather than as an engine of economic growth. This was done purely on political considerations but at a huge economic cost. Further the development of Transmission and Distribution (T&D) system in the state presents an unsatisfactory picture. As a result of poor state of T&D System, the state is seriously constrained by its limited capacity to evacuate power from generation points. This sad state of affairs is even though sufficient allocations were made for the development T&D system under different five year plans thus, raises certain questions about the utilization of plan funds. The Godbole Committee has reported that the poor state of T&D System in the state is a reflection of unsatisfactory planning, inadequacies in project formulation, poor execution and possibly misuse of funds thus calls for scrutiny. The other disquieting feature of the power sector in the state is the huge T&D losses. As per the available records as presented in Table 5.3, the Transmission and Distribution (T&D) losses in the state are unbelievably at 52.6 percent while as, at the national level it is only 21.24 percent. As a matter of fact, it is not only T&D losses but mostly includes pilferage.

The Indus water Treaty is another unfavorable factor for hydropower sector in the state. Under Indus Water Treaty three rivers which flow through Himachal Pradesh and Punjab viz; Sutluj, Beas and Ravi were given to India for utilization. The other three rivers which flow through J&K State namely; Jehlum,

Table 5.3: Power Generated, Purchased, Sold & T&D Losses in J&K State (lakh Kwhs)

Year	Generated	Purchased	Total	Sold	T & D Losses	T & D Losses
1980-81	7737.70	2883.40	10621.10	4199.00	6422.10	60.46
1985-86	8831.52	5876.59	14708.11	8815.20	5892.91	40.06
1990-91	9116.72	18559.31	27676.03	13445.19	14230.84	51.41
1995-96	8834.40	24873.00	33707.40	17280.40	16427.00	48.73
1996-97	8271.11	30529.70	38800.81	20148.90	18651.91	48.07
1998-99	7133.17	47243.80	54376.97	28736.90	25640.07	47.15
1999-00	6383.83	43466.90	49850.73	26376.80	23473.93	47.08
2000-01	5800.70	48083.00	53883.70	25630.70	28253.00	52.43
2001-02	5999.13	49894.80	55893.93	28527.09	27366.84	48.96
2002-03	5156.21	57786.50	62942.71	33101.60	29841.11	47.40

Source: *Digest of Statistics*, Directorate of Economics and Statistics, Planning and Development Department, J&K Government, 2002-03.

Chenab and Indus were given to Pakistan. As per the treaty, on these three rivers, the state is prohibited to build storage dams. As such, the state could undertake only run of the river power projects on these rivers. This in turn is resulting in low utilization during winter when there is low discharge from the rivers. It is being reported that this treaty is resulting in a potential loss of nearly 15000 MWs. This treaty is unfair neither to India nor to Pakistan but only to the state of J&K. The more disturbing aspect about this treaty is that neither the Central Govt. at its own has compensated to the state for the losses caused due to this treaty nor the state govt. has succeeded in seeking compensation from the Indian union. Further, the different governments in the past have failed to negotiate on favorable terms with NHPC for the Central Hydropower Projects commissioned in the state. In fact these projects were battered to the NHPC on cheap terms thus, causing losses to the state (Zabita; 2003).

Although, the problem of power shortages in the state are faced throughout the year yet, it is getting more acute during winter. The acuteness of the problem can be judged from the figures that as against the total demand of 2400 MW, only 1350 MWs of electricity are generated from all available sources during winter. This is due to low capacity utilization during winter because of low discharge in the rivers. The need to supplement hydropower generation by commissioning thermal power plant was not fully taken care off. Huge deposits of lignite have been found to occur in Nichaham, Shaliganga-Lanyalok, sectors in Handwara Tehsil of Baramulla district. Based on the detailed investigation of these lignite deposits, there was a plan to commission lignite based thermal power plant at Handwara, however, could not come till now for unknown reasons, thus leaving this natural resource of great use unutilized.

Entrepreneurial Bottlenecks

Economic greatness of nations is not a result of mere natural resource base but also of the quality entrepreneurial talent with which endowed. The fact of the matter is that natural resource base could only provide a comparative advantage to the nations concerned for industrialization, but it is ultimately the reservoir of rich entrepreneurial talent which matters most. An entrepreneur who is a front line actor in the process of industrial development with his dynamism, ability and ingenuity, he brings a change in the socio-economic order (Butt, 1998). This accords with the opinion of McClelland (1961) that economic development originates and fosters in relation to the strength and health of entrepreneurship, which in turn depends upon the rate of its generation and equally to the intensity of its sense of social responsibility, inventive quotient and index of management capability. The most glaring examples in this regard are some of the most industrially developed nations of the world for example Japan, Taiwan and Hong Kong. These have achieved phenomenal growth because of rich entrepreneurial talent though not rich in natural resources. As compared to these countries, India though being rich in natural resource base is yet to achieve the desired economic growth. While a number of factors could be argued to be responsible for the low economic progress of this vastly resourceful country, but the lack of motivated and talented entrepreneurs cannot be ignored to have not resulted in the under-development of Indian Economy. The state of Jammu and Kashmir has been more unfortunate in this regard as compared to the other states of the country. Most of the entrepreneurs in the state have been found lacking widely accepted Essential Personal Entrepreneurial Traits like, strong urge for achievement in entrepreneurship, initiative, creativity & innovations, focused knowledge etc.

Gamblers instinct and a certain degree of ruthlessness for achieving unusual results is essential ingredient of entrepreneurships. David C. McCleland of Harvard University, who has done a pioneering work in the field of entrepreneurship has established a close correspondence between economic growth and the entrepreneurial ability displayed by the society in terms of motivation. Further studies conducted in India and elsewhere also revealed existence of close correspondence between need for achievement motivation and entrepreneurial success. In fact it makes an entrepreneur to withstand all the onslaughts of challenging business world and to persist to gather necessary resources and energy to achieve unusual results.

The state is not fortunate enough to enjoy historical legacies in industrial entrepreneurship. Added to this, discouraging fact is that the educated youth in the state in particular in Kashmir division are displaying little preference for industrial entrepreneurship and are heavily oriented towards White Collar jobs. The entrepreneurship that emerged so far; one is that most of the entrepreneurs in the state are first generation entrepreneurs and second most of them have assumed industrial entrepreneurship either due to the wave of a particular industry or as were unable to find a job or due to an induced phenomena. The Survey results to this effect have been summarized in Table 5.4. The success rate of such entrepreneurs has been found very dismal due to the fact that these generally lack Personal Essential Entrepreneurial Traits.

Table 5.4: Level of Motivation of Small Entrepreneurs in J&K State

Indicators	Jammu Region (N=92)	Kashmir Region (N=94)	Total State (N=186)
Aim in Life			
• Entrepreneurship	28 (30.43)	21 (22.34)	49 (26.34)
• Govt. Service	32 (37. 78)	41 (43.61)	73 (39.24)
• Other	32 (37.78)	32 (34.04)	64 (34.40)
Motivated towards entrepreneurship			
• Incentives	34 (36.95)	35 (37.23)	69 (37.09)
• Family members	42 (45.65)	31 (32.97)	73 (39.24)
• Unable to get a suitable job	16 (17.39)	28 (29.78)	34 (23.65)

Note: Figures in Parenthesis indicate Percentage Respondents to the Total Sample.

Source: Butt K. A. (2000), 'Modern Small Scale Industries and Industrial Sickness', Anmol Publishers, New Delhi.

Further the industrial entrepreneurship obtaining in the state, apart from being limited, most of it does not appear to appreciate the significance and utility of organizing their units on modern lines. Most of the entrepreneurs have been found not possessing even a rudimentary knowledge of business/managerial aspects and because of which their approach has remained conservative rather than systematic. The other disturbing aspect of the entrepreneurship in the state is that people in the state have displayed a *"Herd Mentality"* with a number of them simultaneously venturing into projects without assessing the demand potentialities. More intriguing part of entrepreneurship in the state is that many entrepreneurs have developed a dependency syndrome, which to a great extent has retarded their confidence and initiative to create and innovate.

It is also that large number of people in the state have assumed entrepreneurship just to obtain institutional finances and pocket away incentives and subsidies. There are many instances where emtrepreneurs people who have installed a few machines for namesake only, have been found to have got subsidies and other incentives. The problem of ghost units (untraceable units) is more alarming in the state than other parts of the country. Current statistics reveal that more than 4000 industrial units are untraceable (Greater Kashmir, 1997). True entrepreneurs do exist in the state though in small numbers, however, these suffer from an attitude called as "Stay Small and Stay Happy Syndrome" Such entrepreneurs do not want to grow big as a result these have also failed to make a worthwhile contribution to the industrial growth. The thing that becomes vividly clear from the above facts that the industrial culture is missing in the state.

Political Bottlenecks

Kashmir is considered paradise on earth because of its scenic beauty, but this paradise on earth has been quite unfortunate with regard to political stability and peace, an essential prerequisite for sustainable economic development. The state of J&K continues to be a bone of contention between India and Pakistan and so far, the two countries have fought three wars over Kashmir. Although the state suffered from political instability and peace right from the beginning yet, its fragile political setup and peace got pulverized in 1990 when political movement aspiring change in the political status of the state took a violent turn. This violent political struggle has taken a heavy toll of the state's economy. Although political instability is bound to adversely affect the states economy yet, the different strategies that the Govt. of India followed at different stages to defeat the political movements seeking change in the status of the state have also played its part in dampening the economic growth and development. The political instability in the state has resulted into the following economic ramifications:

- No sincere effort has been made by the Govt. of India to develop necessary infrastructure and resilience in the states economy perhaps due political uncertainties. An important example to note in this regard is that the Govt. of India made no serious effort to harness the vast potential of hydro-electric power for the benefit of the Jammu & Kashmir. The state is severely constrained by inadequate power supply even though it enjoys huge potential. Further, J&K state is perhaps the only state in the Indian Union where much needed railway networking for a major portion of its area is missing. It is only after 50 years, the Govt. of India could visualize the need for taking Railhead up to Kashmir. More evident fact of their intent is that J&K despite having been declared industrially backward, central investment in central public sector enterprises and the assistance from Central Financial Institutions eludes the state. The state is being deliberately discriminated in the allocation of plan funds as well. The rank occupied by the state in terms of per capita resource transfer from the center to the different states under different plans stood at 18th, 16th, 15th, 16th, 15th, 11th and 12th through first five year plan to 7th five year plan respectively in spite of the fact that the cost of raising infrastructure here is much higher than other states.

Another fact supplementing the above hypothesis is about central financial assistance. Although J&K was eligible to receive 90 per cent in the form of grant-in-aid and 10 per cent in the form of loan yet, J&K was the only state to have been denied this special status till the recent past. This unjustified action by the Indian Govt. has made the state to suffer from the maze of financial constraint right from the beginning. This has constrained the state to spend sufficient sum on the creation of much needed infrastructure.

- Responsible and committed leadership is necessary to set a direction for achieving accelerated economic progress. The committed and responsible political leadership emerges only through the process of real democracy. The state of J&K has been deprived of this necessity, as well. Unfortunately the Govt. of India never allowed true democracy to flourish in the state. Though elections were held regularly but every time these were manipulated to install people of their own choice. As a result various governments formed in the state were least sensitive to the economic and other concerns of the state but were more interested to the concerns of their masters sitting in the power corridors at Delhi. Notable example in this regard is that the Indian union got the Article 370 reduced to ashes through the governments installed soon after the dismissal of Sheikh Abdullah's Govt. in 1953. Lack of accountability to the masses of the land has given them a free hand to plunder national wealth. No doubt Corruption is a national phenomenon but it is more widespread and rampant in the state where it has reached to alarming proportion. It is being argued that the govt. of India deliberately has let the corrupt practices at all levels to flourish as one of the strategies to defeat political movements aspiring change in the status of the state.
- Different governments have tried to woo the big industrial houses of the country to establish industrial units in the state. But failed in this regard largely due to the lack of political stability and peace and less by other extremes like lack of

industrially important infrastructural facilities etc. Till lasting peace returns to the state, there are very bleak chances of getting much needed foreign investment in various potential sectors of the economy.

Policy Hurdles

The role of the government in generating necessary impulse towards industrial growth is immense in particular in the state of J&K in view of its peculiar features. To regulate and promote industrial growth, different governments from time to time have come up with policy initiatives and launched various industrial programmes. Further it floated various promotional agencies and enacted laws and regulations to give necessary flip to the pace of industrialization in the state. A detailed analysis of various policy initiatives has revealed the following shortcomings in various policy initiatives which among other things have impeded the industrial growth.

Although the state is not rich enough in wide variety of natural resources yet it has some proven natural resources which offered huge industrial potential right from the beginning like gypsum, limestone, quartzite, white clay, horticulture produce, skins and hides, willow etc. But the focus on these natural advantages was missing in different policy statements till the recent past. As a result, these natural advantages have remained grossly under-utilized. It is only during the last decade or so that some headway has been made in the utilization of some of these resources. If the state would have focused on these natural advantages and has evolved right type of strategies to capitalize on these resources, the picture of industrial development would have been altogether different.

The Govt. has been pursuing a policy of protective industrial programmes. A number of fiscal and non-fiscal measures were taken to support the process of industrialization with the purpose to help industries to overcome certain inherent difficulties. Given our unique state setting, providing various fiscal and non-fiscal incentives are necessary, but the policy of providing general nature support has led to a situation of a '*Dependency Syndrome*' which in turn has ushered the state in an industrial environment where entrepreneurial class adaptive to competitive and changing business situations has gone dormant. In fact, protection and support of general nature has been confused by many with "mollification" thus has road-blocked the creation of resilient industrial environment in the state (Kuchal; 1989). No doubt fiscal and non-fiscal incentives are necessary given the unique state setting, as such, these have to stay for some more time, but the need is to restructure incentive packages and streamline their delivery system so that these are not misused and delivered in time and with ease to the genuine entrepreneurs.

Industrial sickness, an economic reality is a universal phenomenon and more so in growing economies like ours, where some inefficient and problematic units go out of existence and new units come into existence. But when the problem of industrial sickness becomes widespread and attains serious dimensions, then it is not treated as a normal phenomenon, rather a serious economic problem which needs an immediate attention. There is no statistics available about the problem of sickness in the state, however, there are indications that large number of units have gone sick. The industrial sector in the state is in the *'State of Paralysis'* rather than sickness (Greater Kashmir, 1998), which had the most dampening effect on industrial development. Given the large proportion of industrial sickness and its serious Socio-economic costs, there is a strong case for a well defined policy for the rehabilitation of sick units.

Amazingly the different policy statements announced by the successive governments in the state have not attended this serious socio-economic problem in its entirety and have only evolved a casual and half-hearted approach towards this problem. For example no mechanism has been created to which the sick units should have been referred for the formulation of rehabilitation package. This was very much needed in the state since most of the industrial units in the state are in the small scale sector which does not fall under the purview of BIFR. Further the policy makers in the state have generally viewed rehabilitation as offering financial assistance only. But rehabilitation has two aspects; one to restore the capacity of generating internal surpluses' and the other is *'Mercy Killing'*. Giving mercy killing has been completely overlooked by the policy makers. It seems that the rehabilitation in the state is being viewed as the rehabilitation of humans rather than as a process of strengthening the economic fabric.

Promotional Bottlenecks

Industrial development in effect is the role-play of different role players. The role play of the Govt. is even more pervasive in the promotion of industries that too small scale industries for which the state is well endowed in view of its extreme location in the national setting, missing industrial culture, poor natural resource base etc. The Govt. was aware of the role expected of it as an agency in the promotion and acceleration of the pace of industrial development in the state, thus assumed multi-faceted role. Accordingly it launched number of programmes and incentive schemes to induce the spirit for entrepreneurship and a number of promotional organizations were established to manage these programmes. Further in a bid to cut down multi office hassles a *'Single Window Clearance System'* has been introduced. In sum to blaze a new trial in the state's economy with the proliferation of viable industrial projects, the Govt. has assumed the role of a financer; marketer; supplier; trainer and councilor."

Different industrial progammes and incentive schemes will be of little use unless the institutional set-up created to manage these programmes are effective in their role performance. A healthy institution is not necessarily the one whose activities appear most appropriate but the one that is free from all administrative slants and more importantly manages industrial programmes strategically rather than administratively. Further healthy promotional organization changes its role pattern to meet the changing requirements of industrial economy in today's dynamic business world. However, a close introspection of the role performance of various financial and service organizations in the state has brought to light the role failure on their part (Butt. 1997). Indeed these organizations suffer from various forms of ill-health, like more paper work, inordinate delays, procedural wrangles and corruption which have had the most dampening effect on the industrial development and the spirit for entrepreneurship.

Although the various incentives offered to industries in the state with the purpose to help them in the management of logistics which is otherwise weak in view of peculiar features of the state yet, these are hardly being delivered to the genuine entrepreneurs easily and in time. It is an open fact that the applications are willfully kept pending and problems created in the garb of different laws and regulations in order to compel entrepreneurs to offer some gift. In spite a network of institution that was created in the state to make available raw materials, cheap credit and provide a helping hand in marketing, the entrepreneurs among other things complain about financial problems, the problems of raw material and difficulties in marketing their products. In fact these problems are not due to scarcity of these resources but due to the role failure of various promotional organizations.

The different promotional organizations are administered more than strategically managed and their culture is one of bureaucratic '*Mazo*' than that of *'Risk-taking Entrepreneurs"*. Further these organizations have misconstrued their role of a promoter and are obsessed with a regulatory role. Added to it, these organizations have demonstrated inflexibility in their attitudes and at the same time have shown rigid bureaucratic attitudes. Managers in these organizations lack autonomy and entrepreneurship and the employees in general lack commitment and proper attitudes. Their lack of the concept of industrial promotion makes the things much more worse.

Institutions whether political, social, cultural, economic provide necessary direction for development in all spheres of life. So when these institutions fail to deliver aberrations are bound to take place. As becomes clear from the above discussion like other institutions, organisations looking after industrial development in the state have degenerated into monumental incompetence and malpractices with cascading effect on the health of industrial economy. Interestingly enough the policy makers have totally ignored this fact while propounding strategies for attaining much needed industrial development on sound lines. Unless these promotional organizations are put in right shape, nothing concrete is going to emerge in the sphere of industrial development in the state.

Industrial Sickness

Industrial sickness, an economic reality is bound to exist in one form or the other and more so in growing economies like ours where some inefficient enterprises have to go out of existence and new enterprises have to come into existence. But in a relative slow growing economies like ours when the problem of sickness becomes widespread and reaches serious dimensions, then it is not treated as a normal phenomena rather a serious economic problem which needs an immediate attention. As per the Report of World Development (1988), when industrial sickness becomes endemic and epidemic, it poses serious challenges affecting the whole of the economy in a variety of ways. The industrial sector in the state which mainly consists of small scale industries is gripped with the phenomenon of sickness, a malady which is engulfing a wide variety of industries belonging to large, medium and small scale year after year. The data about the incidence of industrial sickness in the state is not available. As yet, there has been no detailed survey as to the identification of number of sick industrial units in the state by any agency whatsoever, thus making it difficult to give the exact number of sick industrial units in different industrial sectors.

However, there are clear indications that large number of industrial units in the state have gone sick. According to a survey by the State Industries Department, of the 35,641 small scale industrial units registered till March 1995, about 3,500 units in Jammu region and 5,000 units in Kashmir region were untraceable. Another 4,000 units were confirmed to have been closed down. But the ASCI team headed by Dr. B. Y. Raju, which was appointed by the state government to suggest measures for the revival of small scale industries observed that not more than 1,000 small scale units in the manufacturing sector are in actual operation (Greater Kashmir, 1997). As a matter of fact, the industrial sickness in the state is widespread and has reached to alarming proportions. It has not only affected traditional industrial units alone but many more modern industrial units. More disturbing aspect of industrial sickness in the state is that there is no abatement to this serious economic problem but it is growing at a rapid rate. The widespread industrial sickness in the state has caused number of serious socio-economic implications which have had the most dampening effect on the industrial growth and the spirit for entrepreneurship.

Industrial sickness is not only to the disadvantage of entrepreneurs but to the whole economy. It results in huge losses to the economy in the shape of loss of production, employment, revenues etc. Sickness in industries is inviting sickness in banks and financial institutions as well by reducing their profitability. The State Financial Corporation, the only premier developmental financial institution in the state is passing through difficult times due to poor recovery of dues and more bad debts caused more by the widespread sickness and less due to other extremes. As on 2002-03, the amount of loans outstanding including interest liability was Rs. 68,801.21 lakh. Out of this, Rs. 65,917.12 lakh were overdue, accounting for more than 95 percent of the total amount of outstanding as on 2002-03. (Annual Report, 2002-03) More default rate has reduced the loaning activity of the state financial corporation considerably (Table 5.5).

The industrial sickness in the state has not only caused economic losses but has resulted in socio-psychological crisis to the individuals. The study on socio-psychological crisis of sickness has revealed that the state of extreme poverty faced by the workers of sick textile mills in Kanpur reached to its culmination when some of the workers were found involved in Beggary, Starvation and Prostitution (Panchakasharia, 1981). Industrial sickness is also eating the precious time of judiciary as

Table 5.5: Position of Sick SSI Units & Sick/Weak Non-SSI Units Financed by Scheduled Commercial Banks in India (Rs. crore)

Year	No. of SSI Units	Amount Outstanding (Rs.)	No. of Non SSI Units	Amount Outstanding (Rs.)	No. of Non SSI Weak Units	Amount Outstanding (Rs.)
1987*	158226	1542.25	1057	2680.44	655	1515.19
1990	218228	2426.94	1455	4538.82	814	2386.77
1995	268515	3547.16	1915	8729.61	476	1452.2
1996	262376	3721.94	1956	8823.19	418	1203.12
1997	235032	3609.2	1948	8613.95	420	1563.86
1998	221536	3856.64	2030	9861.67	446	1963.58
1999	306221	4313.48	2357	13113.87	435	2036.54
2000	304235	4608.43	2742	16748.08	422	2299.21
2001	249630	4505.54	2928	18478.17	389	2792.09
2002	177336	4818.95	2880	17591.12	381	3654.52

Note: SSI = Small Scale Industry.
Figure related to end –June
Source: Reserve Bank of India.

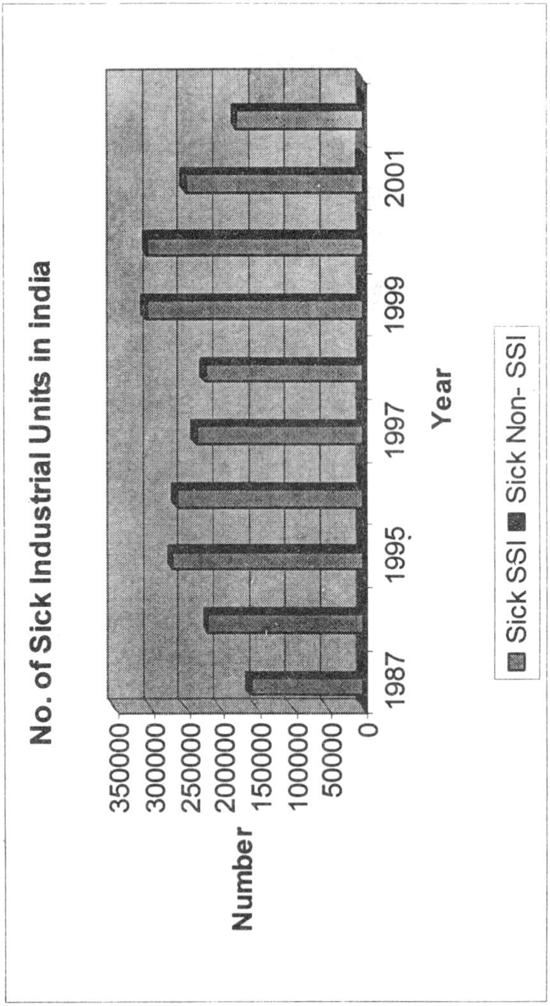
No. of Sick Industrial Units in india
Number
3500000
3000000
2500000
2000000
1500000
1000000
500000
0
1987
1995
1997
1999
2001
Year
Sick SSI
Sick Non- SSI

sickness generally results in litigations, thus forcing it to cut short its time on productive and more serious matters. Industrial sickness in the state has lead to an unhealthy notion in the minds of youth that no industry can be run successfully in the state, more particularly in Kashmir region. It is because of this undesirable notion educated youth have got little or no preference towards entrepreneurship which in turn is adding to the burden on the state sector to create more jobs. If the industrial sickness is not checked, it may stagnate industrial growth and vitiate the entire socio-economic atmosphere in the state. So to usher in a healthy and self-sustaining industrial economy in the state, there is a fervent need to unfold the malady of sickness in the state for framing pragmatic policy measures. More appropriate would be to evolve a comprehensive and wholestic redress rather than inventing quick fixes as the practice goes presently.

Summary

What emerges from the above discussion is that the industrial development in the state is constrained more by political, entrepreneurial, infrastructural and promotional bottlenecks and less by other extremes operating in the environment of industries. Until these bottlenecks are removed, all efforts towards industrialization in the state are going to yield very little as has been the case in the past. Lack of peace and political stability has done most of the damage to the fabric of industrial development in the state, particularly since 1990 when militancy erupted in the state which has had the most dampening effect on all spheres of life. However, the silver lining in the cloud is that things on the political front are improving. But till the problem of Kashmir dispute is resolved to the satisfaction of the people of the state, the peace and stability will continue to remain fragile. The other serious impediment to the process of industrialization in the state has been the lack of requisite infrastructure in particular electric power. Industries in the state are likely to continue to suffer for want of adequate infrastructural facilities.

The infrastructural development in the state in particular

power generation calls for a *'Big Push Strategy'* which is not in the offing at least in the near future on account of financial and other constraints. The absence of an ambitious entrepreneurial class with outward looking approach is also affecting the growth of industries in the state. The educated youth in the state are displaying little preference towards industrial entrepreneurship and are heavily oriented towards white collared jobs.

However, the state government is now making all out efforts to defeat this undesirable phenomenon. For this purpose in the recent past, the state government has established Entrepreneurship Development Institute and is also seeking collaboration of different agencies of repute in the country to guide and help the state towards entrepreneurship development. But the outcome of all these and other initiatives would depend upon the serious and conscious efforts made to strengthen and improve the role performance of different organizations that have been created to promote industrial growth in the state. There are no two opinions that the different organisations looking after industrial development in the state have degenerated into monumental incompetence and malpractices with cascading effect on the health of industrial economy. Unfortunately nothing is being done to set these organizations in right shape and direction so as to make them to manage industrial programmes strategically and with vigor.

References

43rd Annual Report (2002-03), J&K State Financial Corporation, Srinagar, Kashmir.

Butt K. A. (1998), "Small Entrepreneurial Education: Approach and Methodology", Abhigyam, Fore School of Management, New Delhi, Volume XVII No. 04.

Butt K. A. (2000), 'Modern Small Scale Industries and Industrial Sickness," Anmol Publishers, New Delhi.

Butt K. A. (2003), "Performance of Promotional Institutions in the Development of Small Scale Industries," The Business Review, Faculty of Commerce and Management Studies, volume 06, No. 1.

Digest of Statistics, (2002-03), Directorate of Economics & Statistics, Planning & Development Department, Govt. of Jammu & Kashmir.

Godbole, M. et al (1998), "Report on Economic Reforms for Jammu and Kashmir", The govt of Jammu and Kashmir.

Kuchal S.C. (1998), "The Industrial Economy of India" Chaitamiya Publishing House, University Road, Allahabad.

Mishra. R.K. et.al. (1998) "Sickness in Small Industries" Himalaya Publishing House, New Delhi.

Nazim A. (1978)," The decadent Industrial Culture" The Daily Greater Kashmir, Jan. 08, P 02.

Panchakasharia, H. M.(1981), "Problems of Sickness in Small Scale Industry: A Comparative Sociological Study of Small Units" Unpublished Ph. D. Thesis.

Staley, E. (1963), "The Future of Underdeveloped Countries",

The Daily Greater Kashmir, Srinagar, Wednesday, Nov. 5, 1997, page 01.

Zabita K. (2003), "The Right Road to Performance" Greater Kashmir, October 23.

6

Strategies for Industrial Growth and Development

Introduction

Knowing the importance of industrialization as a means to achieve rapid economic growth, like other parts of the country, the state of J&K emphasized on the process of industrialization. Although it evolved different policy initiatives, created a number of promotional agencies, offered wide variety of incentives to generate necessary impulse for industrial growth yet, a worthwhile change in the transformation of the states economy is not noticeable. The less developed nature of the states industrial scene is obvious from the composition of its State Domestic Product (SDP). It exhibits all the characteristic features of an underdeveloped economy. This is because that the state has witnessed very little industrial activity and lags behind to other parts of the country. As a result, agriculture continues to be the main stay of the people in the state. About 60 percent of its people derive their substance from the pursuits in agriculture and allied sectors. However, the agriculture sector in the state is constrained with low man-land ratio severe agro climatic conditions resulting into mono cropping etc. as such the development of agriculture alone is not enough to take-off the state's economy to a higher growth path.

As a result of industrial backwardness, the state suffers from various socio-economic problems like large-scale unemployment, low per capita income etc. As such, the development of industrial base on sound lines is very much needed to raise income, absorb surplus labour and strengthen economy. With vast unexploited potential for industrial development and a huge reservoir of manpower, the pace for industrialization can considerably be stepped up in the state. But to achieve this cherished goal, the need is to address the basic issues confronting industrial sector in the state by evolving suitable strategies to help this sector of crucial importance in overcoming the impediments and provide all necessary resources to meet the challenges and threats. However, the strategies aiming at industrial growth in the state should be based on the ground realities and the demands of the new economic system that is fast evolving in the country.

New Economic System

As a consequence of globalisation, privatisation and liberalization, a radical transformation has taken place in the competitive intensity of Indian markets. In the post-liberalized markets, the number of competitors have expanded manifold in every industry. Take the case of television market which at one point of time was represented by a few Indian players like, BPL and Onida, is today crowded with a number of global brands viz. LG, Samsung, Sony, Hitachi, and Panasonic. Similarly automobile industry has seen the entry of many new manufacturers like, Toyota, Opel, Honda, Mercedes, and others. Same is the case with other segments of the Indian market. Collapsing of tariff walls under WTO agreement by 2005 will further accentuate the competitive intensity of Indian markets, which were so far to a great extent protected. As a result of which Indian entrepreneurs have to come face to face with global players, thus making their position vulnerable.

The emerging economic environment is not only throwing open great challenges but innumerable opportunities as well. Aggarwal (1999) observed that the opening up of the Indian economy has unfolded vast opportunities for growth and also an unnerving uncertainty for Indian entrepreneurs. Indian entrepreneurs will have to operate in a totally new business landscape where only fittest can survive. So the message from the changing scenario is very clear for the Indian entrepreneurs i.e. *"To Improve or Perish with the Winds of Change* ". The Indian entrepreneurs need to evolve a different outlook to mobilize and utilize resources with an objective to build competitiveness in national and international context. In this direction they need to unlearn the traditional beliefs and methods and relearn them in the light of new dynamic business environment. In today's competitive and dynamic business environment delighting customers all the times by delivering superior value is the hallmark of excellence.

LPG and Small and Medium Enterprises

Owing to inherent weaknesses, small enterprises in the post-liberalized era are the most unsettled (Raju, 1997). The government protection and support in the form of concessions in interest rates, protection from large scale industries, marketing and raw-material support etc. will be of little help in this era of borderless trading, In the post Quantitative Restrictive Regime (QR), all the items which are reserved for exclusive manufacturing by the Small Scale Industries, can be imported into the Indian markets, thus making them vulnerable. Thus, Indian small and medium enterprises will have to face severe competition from the global players even in such areas where till now they had some protection (Roa, 1996). However, small enterprises in the country in general and of the state in particular have failed to appreciate that the world around them is changing rapidly, throwing open great challenges and innumerable opportunities. This is the high time for the small enterprises to understand the emerging realities and prepare to withstand the onslaughts of new and hostile environment These enterprises can no more afford to live with the traditional mindset but need to plan and manage their businesses on modern lines To survive and prosper in the emerging borderless markets, small enterprises would require a metamorphosis of their Vision, Mission, and Strategy (Butt, 2005). Their vision should be *"to be one of the best"* and mission to achieve competitiveness both in national and international context. (According to Roa, (1996), under the new and non-protective environment, a different outlook with competitive attitude to mobilize and utilize the resources is needed by the small entrepreneurs in their struggle for existence in this age of' survival of the fittest'.

Strategies for Growth

Literature is abound of different strategies propounded to accelerate economic growth in underdeveloped countries. Most important strategies include Big Push Strategy (BPS), Critical Minimum Effort Strategy (CMS), Balanced Growth Strategy (BGS) and Unbalanced Growth Strategy (UGS). Big Push Strategy is propounded by Rosenstein-Roden in early forties and was designed in the context and aimed at the industrialization of Eastern and South Eastern Europe. Instead of small amount of investment, the strategy envisages a very large amount of investment in the industrial sector over a short period. This strategy is based on the rationale that the massive investment in wide variety of industries simultaneously will result into many external economies to the industries which in turn will stimulate growth. Another strategy namely Critical Minimum Effort Strategy (CMS) which was formulated by Leiberstein envisages the deployment of investment of a size that is needed to attain a substantial increase in the per capita income to meet the needs of fast growing population. An investment less than the critical minimum will result in low per capita income which in turn will cause decline in demand for industrial products thus low growth.

Balanced growth strategy has been evolved by H. Leiberstein; R. Rodan and W. Lewis. This strategy contemplates balanced development of different sectors with the rationale that the investments in diverse directions will create demand for the products as the different sectors become each others customers. Contrary to balanced growth strategy, Hinchman, Singe and Fleming advocated for a totally opposite strategy which is called as Unbalanced Growth strategy. This strategy stipulates that for achieving sustainable economic growth, initial investment be made in certain strategic industries only. This they believe will result in imbalance which will stimulate efforts to meet this imbalance, thus will constitute steps towards economic progress.

Each one of the strategies discussed above has been designed specifically for under-developed economies like ours. These strategies focus on two aspects of industrial development; one about the magnitude of investment and the other where to invest? These strategies assume that all other pre-requisites like infrastructural facilities, support system etc. necessary for industrial development are there. But the problem of industrial development in the state is not constrained by the lack of investments only but more by other extremes operating in the environment of industrial economy. Therefore, the state of J&K is not a fit case to use these strategies to accelerate industrial growth. Given the unique features of the state and the problems confronting the industrial economy the state needs an altogether a different prescription for attaining industrial development on sound lines.

Industrial Development Model

The contours of industrial development are based on three pillars viz. Entrepreneurial Abilities, Infrastructure Capital and the Efficiency of Support System. However, the role of the Govt. is vital in creating entrepreneurial class adaptive to changing market initiatives, developing requisite infrastructure and offering various incentives and at the same time in improving the role performance of various promotional agencies created to promote industrialization. To accomplish all this there is a need for a strong political leadership with a clear vision and mission. As is evident from the previous chapter that the states industrial economy is constrained more by the lack of industrial culture, infrastructural bottlenecks, inadequacy of role performance of various promoting agencies and more importantly by political instability and less by other extremes operating in the environment of industry economy in the state. It is in view of these facts that the strategies aiming at achieving sustainable industrial development in the state, among other things should focus on improving upon the role performance of various agencies created to promote and regulate orderly development of industries, developing self-motivated entrepreneurs; evolving big push strategy in infrastructure development in particular power generation; and in tackling the problem of industrial sickness which is wide spread and rampant in the state. The specific strategic interventions propounded in this chapter for putting the industrial economy on the track of growth and prosperity are based on the following facts:

- Corruption is deep rooted in the state's social fabric, as such; it is difficult to root it out. Also the political will needed to check it is missing in the state. As such, the need is to rewrite the promotional methodologies with the purpose to provide less scope for corrupt practices.
- State is more suitable for small-scale industries which are weak thus vulnerable in today's highly competitive business world. Thus necessitating for supporting these industries particularly in early stages of their growth.
- Given the new business landscape that is emerging fast in the country, the world is for modern small enterprises, the essential features of these enterprises are modern technology, professional management cadre with outward and forward looking approach.
- The blue print of specific strategies needed for attaining sustainable industrial development under the unique state setting are exhibited in figure 6.1

S I: Adequacy of Role Performance

Institutions whether, political, social, cultural, economic provide direction for development in all spheres of life. When these institutions fail to deliver, aberrations are bound to take place. Unfortunately, almost all the institutions in the country have degenerated into monumental incompetence and malpractices. As Gita Mehta in her book "Snakes and Ladders" argues passionately that there was "lightness in India's leaders, fighting for independence was a game for them but a very pure game. Now we are clawing our way back 25 years of institutionalized corruption." It is in view of this fact it is being

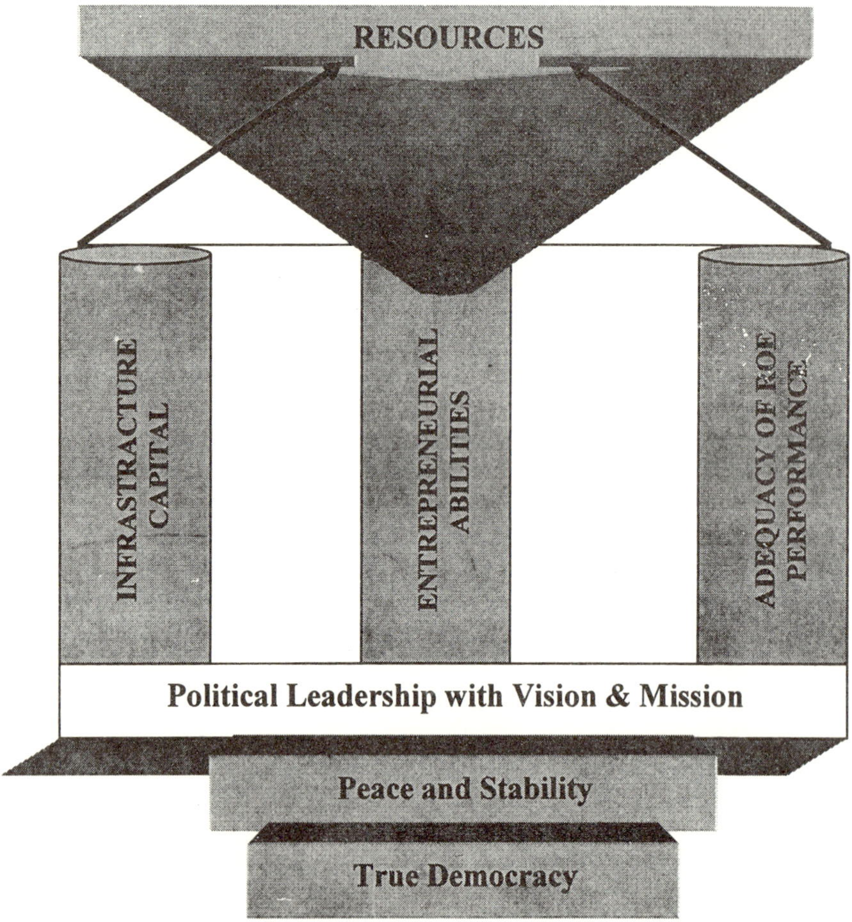

Figure 6.1: Essentials for Industrial Development in J & K State

argued that the development in different spheres of life in the country is constrained more by the widespread corruption and less by other extremes plaguing the country. India is being rated among the most corrupt countries of the world. The annual corruption perception Index (CPI), put out by transparency International, out of 99 countries, India is 73rd with a rating of 2.9, which indicative of the degree of corruption to which different officials in the country are perceived to abuse their official positions. The wide spread corruption to a great extent is being held responsible for the underdevelopment of different sectors of Indian economy. The state of J&K is no exception to this undesirable phenomenon of degeneration of systems and institutions. In fact the state is more unfortunate in this regard.

A close introspection of the role performance of various promotional institutions in the state brings to fore the inadequacy of role performance. Different institutions suffer from obesity and various other forms of administration ill-health which had the most dampening effect on the process of industrialization in the state. Corruption and other administrative slants which are rampant in the administrative machinery in the state have rendered different endeavours towards industrialization ineffective. Major factors contributing to the role failure of promotional agencies include:

- Employees in general in different promotional organisations lack commitment, proper attitudes. Their lack of understanding of industrial promotion adds to the problem.
- Lack of accountability is the root cause of many ills and weaknesses. People working in these organisations are not paid for performances but for longevity and for conventionality.
- Government inaction has aggravated the problem of corruption. Unfortunately different governments in the state have acted as mute spectators to the social evil of red-tapsim, favouritism and corruption. Governments resolve to put a break on these social evils would depend upon the political-will which unfortunately is missing in the state.

- More procedures and ambiguity in rules and regulations has enabled the unscrupulous employees to play the cards of corruption through procedural wrangles.
- Nature of management in these institutions does not correspond with their role profiles. These organisations are administered more than strategically managed. Their culture is one of *'Bureaucratic Mazo'* than that of risk-taking entrepreneurs. In fact, these have misconstrued their promotional role and are obsessed with regulatory role. Managers in these organisations lack autonomy and entrepreneurship. These organisations have failed to abandon the *'spanner set system'* of procedures and rules in favour of flexible organisational structures.
- .Absence of coordinated efforts of various organisations is also reported to be one of the causes of aberration.
- In view of the above facts, any action aiming at the acceleration of industrial growth in the state in the first place should set various organizations looking after industrial development in the state in right shape by rewriting their promotional methodologies and merge some of these organizations to avoid duplicity of roles. Further given the demands of the new economic system and the unique environment in which different types of enterprises will have to operate in the state, there is an equal need to create new roles and redefine the roles of the existing institutions.

Debt Recovery Tribunals and Entrepreneurial Grievance Cells will help greatly in disciplining both the erring entrepreneurs and irresponsive financial and service organisations. SSI Specialised Bank branches would provide an opportunity to the banks to have better understanding of Small Scale Industries and also in effective monitoring of the cases sanctioned. Entrepreneurship Development Institute would be an ideal set up for developing competent entrepreneurs. Far greater need is of the on-site advice and support than classroom training, which calls for a paradigm shift for creating a Task Force of Sponsored Consultants. Creation of Small Industries Reconstruction Board either at the state level or at the level of centre with state level branches would help in the identification of sickness at an early stage and to deal with the problem of rehabilitation of sick units.

The following steps are suggested in improving the role performance of existing institutional network in the state:

Remove Corruption: Nations become great not because of their natural resources but through morality and inspired vision; both of which unfortunately, it seems to have been lost in the state. Today menace of corruption and other malpractices have pervaded all the sectors, organizations and classes of society which are eating the vitals of economic development. So if we have to march towards better future, an immediate need is to contain corrupt practices at all places which would require some bold initiatives. But the menace of corruption which has become a social stigma is difficult to contain as being widespread and deep-rooted in our socio-political and administrative set-up. The existence of political-will and resolve is important to contain it which unfortunately is lacking in the state. Lack of accountability is considered to be one of the important causes of corruption. An old saying goes *"as you sow, so shall you reap"*.

In fact it is not simply a saying but a reality of life. God has created man and this fascinating universe for him but at the same time made him accountable for all his deeds on the day of judgement. Contrary to this the systems that we have created to govern development in the state for that matter in the whole country are not based on this fundamental law of nature. Different institutions and the positions created therein are being provided with sufficient authority but without any accountability. Under the present system, people working in different organisations are not paid for performance but for longevity and conventionality. It is also that people are elevated to higher positions not because of their achievements and morality but for their affiliations etc. Further, the present system believes only in competence rather than both in competence and character. It is because of these unrealistic and unwarranted foundations of the systems that govern our lives, different organisations have degenerated into monumental incompetence and malpractices. So if we have to check different malpractices, there is a need to make difficult institutions accountable for the results and give credit to achievement, competence and character rather than affluence and affiliations.

Single Window Clearance System: Political-will an essential pre-requisite to check corruption in the state, unfortunately, is missing. But industrialisation cannot wait till the menace of corruption is removed. We are already late in the race for industrial development. So what is immediately needed is to evolve such a promotional methodology that will provide very less chances for corruption and other administrative slants. It is an open fact that entrepreneurs in general are subjected to red-tapism, inordinate delays and procedural wrangles. Entrepreneurs, who come with great zeal and enthusiasm, find themselves entangled in the maze of red-tapism and procedural wrangles which the very administrative system has set-up for them. As a result, they finally loose interest and some of them leave half way while others submit to the system. So to protect the entrepreneurs from the maze of procedural wrangles and multi-office environment, the introduction of "Single Window Clearance System" is the need of the hour. This will facilitate new entrepreneurs in getting registration, allotment of land, clearance of Pollution Control Board and certificate of power and water availability in a short time and without any hassle. The Single Window Clearance Cell should meet once in a month to approve new sanctions and also review the progress on earlier cases.

Entrepreneurs are also made to suffer for want of adequate and timely financial assistance. An average entrepreneur faces great difficulty in getting loans sanctioned and disbursed. In view of this fact, it would have been in the fitness of things that the sanction for financial assistance be also made to fall within the ambit of Single Window Clearance System. To enable financial agencies to take decision about the financial viability of the proposed project in due course of time, the prospective entrepreneur can be asked to submit his application along with a project-cum-feasibility report detailing out all the aspects of feasibility and project cost, and the same be passed on to the State Financial Corporation (SFC) by the Directorate of Industries and Commerce for analysis and final decision. In this way the corporation will have no difficulty in taking the decision about the proposed financial assistance in due course of time. The proposals for modernisation, expansion and diversification can also come through this system.

The above methodology is not complete in itself; It is expected to rescue the entrepreneurs from the maze of complexities which the administrative system has set-up for them during the pre-operational stage only and not post-operational stage. So to make the post operational living of industrial units easier and smooth, the following few suggestions are offered:

- Minimise paper work and have less controls which would require simplification of rules, procedures and substantial deregulation.
- Avoid duplicity of paper work which is largely being caused by the lack of co-ordination between different agencies. Lot of problems of small and medium enterprises (SMEs) will get solved when there are co-ordinated efforts of all agencies involved in the promotion of industries in the state.
- Streamline the flow of different incentives and concessions to the entrepreneurs. Better approach would be to replace cash incentives with non-cash incentives.
- Introduce "Time frame" into different approvals and sanctions by different promotional agencies. This will make administrative system quick in processing the requests of the entrepreneurs.
- Make entrepreneurs to know and understand the different laws and regulations so that they are not exploited.

Restructuring of Financial and Service Organisations: It is an open fact that the institutions that were created to promote sustainable industrial development in the state, suffer from various forms of administrative ill-health. These organisations are administered more than strategically managed and their culture is one of '*Bureaucratic Mazo*' than that of risk taking entrepreneurs. This is because these organisations have misconstrued their role of being regulators rather than promoters of industrial growth. Add to this, the employees working in these organisations lack right attitudes and commitment. As a result, these organisations are being feared more than respected as their partners and guide by the entrepreneurs. So to provide right type of institutional set-up for the promotion of industries, there is an equal to restructure and reorganise the existing institutional set-up which among other things should focus on the following:

Memorandum of Understanding (MOU): To revamp the different promotional corporations, one time financial assistance may be given to them only after signing the memorandum of understanding wherein it would be specified that a corporation has to meet certain financial and service targets during a year fixed in the MOU. To make them to serve professionally and effectively, more autonomy may be granted to them and at the same time make them accountable for results/and not targets.

Professionlisation of Management: In the first place, the practice of short tenure of bureaucratic heads should be replaced by permanent heads having some sort of specialisation in the field of industry/finance. However, such appointments should be backed with greater degree of autonomy in decision-making, otherwise they will get frustrated and will ineffective. Further, technical skill base of these organisations need to be strengthening on all fronts. The goals and the methodologies of these organisations also need to be redefined in the light of changing business realities. Such organisations should be made to understand that there role is basically to promote industrial development and their regulatory role is subservient to the promotional role.

Attitudinal Reorientation of Employees: It is an accepted fact that people with right attitudes, total commitment and right conception of things can do undo things. As already stated that people working in various organisations looking after industrial development in the state lack commitment, right attitudes and industrial conception which to a great extent has marred their efficiency in managing the programmes for industrial development. So to put these organisations in right shape, it is equally important to create right attitudes, attain total commitment and broaden the industrial conception of the employees at all levels. Commitment of the top management is essential that can bring commitment in all other levels. Top leadership should demonstrate its commitment visibly and consistently so that the remainder of the organisation has a role model to follow. Seminars, workshops and training programmes will help in shaping right attitudes and in broadening the industrial conception. Among other things, the organisations need to develop among their managers an art of forgoing closeness and to develop confidence and faith in entrepreneurs; encourage autonomy and entrepreneurship and abandon the '*spanner set system*' of procedures and rules' in favour of flexible organisational structure. The managers should be made to realise that they need to manage industrial programmes strategically. The employees should be send to attend training programmes so that they are also exposed to the changing realities of business and learn emerging practices.

Entrepreneurial Grievance Cell: Under the present institutional set-up, the entrepreneurs have no means of redressal of their grievances. The only way out with them is to approach top bureaucrats, unfortunately, bureaucracy has developed perfunctory attitudes, as such does not pay any attention to the administrative slants in their respective departments. A situation like this if allowed to continue would further vitiate the otherwise weak industrial environment in the state. To provide a forum for the immediate redressal of the problems imposed upon entrepreneurs, it would be appropriate to create a redressal cell under the nomenclature '*Entrepreneurial Grievance Cell*' to be headed by a retired High Court Judge. The grievance Cell should have independent existence working under the banner of Ministry of Industries and Commerce. To allow the Grievance Cell to discharge its responsibilities effectively, it needs requisite empowerment. Among other things, the Grievance Cell will help greatly in disciplining the administrative machinery.

S II: Entrepreneurship Development

Industrial Development in the state is also constrained by the absence of right type of entrepreneurial class, more so in Kashmir Division. It is really a paradox that in spite of being rich in some natural resources and with plentiful human resources, the state could not witness the emergence of sufficient quality entrepreneurship. The other disturbing aspect is that the entrepreneurship obtaining in the state, apart from being limited, most of it does not appear to appreciate the significance and utility of the modern business practices. Many units in the state die as a *'Still Born Child'* largely due to the absence of right attitudes on the part of entrepreneurs. This is being largely attributed to two facts; one that the state has first generation entrepreneurs, most of them without proper motivation, financial base and more importantly an understanding of an industry and entrepreneurship; second that the educated youth are lacking preference for industrial entrepreneurship and are heavily oriented towards Govt. jobs.

Given the above facts, if the state has to witness emergence of quality entrepreneurship in a big way, among other things it needs to emphasize on the development of highly motivated and result-oriented *'Entrepreneur Manger Cadre'*. The development of sustainable entrepreneurship is a three tier process viz., Creating Achievement Motivation; Training and Development; and Sponsoring. Each group of activities are highly interactive and crucial to one another. Therefore, under-emphasis on one or the other activity will render the whole process of entrepreneurship development infructuous and the end result would be birth of large number of enterprises with equally growing percentage of sickness.

Achievement Motivation: Motivation is nothing but a strong *'Desire'* to achieve an entrepreneurial *'Goal'*. It is this strong urge for achievement that acts as a true motivator to persist and mobilise resources to face unnerving challenges. The most potent strategies for creating achievement motivation in industrial entrepreneurship include entrepreneurising the system of education and organise on regular basis entrepreneurial awareness programmes.

Entrepreneurising of Education: Colleges and Universities are ideal places to rear the budding entrepreneurs. However, the present system of education in the state is not attuned to foster entrepreneurship rather, it is oriented to produce an army of white collared job seekers. Curriculum in Polytechnics and other institutions does not enthuse and prepare students to opt for entrepreneurship (Saini, et. al., 1996). To generate taste for entrepreneurship at an early stage, the need is to restructure the curriculum both in technical and non-technical institutions in a way to entrepreneurise the educational system. The introduction of management of entrepreneurship as one of the compulsory subjects in three year degree programme would provide sufficient basis for the development of entrepreneurial zeal and skills among the educated youth. More appropriate would be to introduce vocational course on entrepreneurship in all the colleges of the state and the interested students from all streams be allowed to take-up this course. Initially counselling to the students should attain top priority.

Entrepreneurship Awareness Programmes: Entrepreneurs can be found in any strata of the society. However, in Japan entrepreneurs mostly emerge from the under privileged classes. This is because of the fact that this class of society has got a strong urge to achieve economic affluence (Desai, 1995). But the middle and lower middle class in the country and more so in the state have demonstrated little preference for entrepreneurship. One of the dominant factors responsible for this undesirable behaviour is the lack of information about the entrepreneurial opportunities, schemes, incentives etc. (Mehta, 1996). Current state of affairs in the state is that many of the entrepreneurs have chosen it a career of last resort. The current method of waiting for the prospective entrepreneurs to come forward, the practice of organising entrepreneurial awareness programmes to enthuse entrepreneurial zeal and selecting the potential entrepreneurs at their doorsteps should be followed. The entrepreneurial awareness programmes should be conducted on continuous basis. To supplement the efforts of Entrepreneurial Awareness Programmes, it would be appropriate to create "Entrepreneurship Development Cells" in various colleges and universities to act as data banks councillors. But such cells should be sponsored by the promotional agencies so as to make them meaningful rather than mere academic formality.

Training and Development: Are entrepreneurs born or made? Earlier economists were of the opinion that entrepreneurs are born and not made. However, this is regarded simply a myth today. In this regard, one of the architects of Gujarat EDPs which are regarded as the most successful programmes in India, comments, "Over the years, the programmes have successfully demolished the erstwhile belief that, entrepreneurs are *'Born and not Made'*. There is no denying the fact that the achievement motivation and creative behaviour are the most important Essential Personal Entrepreneurial Traits but, the other traits notably focussed knowledge has to be there as well (Butt, 2005). This is because entrepreneurship is not a chance factor but an extraordinary work, commitment and knowledge that go into it. Entrepreneurship demands uncanny ability and focussed knowledge to spot and exploit an opportunity. In fact it is the focussed knowledge that provides a feel of what will make an enterprise to succeed through an insight into the challenges and opportunities. Focussed knowledge can be gained by working for others or by attending some well-structured specialised Entrepreneurship Development Programme. The small entrepreneurs are required to discharge twin functions of 'an entrepreneur' and 'multifarious manager', therefore entrepreneurship development programmes should focus on:

- Making the prospective entrepreneurs aware of the challenges and opportunities thrown open by the new economic system so that they have a clear vision and mission to follow.

- Educating them of different incentive schemes and the rules and regulations thereof.
- Developing in them entrepreneurial values and attitudes and making them to understand what behavioural competencies are important for success in entrepreneurship.
- Educating prospective entrepreneurs about different stages of growth of an enterprise and more importantly how to develop markets and meet competition.
- Developing in them workable technical managerial skills. More emphasis has to be on the transformation of potential entrepreneurs into a disciplined management knowing persons.
- Unless a marriage between theory and practice is not attained, training programmes are unlikely to deliver the best results. To make the entrepreneurship development programmes meaningful and result-oriented, the potential entrepreneurs should be exposed to real life experiences during the training programme on the pattern of British Training Model.

Training by itself is not development. Training may result in entrepreneurship but does not guarantee success unless and until it is backed by a conducive external environment. Entrepreneurship development is to be viewed in the context of *'socio-economic'* environment as it is not a process of individual development alone but it is a movement that requires the support and involvement of all. As for the present state of affairs goes, that once entrepreneurs comes out of entrepreneurship development institutes with all sorts of knowledge and zeal then they suddenly find themselves caught in the administrative red-tap etc. So the entrepreneurship development should encompass a total perspective of the entire process i.e. to set the administrative machinery in right shape and strengthen the induced phenomena.

Sponsorship: The Entrepreneurship Development Institute in no case should feel that it is absolved of its duties and responsibilities once the training programme is over. Now the time has come to think seriously that their role is extended to provide backup support to the extent possible. To rescue the potential entrepreneurs from the administrative red-tap etc. Entrepreneurship Development Institute may be allowed to sponsor. To allow the institute play its role of a sponsor effectively there is a need for some empowerment which may be in the manner that the institutes sponsor or act on behalf of the trained entrepreneurs. A person who gets training from the institute should be treated as a member of the institute for the purpose of sponsorship. Added to this the institutes should act as key 'consultant' to the trained entrepreneur in the initial stages of development.

Entrepreneurship Development Institute: Entrepreneurship Development Institute is an ideal agency to organise entrepreneurial awareness programmes, conduct entrepreneurship development programmes, and act as a sponsor and key consultant to the entrepreneurs. However, the broad objectives of the institute shall include:

- Propounding industrial planning methodologies
- Organising and arranging research to identify the problems that the different industrial sectors are facing and to provide plausible solutions thereof.
- Preparation of project profiles to be taken up in the state.
- Conducting entrepreneurial awareness and development programmes.
- Helping potential entrepreneurs in preparing project-cum-feasibility reports.
- Conducting management development programmes of the entrepreneurs and their employees.
- Arrange interaction with the outside entrepreneurs.

Although in the recent past the state has established Entrepreneurship Development institute, yet it needs to be equipped with all necessary resources and organised on sound lines. Keeping in view the expected role profile of the institute, the institute should be organised into three divisions, viz., Research and Development, Trainings and Statistics and Evaluation. Further, the institute on the lines of developed countries like US should work in close association with different promotional agencies and enter into partnership with the universities, engineering colleges and research institutes in the process of creating sustainable entrepreneurship. Apart from the traditional role, universities can be made to play an important role in promoting entrepreneurship by organising *'incubators'* etc. In US state universities are contributing significantly in the promotion of industrial activity by helping in innovations and by organising incubators.

S III: Big Push Strategy for Infrastructural Development

Adequate infrastructure is necessary to exist to generate necessary impulse towards industrial growth. Although some progress has been made in the development of industrially important infrastructural facilities yet, the state's industrial economy is suffering on account of inadequate infrastructure facilities, in particular, electric power. Till the infrastructural index, in particular the position of power supply improves in the state all efforts towards industrialisation would fail to yield desired results. So the urgency in the state is to evolve a 'Big Push Strategy' towards the development of requisite infrastructure on priority basis.

Electric Power: The electric power which is of crucial importance for furthering development process, more so in the present day living is in short supply in the state. This is despite the fact that large part of successive plan investments were made towards power sector. But most of the Plan allocations were spent on rural electrification as was being used as a social service rather than a tool to accelerate economic growth. However, the policy makers argue that the power generation did not get much attention due to competing claims from the social services sector, and now the basic infrastructural facilities in social services sector have been made available, therefore, it will be possible for the Govt. now to devote greater attention towards power generation. But given the demands of the power sector and the state of financial health of the state, it seems quite unlikely it can do much at its own. In fact the need of the hour is to invite foreign or private investment and for the purpose the first thing that needs to be done is to treat power sector as an industry for the purpose of availing incentives offered to other industries in the state.

Private/Foreign Investment Promotion Brand: The state is fortunate enough to have huge potential for hydro electric power. It is being estimated that the state has potential for 15,000 MWs. Less than 4 percent of this potential has been exploited so far. Much hopes were pinned on National Thermal Power Corporation of India (NHPC) to harness this natural gift for economic upliftment of the state. However, NHPC has failed miserably to harness the huge potential for hydel power with which the state is endowed. So far it could commission only two power projects in the central sector and has failed to undertake Dulhasti (390 MW), Baghliha (450 MW), Kishenganga (330 MW) and Savalkote (600 MW) projects. The state has taken back Baghlihar project and is contemplating to take back other projects as well.

However, to commission these projects, the state would need to make investment of huge magnitude. But given the precarious financial health of the state, it seems unlikely that the state would be able to make investment of required magnitude on priority basis at its own. But the commissioning of these projects within the shortest possible time is needed. The only viable option available to the state is to seek foreign or private investment in the power sector. Given the new economic system that is emerging fast in the country, the private or foreign investment in this sunrise sector will be forthcoming but, the states needs to devise specific strategies in this regard. Presently, the number of private companies are operating in the power sector which so far have made investment in different state of the country worth thousands of crores. To promote foreign/private investment in the power sector, creation of a Foreign/Private Investment Promotion Board will be needed to aggressively promote investment in this sector of crucial importance to the economic development of the state.

Lignite-based Thermal Power Plant: As per the Indus Water Treaty, the state can not construct storage dams on three river basins flowing from the state of J&K to the Pakistan beyond a particular height. As such on these rivers, the state can undertake only run-of-the-river projects. This in turn is resulting in low utilisation during winter when there is low discharge from the rivers thus, further aggravating the problem of power shortages. Against a background such as this, the state government has no option but to develop some thermal power plants as well to supplement hydro power generation during winter months. Two thermal power plants were commissioned namely, Kalakote Thermal power plant and Gas Turbine at Pampore, however, the Kalakote Thermal power plant has been shut down whereas, out of 4 units, 3 units of Gas Turbine have been out of order for long. Such a situation makes the case for setting some large thermal power plant in the state to supplement hydro power generation during winter when the capacity utilisation of hydro projects remain significantly low due to low discharge from the rivers. The state is fortunate enough to have huge deposits of lignite which have been found to occur in Nichahom-chowkibal, Odurand Reitha-Langalab areas of Baramulla district. The lignite found in Baramulla has been found not suitable for use by the manufacturing industries as a source of energy but can be utilised for thermal power generation. As such, commissioning of lignite based thermal power plant will be a step in right direction. In the past, studies were conducted on Lignite found at Nichahoma area which has revealed that the lignite found there is very much suitable for thermal power generation.

Metering and Tariffs: As per the available records, the Transmission and Distribution (T&D) losses in the state are unbelievably at 52.6 per cent while as at the national level it is only 21.24 per cent. As a matter of fact, it is not only T&D losses but mostly includes pilferage. As a result of large scale pilferage, the State Electricity Board (SEB) is in an extremely bad state of financial health. To check large scale pilferage, the State Electricity Board in the recent past has started installing digital meters. However, the department will have to face lot of opposition of the vast majority of people against installing digital meters particularly in downtown and rural areas of the state. This is because that the people are aware of the fact that at present they are paying much less than they consume and with the installation of digital meters they will have to pay more. The other side of the story is that most of the people in these areas would be unable to pay more. In such a situation, it would be more appropriate to install digital meters but charge different rates for different types of customers on the basis of their area of residence. This way the large scale opposition to the installation of digital meters will subside to a great extent. For this purpose, it is suggested to follow the following three tier classification of customers:

- Commercial and non commercial customers
- Customers of Non-backward districts
  - ✓ Customers residing in up-town
  - ✓ Customers residing in downtown
  - ✓ Customers living in rural areas
- Customers of Backward districts
  - ✓ Customers residing in the towns
  - ✓ Customers residing in rural areas

The commercial customers should be charged more than the non commercial customers. The customers of backward districts should be charged less than that of non-backward districts. Within the backward districts, customers residing in rural areas should be charged less than the customers living in town areas. Similarly in other districts, customers residing in rural areas are charged less that the customers of downtown city and the inhabitants of downtown be charged less than the customers of uptown. If the State Electricity Board goes ahead with its campaign of installing digital meters without opting for *'Differential Pricing Mechanism'* then most likely it would be unlikely to check the pilferage to a considerable extent. Like in the past, the people in general in connivance with the field staff of SEB will resort to the alternative means of pilferage. It is an open fact that large scale pilferage is taking place in due cooperation of the field staff of the SEB. More appropriate step would be to privatise Transmission and Distribution with Tariff Regulatory Commission on the pattern of western countries.

Comparatively very low tariffs are charged in the state. The non-commercial customers in the state are charged 50 paisa per Kwh. which is lowest in the country? The disturbing feature about tariffs in the state is that even commercial entities are charged abnormally low tariff. As a result of low tariffs, the State Electricity Board is suffering from financial losses worth hundreds of crores. As a result of mounting losses due to low tariffs and large scale pilferage, the government faces great difficulty in paying for the power purchased from the central sector thus, putting severe strain on the already constrained state exchequer. The revenue realised from the sale of power is even not sufficient to pay for the purchases not to talk of paying for the maintenance of existing T&D System. Such a situation calls for revision of tariffs in the state marginally in a phased manner. However, increasing of tariffs should be avoided till metering of all the categories of customers is completed.

Over and above the measures discussed above, the following few steps are also needed to improve the position of power supply:

- Policy of establishing smaller hydro power projects at various potentially viable *Nallahs/Streams* to meet the local demand by the state should be followed. Such projects can be commissioned within a short period of time and at the same time reduces per unit cost of generation and distribution. Such experiments have been successful in china and other similar countries of the world.
- While seeking compensation from the central government for the disadvantage that the state has been put under Indus water treaty, the state should seek the transfer of Uri hydro project to the state or at least renegotiate the power sharing agreement. Instead of 80:20, the ratio of 20:80 may be asked at least till the power supply improves in the state.
- Revamp the State Electricity Board so as to make it administratively effective and operatively viable

- Privatisation of power distribution may be considered on the lines of other states to improve the financial health of the state electricity board

Development of Industrial Estates: Proposals for the development of industrial estates have been envisaged in the new industrial policy. The government has contemplated huge investments in the development of industrial estates and growth centres. Emphasis on the development new estates is a step in the right direction. But before contemplating any new investment more appropriate for the government would be that in the first place, the necessary steps are taken to utilise the closed/abandoned sheds in the industrial estates. Large number of units in different industrial estates stands closed/ abandoned. So the need is it to make necessary arrangements with those units' holders whose units are chronic sick and not viable for revival and who have abandoned their units due to one or the other reason for sale and allotment to new entrepreneurs. Such an arrangement would enable to put these idle assets into productive use and at the same time save scarce financial resources.

At present entrepreneurs are allowed to transfer plot of land allotted to them in an industrial estate on a 90 year lease at subsidised rent, however, subject to the condition that it is used for industrial purposes only. Such a policy is likely to result in trafficking of land. As such, it will be in the fitness of things that entrepreneurs may not be allowed to transfer plot of land/shed to the third party. But if an entrepreneur intends to exit, in that case the lessor should take-over the property and the entrepreneur compensated for the expenses incurred on the development of land. If due to some technical of financial constraint, it would not be possible for the lessor to take-over the land, then at least the lessor should involve itself in the transfer deal so that an entrepreneur is not allowed to charge more than the expenses incurred in its development.

Industrial Processing Zone: The new economic milieu fast emerging in the country makes to view industrialization as the means to attain economic development and not in the context of employment and removing regional imbalances. Given this fact, the policy of developing smaller industrial estates at dispersed places should be given up in favour of establishing fully equipped a few large industrial processing zones at an ideally located places preferably away from the urban and populated areas. The processing zone should be developed on most modern lines and commissioning of a captive power plant in the zone may also be considered. The construction of residential quarters for the workers may also be taken up in the estate which the management of the processing zone will let out to the firms or directly to different workers working in the processing zone. The zone should be kept open for the establishment of all types of industries to develop linkages between different industries types. However, for sports goods, leather tannery and leather goods, there is a need to develop separate industrial estates. Leather tannery requires a location at an isolated place particularly near some water canal.

Infrastructure Development Corporation: To generate necessary impulse towards industrialization, number of promotional Corporation were created in the state. However, one disturbing aspect about the se corporations is the overlapping of some their assigned roles. For example, the task of Developing and Managing industrial estates figure in the role profile of three corporations viz, Small Scale Industries Development Corporation (SICOP), State Industrial Development Corporation (SIDCO) and the Directorate of Industries Commerce. Though it does not hamper the process of industrialization in the state but more appropriate would have been to assign the responsibility of developing and managing industrial estates to one agency only. Accordingly it is suggested that the development and management of industrial estate is suggested to be entrusted to SIDCO, however, its name may be changed into 'Infrastructure Development Corporation'. Such corporation should be allowed to develop industrially relevant infrastructure only and the financing of medium and large scale industries which presently falls within the ambit of the assigned roles of SIDCO be entrusted to State Financial Corporation. This sort of rationalization would enable SICOP and Directorate of Industries and Commerce to channelise its energies and resources on their main activities which are much more important in the industrial development of the state. The role profile of Infrastructure Development Corporation should include the following:

- Developing and managing industrial estates on modern lines.
- Create common testing facilities in different estates.
- Seeking partnership with private entities in the development of industrial estates
- Commissioning capitalize power plantation leading processing zones.

S IV: Timely and Sufficient Credit Flow

Industries in the state have been made to suffer for want of adequate, timely and varied type of finances. The problems of under-financing, diversion of funds, cost and time over-run and above all *'Promisory Estoppel'* by the banks are being faced by the entrepreneurs (Butt, 2000). In fact the problem of working capital is more widespread and one of the major financial problems being faced by the industrialists in the state. This fact has also been emphasized in the Industrial Policy, 2004. To improve the credit flow, the new policy statement stipulates to activate and strengthen the present arrangement of monitoring credit flow through State Level Banker's Committee (SLBC) and State Level Inter Institutional Committee (SLIIC). Further, it offered that the Divisional and District Level Committees will be constituted to monitor expeditious settlement of the loan cases within prescribed time limit. Such measures are welcome steps but it would be highly unrealistic to expect much from these committees given their past track record. So if the state is serious about industrial development the following steps are equally important to mitigate the financial problems of different industrial sectors:

Term Loans: State Financial Corporation suffers from both administrative as well as financial ill-health. Industry circles have persistently been representing about the administrative red-tap and other malpractices plaguing the Corporation. One way to free industries from the red-tap and the problem of under-financing as already suggested is to explore the possibility of including sanction for financial assistance by the SFC under the ambit of proposed Single Window Clearance System. Further, to improve the loaning capacity of the SFC, it needs to improve its financial health which among other things would require to recover overdue loans. As on 2002-03, the total amount of loans including interest liability outstanding was Rs. 68,801.21 lakh. Out of this, Rs. 65,917.12 lakh are overdue accounting for more than 95 percent of total loans outstanding. It is quite pleasing to note here that the SFC has started aggressive Recovery Drive in the recent past and has set-up a monitoring cell to improve the recovery of arrears. As a result of this special drive, the NPA portfolio of the SFC has come down by 1.5 percent. However, given the various complexities involved in the recovery of debts, it is unlikely that it will have much success unless 'Debt Recovery Tribunals' one each at Srinagar and Jammu are set up, otherwise, as usual, most of the cases will end-up in long drawn court cases. There are 115 cases pending disposal in various courts of the state involving an amount of Rs. 2,151.15 lakh at the end of 2001-02. The average age of these cases is a little over 4 years.

As a matter of fact, it takes lot of time for the courts to dispose-off the cases for recoveries. By the time the court makes a final disposal of the case, the mortgaged assets get rusted thus the amount realised from the sale of mortgaged assets is usually much less than the amount due. This gives rise to a *'Million dollar Question'* that for whose benefit is all this; surely for the benefit of none. Such a situation makes the case for an alternative mechanism like Debt Recovery Tribunal all the more strong. The tribunals should be given adequate statutory and administrative powers. In fact more appropriate would have been to amend the SFC Act to give powers to the tribunals to even utilise the personal properties of the wilful defaulters to recover debts so that a right signal goes across the board. This will not only help in quick recovery of dues but also in putting a stop to the entry of ill-motivated entrepreneurs and in imposing financial discipline. The other viable option is the creation of Asset Reconstruction Company (ARC) which would buy non-performing assets of the corporation and other financial companies. The ARC would then evolve different options available to recover the dues from the defaulters.

Working Capital: Banks which are profit-making organisations, consider lending to small-scale industries highly risky due to the lack of information to judge credit worthiness and lack of suitable security. It is because of this, a lot of difficulty is being faced by the small entrepreneurs in getting working capital from the banks. Although due to growing competition in the banking industry in the country, the situation is likely to improve yet, small entrepreneurs in view of their peculiar features will continue to face difficulty in getting credit from the banks. Supporting SSI carries a feeling of social obligation and banks deny to accept it as a viable investment (Butt, 1998). To ease out the problem of working capital, the following few steps are suggested to be taken in the state:

- To make SFC to evolve a "Composite Loan" Scheme to provide both fixed capital and Working capital. If it is not technically possible then the SFC should tie-up with few banks for joint lending.
- Banks should be prevailed upon to simplify appraisal procedures and norms and also give more powers to the Branch Managers for sanctioning working capital to SSI.
- Where entrepreneur fails to bring additional contribution, a working capital term loan will have to be provided to such borrowers at an enhanced rate of 1 per cent as recommended by Chore Committee.
- Banks should take immediate steps to ensure complete adherence in letter and spirit to the RBI guidelines in the matter of financing of working capital.
- Banks be made to adopt the Single Window Clearance Scheme of SIDBI for meeting the credit needs of small scale industries.

- As per the recommendations of the Kapoor Committee (1998), the banks may be impressed upon to establish 'Specialised SSI Bank Branches' district-wise. This would go long way in improving the flow of credit to the SSI. Such branches among other things should monitor the working of assisted units so as to arrest the signals of sickness at an incipient stage and at the same time help and guide such units in turnaround strategies. For all this, such branches need to be well equipped with requisite resources and suitably empowered.

Venture Capital Fund: As already stated that the youth who are technically and professionally qualified are showing very little rather no interest towards entrepreneurship in the state. Added to this, entrepreneurs in the state are not trying new ideas or new technologies. So to encourage entrepreneurs to specialise in new ideas or new technologies, the establishment of *'Venture Capital Fund' by the SFC* is suggested with the following broad objectives:

- To provide seed financing to support a new concept or new idea.
- To finance R&D aiming at new product development to research institutes and other entities.
- To provide financial assistance to new small entrepreneurs with somewhat new ideas and who are professionally and technically qualified, but with inadequate resources or backing to finance the project.
- To finance existing enterprises for diversification in unrelated and untried lines of activity.
- To provide turnaround financing for turning around a sick unit.

The method of venture financing may be in the form of *'Conditional Loan'* or *'Income Note'*. A conditional loan is repayable in the form of royalty after the venture is able to generate sales and no interest is paid on such loans. Income note is a hybrid security which combines the features of both conventional loan and conditional loan. Under this loan scheme, entrepreneurs have to pay both interest and royalty but substantially at low rates. The critical aspect of venture capital funds in developing countries is their participation in the management of assisted enterprises. Therefore, venture capital organisation of SFC should also guide and help the assisted units in the management of operations. For the growth of venture capital business in the state, initially it would be necessary for the SFC to organise venture fairs, venture clubs, venture networks, etc.

Effective Project Planning and Evaluation: The activity so identified has only a prima facie feasibility. So before moving to the next stage, a project warrants a detailed research and evaluation. It would be better to drop the idea at an early stage than moving ahead to pursue unviable idea as it will be extremely expensive rather traumatic to abandon it at a later stage. However, it is intriguing to state here that the need for systematic project planning and evaluation is largely being overlooked in the state both by the entrepreneurs and the financial institutions. The entrepreneurs in general follow a practice of *'Going Straight into Action'* without completing preliminaries which among other things would have given them a picture of the prospective returns, problems of procuring inputs and selling the product.

More disturbing part of this is that the State Financial Corporation (SFC) which is expected to allow only viable units to come into existence, has miserably failed in this regard. Hardly project reports submitted for sanctioning term finance to the SFC are being checked for accuracy of estimates made in it. More importantly, while evaluating projects to determine their financial viability, technical and market analysis is being grossly ignored. In fact the SFC follows a conservative and traditional *'Touch Stone Theory'* approach to project evaluation. Political patronage has also been used to get loans sanctioned and disbursed by the SFC in total disregard to project feasibility. This undesirable phenomenon has resulted in the problem of born sickness in the state, which in turn has caused the problem of bad debts to the financial institutions.

The Godbole Committee report on economic reforms has observed that 'the lack of proper appraisal of the viability of the projects and the credit worthiness of the applicants have resulted in careless lending practices by the SFC. The absence of care and caution in the earlier years compounded by the difficulties in recoveries because of disturbed conditions in the state has resulted in the accumulation of huge arrears'. Given the above facts, the financial institutions need to evolve a systematic project evaluation mechanism and take all the necessary care and caution while analysing projects for financial feasibility. In this direction, the following few suggestions are expected to go a long way in preventing non-viable entities to come into existence which later on became recurring parasites for the economy as a whole:

- The prospective entrepreneurs be educated about the utility of proper project planning and evaluation and of the focussed knowledge of the proposed business that will provide a feel of what makes business successful through an insight into the opportunities and the challenges. Entrepreneurship Development Institute has to play a key role in this regard and has to prepare project profiles for the projects suitable to the state. For this purpose it needs to conduct industrial potential surveys.
- The financial institutions have to give-up a policy of sanctioning loans liberally and evolve a highly systematic project appraisal mechanism. The project appraisal should encompass financial, commercial, technical and managerial feasibility. For this purpose, it needs to strengthen its technical skill base on professional lines. To allow them to discharge their duties of project appraisal professionally and efficiently, they need some autonomy and empowerment in their professional decisions

Flow of More Institutional Finance from All-India Financial Institutions: Institutional finance from All-India Financial Institutions eludes the state. This is despite the fact that the state having been declared an industrially backward state. As on 1998-99, cumulative financial assistance to the state from All-

India financial Institutions was only about 0.9 per cent of the total assistance to the different states. Such a sad state of affairs is partly due to the unwarranted and discriminatory approach of the Central Financial Agencies towards the state and partly due to the fact that the state owned Development Financial Institutions have failed to utilise the funds provided by the Central agencies optimally. It is also that the State Developmental Financial Institutions have failed to make the best use of different schemes offered by the Central Agencies. Therefore, the immediate need is to improve the operational efficiency of the State Developmental Financial Institutions so that such institutions will be able to seek more assistance from All-India Financial Institutions.

Variable Interest Rate: Most of the people who assume entrepreneurship in the state are first generation entrepreneurs with limited financial resources. As a result their units characterise with high Debt-Equity Ratio which is causing more burden of interest liability on such unit's right from the beginning. The increased interest burden starts pressing the backbone of the industrial unit from day one thus making them vulnerable to the forces of competitive business environment. Hence, to reduce the pressure of more interest liability in the initial stages of growth, *'Variable Interest Regime'* to be followed by Developmental Financial Institutions is suggested. Under the Variable Interest Regime, less rate of interest is charged in initial years and more rate of interest at the later years. This will provide some breathing time to the industrial units to consolidate and grow.

S V: Market Support

Ability to produce quality products/services at minimum possible cost is a necessary condition but not the only condition to succeed. The other important condition is to have a well-defined marketing plan. The marketing happens to be the most important weaker line of small and medium enterprises; partly due to their poor understanding of the significance of a well-defined marketing plan and partly due to their lack of marketing intelligence and resources needed for market development effort.

Poor marketability which arises either due to unscientific and primitive marketing practices or due to poor product quality or due to poor market development effort has greater influence on the incidence of industrial failures in the state of J&K.

Knowing the role that is expected of the Government to help small and medium enterprises in marketing their products, the Government has taken various steps from time to time to help small and medium enterprises in marketing their products. In 1975, Small Industries Development Corporation was established among other things to provide marketing support to small enterprises. In the recently announced industrial policy, the incentive for *'Brand Positioning'* is being offered and with the price preference scheme in Government purchases continued. If the scheme for brand positioning is implemented properly, then it is expected to go a long way in improving the marketability of the industrial units in the state. However, the past experience about the scheme of price preference reveals that it has proved of very little help to the small enterprises in the state.

The most disturbing aspect of the marketing support provided to small enterprises in the state is that the Small Industries Development Corporation (SICOP) has failed in its purpose performance to a great extent. The Corporation has unfortunately misconstrued its role of a marketer to the extent of getting orders from the Government and Semi-Govt. departments and distribute the same among the bonafide unit holders, however, that too not equitably. Though the concept of marketing has changed significantly over the time yet, it could not change its role pattern with the changing requirements of industries. Against this background, there is an equal need to restructure and redefine the goals of (SICOP) to make it more relevant and useful to the growing demands of the industrial sector. Towards the same direction the following few suggestions are offered which are expected to go a long way in strengthening the marketing support provided to different types of enterprises in the state:

- Professionalisation of Management at all levels be given top priority. Rigorous training for the executives of the

Corporation may be undertaken so as to broaden their marketing intelligence.

- The Corporation may be reorgnised into four division's viz. Marketing Division; Export Promotion; Research and Evaluation; and Raw Material Division. The role profile of research and evaluation division should include conducting research to know the customer preferences and demand potential of different products of potential sectors in different markets.
- In no way the Corporation should be allowed to deal with the activities which are not provided in its Articles of Association. It should be made to focus its energies and resources only on improving the marketing and raw material support system as envisaged in the Industry Policy Resolutions.
- An equal need is for changing the attitude of the management of the Corporation towards marketing from Conservative to modern and dynamic. It should not restrict its role to the extent of seeking orders only from different departments but should also help enterprises to explore markets within the country and in foreign countries to the export oriented units.
- Guide and Support Enterprises in getting ISO 9000 certification.
- Make entrepreneurs aware of the emerging marketing trends. Also providing a helping hand in marketing tie-ups, franchise, collaborations and help in vendor development.
- Arrange market information for the entrepreneurs, conduct trade fairs/exhibitions and help entrepreneurs to participate in National and International trade fairs.

Market Development Equity Fund: With the Globalisation, Liberalisation and Privatisation of Indian economy, the Indian markets underwent metamorphosis from protected and less competitive to highly competitive. In the wake of liberalisation and other structural reforms, enterprises of all sizes are likely to face an altogether different market environment. Now no more the small and medium enterprises can afford to compete in the market with the present level of effort towards market development. In the changing business scenario, the enterprises need to evolve modern marketing practices, employ dedicated sales force, and invest in vendor development and use advertising and other promotional tools to supplement the efforts of its sales force. For all this, enterprises need finances and marketing intelligence and skills.

As already stated that the small and medium enterprises are constrained by their inability to muster sufficient financial resources for investment in market development effort. Given this fact, there is a need to provide financial assistance at confessional rates to small and medium enterprises to promote their products through the means of modern promotional tools. Towards this end, the Government offers subsidy to the enterprises in promoting brands within and outside the state. Though subsidy for brand positioning is a welcome step but given the past experience about the large-scale misuse of subsidy and other incentives, the new scheme is likely to meet the same fate. As such, instead of offering Subsidy for brand positioning, it would have been more appropriate to offer equity loan with a moratorium of 4 years and repayable in easy instalments. If the entrepreneur fails to pay on due date, in that case interest should be charged though at a lower rate. For this purpose the creation of "Market development Equity Fund" is suggested.

S VI: Rehabilitation of Sick Units

Industrial sickness is a universal phenomenon and more so in growing economies like ours where some inefficient and problematic enterprises have to go out of existence and new units have to come into existence. But when the problem of industrial sickness becomes widespread and reaches to serious dimensions, then it is not to be treated as a normal phenomenon, rather a serious economic problem which calls for an immediate attention. The industrial sickness in the state in particular in small scale industries is rampant and has reached to serious dimensions. It has not only affected the traditional industries but many more new industries in large proportion. The more disturbing feature of the problem is that it is growing at a rapid rate and eating away the vitals of an economy which is already constrained by insufficient capital base etc. The database regarding the incidence of industrial sickness in the state is almost missing. As yet, there has been no detailed survey as to the identification of number of small scale sick units in the state. However, there are indications majority of small scale units in Kashmir region are sick whereas, in Jammu division, the sickness may be as high as 60- 70 per cent.

As per the Second All India Census (1988) of small scale industries conducted by the Development Commissioner (SSI), out of 13000 units surveyed, 4000 units or 31 per cent units were found closed. According to a survey conducted by the State Industries Department, of the 35,641 SSI Units registered till March, 1995, about 3500 units in Jammu division and 5000 units in Kashmir division were untraceable. Another, 4000 units were confirmed to have been closed. But the ASCI team appointed by the State Government in 1996 to suggest measures for the revival of small scale sector feels that not more than 1000 SSI units in the manufacturing sector are in actual operation (Greater Kashmir. Wednesday. Nov.5, 1997). The fact of the matter is that the industrial sector in the state is in the state of 'paralysis' rather than sickness which had the most dampening effect on industrial development and the sprit for industrial entrepreneurship. So given the extent of industrial sickness and its serious socio-economic costs, the rehabilitation of sick units should also figure prominently in any agenda for industrial development.

Industrial Revival: It is evident that industrial sickness in small scale industries in the state is wide spread and has reached to alarming proportion. Given the importance of this sector to the state's economy, It becomes imperative to undertake concrete and long-term measures to tackle this problem in its entirety and right perspective rather than to evolve adhoc and quick fix measures as the practice goes on currently. To rejuvenate the industrial sector, the role play of everyone viz. government, entrepreneurs, promotional agencies, banks, etc. is essential, however, the role-play of the Government in this regard is more important and widespread.

In fact, it is the responsibility of the Government and its sponsored agencies to create conducive industrial environment and encourage others to play their roles more seriously and effectively. It is disheartening to note here that in spite of alarming proportion of industrial sickness in the state, no worthwhile step has been taken to check this malaise. The Government has remained indifferent to the rising scenario of industrial sickness. The rehabilitation programmes are being carried out in an adhoc and a haphazard manner. Rehabilitation is viewed as the rehabilitation of humans and not as a process of strengthening the economic fabric. The adhoc remedies and open-ended commitments to keep the Units alive have only aggravated the situation (Economic Survey 1984-85). In fact, there is a fervent need to treat this economic problem in its entirety rather than to evolve casual and half-hearted approach. The industrial revival requires not only the rehabilitation of the sick Units but also removing all the obstacles that coming are in the way of sustainable industrial development.

Rehabilitation: Policies and Programmes: Rehabilitation of sick units gives rise to three policy decisions: *'Should Sick Units Be Rehabilitated'? 'What Rehabilitation is All About'?* and *'How to Rehabilitate'?* A resolution to these three questions will help us to rationalize our mindsets towards the problem of rehabilitation, thus will lead towards better future.

Should Sick Units be Rehabilitated? An industrial unit is not a mere factory producing goods, but it has got a human face as well. It is a social endeavour involving the lives and social aspirations of many persons. Thus, a failure of an industrial Unit gives jolt to the lives and future aspirations of many individuals. There are studies which have brought out the miseries, privations and mental agony and depression of the entrepreneurs, creditors and laid-off workers caused by the sickness of industrial units in the state of Jammu and Kashmir as well. Industrial sickness in the state has led to an unhealthy notion in the minds of youth that no industrial enterprise can be run successfully in the state, particularly in Kashmir Valley. It is because of this undesirable notion; the educated youth have got no or very little preference for entrepreneurship which in turn is adding to the problem of unemployment among educated youth.

Over and above the socio-psychological crisis, the industrial sickness carries huge economic costs which would be unbearable to the resource constrained state of ours. It leads to the loss of employment, loss of production and blocks huge funds in assets which are loosing their commercial value day-in-day-out. Further, sickness in industries is inviting sickness in banks and financial institutions by reducing their profitability considerably. The J & K State Financial Corporation, for instance is passing through difficult times due to poor recovery of loans and more bad debts resulting on account of wide-spread industrial sickness in the state. As a result, it has curtailed its loaning activity considerably. So by pending the decision on rehabilitation, we are not serving the cause of economic development but wasting scarce economic resources.

Industries which are social entities engage in role interaction with the promotional organisations operating in their environment. So the health of an industrial unit to a great extent depends upon the health of these organisations as well. Therefore, an industrial enterprise goes sick not due to the fault of an entrepreneur alone. In fact, sickness of industries in the state has been found more due to the inadequacy of role performance of service and financial organisations and less by other extremes operating in their environment. There are clear indications that the different industrial promotional organisations are suffering from various forms of corporate ill-health like, red-tapism, procedural wrangles, corruption, rigid bureaucratic attitudes etc. which had the most dampening effect on the process of industrialisation.

So in view of the above facts, there is a strong case for the rehabilitation of sick industrial units which would certainly benefit the economic process. In principle, rehabilitation should be used as a process of strengthening the economic fabric by improving upon the weaknesses in the system and not a mere process of human rehabilitation or putting the idle assets into productive use.

What Rehabilitation is all About? Rehabilitation has two aspects; one to rehabilitate by helping to restore the capacity of generating internal surpluses and the other which is usually overlooked; is to discharge the entrepreneur from the liabilities. The terms of the exit policy may vary from case to case. Thus rehabilitation should not be viewed only as *'Nursing'* but also giving *'Mercy Killing'* which may depend upon the merits of the case and will of the entrepreneur.

Nursing or Mercy Killing: To nurse or to give mercy killing would largely depend upon the viability of such units for revival and will of the entrepreneurs. Rule is *'Nurse'* the potentially viable units and give *'Mercy Killing'* to non-viable units". Potentially viable units are those:

- Whose business has prospects for future growth?. Which does not require total revamping?
- Where the bonafides and character of the entrepreneur are beyond doubt and the entrepreneur is compatible.
- Where the situation is not completely out of control and the entrepreneur is willing to submit to the discipline laid down by the rehabilitating agency.
- Which does not involve more risk?

Determining the viability of sick units is a case-to-case problem and of specialist's job, which among other things would require taking into account future perspectives. The units, which are not viable for revival, should be liquidated with immediate effect in co-operation with the entrepreneurs. Entrepreneurs with poor economic background and where the size of the liability is not large enough, should be discharged from all the liabilities and the unit is taken-over by the trustee appointed by a proper authority. The decision matrix identifying the possible decisions under varying situations of sickness is given in table 2. The table gives a general framework which provides broad spectrum hypothesis, which, however, need to be tested time and again

(Bhat, et al., 1988). The final decision regarding the revival of sick units will be guided by the ground realities. However, the universally accepted fact is that the revival of the sick unit would depend upon the will of the entrepreneur and the stage of sickness.

New Entrepreneurial Culture: It is a fact that large number of entrepreneurs in the state have resorted to diversion of funds and misuse of different incentives. Their main aim has remained to pocket away the loans and incentives and not to contribute to industrial activity. The survival strategies followed by these entrepreneurs hint at a new entrepreneurial culture which has emerged over the time and which has vitiated the overall industrial environment in the state. Such unit holders have also been found in the forefront to claim the benefits of rehabilitation. If the state has to usher in a healthy industrial environment, it needs to identify such entrepreneurs who have resorted to diversion/ misuse of loans, incentives and have amassed huge wealth which is either in their own names or in the names of their family members. In such cases their personal properties should be utilised to recover the dues so that a right signal goes across the table. This would require creation of special courts. However, for such a bold initiative there is a need of a political-will, which unfortunately is missing in the state.

Approach to Rehabilitation: Rehabilitation of sick units is a complex and riskier task, demanding patience, firmness and sympathy. To be successful in the rehabilitation of sick industries, the action needs to be timely. Once the potentially viable units are identified and a decision is taken to assist them, then a revival program should be evolved in the shortest possible time. The revival programme would involve to diagnose the root causes of the problem; a revival package and monitoring of the revival process for better results.

Diagnosis: Rehabilitation begins with the diagnosis of real causes of ill-health of an enterprise. To identify the originating factors of sickness, a system of pruning the dead wood and watching the bottom line be followed. Diagnosis of the causes of sickness is a specialist's job and the co-operation of an entrepreneur is all the more important to root-out the real problem. Industrial sickness in the state has been also found due to the lack of entrepreneurial skills and wherever quality entrepreneurship is available, the same has been marred by the inadequacy of role performance of financial and service organisations. Infrastructural bottlenecks, infructuous government policies, incorrect promotional methodologies, management deficiencies and the lack of working capital have also contributed to the industrial ill-health in the state (Bhat, 1997). Present state of affairs in the state is that the rehabilitation of sick units is being carried-out without knowing the real causes of sickness. It is also that the sickness is not detected at an early stage and the unit is allowed to reach to an advanced stage of sickness which in effect renders the revival of sick units all the more difficult, rather impossible.

Revival Package: It is unfortunate to note that the rehabilitation of sick units is not planned and executed in a systematic way. The piecemeal approach to rehabilitation is followed just to meet the targets by ignoring the net likely outcome. The irrational mind set of banks and financial institutions of throwing good money for bad money needs to be rationalised by the fact that all sick units are not fit for revival; some are potentially viable and some are unviable. However, the approach to deal with the task of rehabilitation should be realistic, systematic and complete. Preparation of a detailed blue print of the reconstruction programme, detailing-out all the necessary steps and requirements for putting the enterprise back on the track of growth and prosperity is necessary. Prescription for reconstruction should include both financial as well as non-financial measures.

Financial Measures: Financial package is the focal point of the rehabilitation programme. The actual need for additional funds for achieving desired level of operation and efficiency shall have to be carefully assessed. The practice of under-financing shall have to be avoided at all costs. Much of the industrial sickness in the state has reached to its advanced stage. It is also that the eruption of militancy since 1989 has had the most dampening effect on the industrial sector, in particular, in Kashmir region. Given the stage and extent of sickness, the rehabilitating agencies shall have to be sympathetic, generous and patient to the revival of sick units. The financial package should consist of the following reliefs and concessions:

- Infusion of further capital both by the promoter and financial institutions in the ratio of 30:70 respectively at confessional rates of interest.
- The seed capital should be sanctioned to cover the margin money contribution wherever required.
- Rescheduling of payments and matching repayment schedules with future inflows is equally important. Also moratorium both for interest and principal repayment is called for.
- Waiver of outstanding interest liability or at least converting it into equity or instead of charging compound interest, simple interest at the rates payable to SIDBI/ IDBI by the Financial Institutions against refinancing at the time of sanction of the loan may be considered. However, no interest may be charged from 1990-2000 because during this period, the normal life in the Kashmir region remained nearly paralysed due to disturbed conditions. The units located elsewhere, the interest may be charged beyond 1990 as well. The interest liability so worked out be treated as a interest free loan repayable in ten yearly instalments with a moratorium of four years.
- Enhance the amount of margin money given under *'Margin Money Scheme'*.
- Reassessment of working capital to be provided by the bank at a reduced margin and less rate of interest.
- Withdrawal of all cases pending in the courts against such units and no penal interest is charged.
- The units which were in operation till 1989, but were closed after the militancy started in the state and whose units got destroyed, be treated as non-entities and freed from all the liabilities. Whatever, property/assets remains, the same should

be taken over by the State Financial Corporation for sale. No further financial assistance be given to them as such unit holders are unlikely to return to the valley for reviving their units.

Small Industries Reconstruction Equity Fund: Many sick small-scale units in the state fail to bring margin money. Also the infusion of additional funds causes BEP to go-up, thus causing further strain on the viability of such units. Such a situation is calling for a support of margin money and interest free or soft loans which the banks and Financial Institutions are not willing to contribute happily. To ease out this problem, creation of "Small Industries Reconstruction Equity Fund" is suggested with the following features:

- The initial, contribution from the State Government may be few crores and the amount received under different central schemes like Margin Money Scheme etc. be credited to this fund as central contribution.
- The fund should be exclusively used for the rehabilitation of sick units. The financial assistance given from the fund be treated as repayable equity with a moratorium of 3 years. The amount to be provided under the equity participation scheme should equal to 30 per cent of additional fund required.

Rehabilitation in Totality: Unfortunately rehabilitation of sick units is being viewed only in financial terms in the state and elsewhere in the country. It has been found that the rehabilitation package provided to the sick units only consists of financial measures and no concrete measures are taken to improve-upon the other weaknesses (Panda et. al., 1995 and Samson et al., 1991). In fact, the problem of industrial-ill heall in the state is more by other extremes operating in the environment of industries. So any action aiming at rehabilitation should encompass all the aspects of sickness. If the state has to succeed in rehabilitation efforts, it should emphasize on strengthening different agencies, streamline administrative machinery, minimizing and simplifying official procedures, improving infrastructure, developing competent entrepreneur -managers and assuring the availability of different resources for smooth conduct of business operations. In addition to the above measures, the rehabilitator should also focus on the following aspects of an enterprise:

- Help in improving productivity which requires correcting the work Culture and improving labour relations. Modernisation may also be needed to work at.
- Help in improving the management practices of the enterprise which would require the transformation of an entrepreneur into a disciplined and management knowing person with outward and forward looking approach.
- Most of the small-scale units in the state have been found to have been beaten at the marketing front largely due to low key market development effort. Majority of the small and medium enterprises have been found lacking marketing intelligence. Therefore, any endeavour aimed at the rehabilitation of SSI, should also focus at improving their marketing intelligence and ability. They need to be guided and helped in market development effort
- Make entrepreneurs quality conscious and simultaneously guide and help them in turning-out quality products at lowest possible Cost.

Monitoring: There is a strong point for close monitoring after blood transfusion, thus calls for having set standards for post revival performance (Desai, 1980). However, monitoring is not that important as that of bringing attitudinal changes in management and curbing malpractices (Naidu, et al., 1987). Both monitoring and reorientation of attitudes of entrepreneurs is required for making revival programmes a success. To make the rehabilitation programmes a success in the state, appropriate steps need to be taken for careful monitoring of key performance indicators during the nursing period. For this purpose necessary information system is required to be devised and regularly reviewed. Further, during the period of nursing, the management of the enterprise should be guided in the management of logistics and other operational aspects of management. It would be better to contract with some management consultants under whose guidance the nursing of industrial units be carried out and the compensation package of the consultants may be linked to the performance of the units under their supervision

Whose Responsibility is this Anyway? The detection of sickness at an early stage has remained the responsibility of none. Because of this, most of the industrial sickness found in the state or elsewhere in the country is of chronic nature which is making the revival of sick units a difficult proposition. Same situation is prevailing with regard to rehabilitation of sick units. A lot of time is being wasted in deciding whether the enterprises be rehabilitated and what sort of financial relief and concessions be given to it largely due to differing views offered by the banks, financial institution and other related agencies. This is really a sad situation that ought to be improved at all costs. The other sad state of affairs is that the rehabilitation is viewed as the responsibility of banks and financial institutions alone. As being commercial entities, these should not be asked to rehabilitate sick units. However, these need to be sympathetic enough with regard to rehabilitation of sick industries and provide financial assistance at confessional rates for which these need to be flexible enough in their procedures which so far they have not demonstrated. To make things better and easier with regard to rehabilitation of sick units, there is a need to create a specialised agency specifically meant for the purpose of rehabilitation enjoying some statutory powers. The support and co-operation of all viz. banks, financial institutions, government, entrepreneurs etc. is all the more essential.

J&K Small Industries Reconstruction Board: To ensure the timely and proper rehabilitation of small and medium enterprises, number of committees were constituted in the state. Unfortunately, the performance of the SLII C etc. has not remained satisfactory owing to the fact that the decisions taken by these committees are not binding-upon financial institutions. The SLIIC deals inter alia with, problems relating to co-ordination between Banks and the Financial Institutions etc. It is strange to note that banks do not follow the guidelines issued from time to time by the RBI in true spirit for identification and rehabilitation of sick small and medium enterprises. Further, there is no mechanism to arrest sickness at the earliest stage. In fact, the cases that are being referred to SLIIC, are of chronic nature. These and many other weaknesses have zeroed the effectiveness of these committees. To deal with the problem of sickness and subsequent revival of small-scale sick units effectively, the establishment of *"J & K Small Industries Reconstruction Board"* or on the pattern of BIFR at the central level with state level branches is suggested. The board should have statutory powers with the following features:

- To conduct surveys for the identification of sick units; potentially viable and non-Viable. Once the board completes the backlog, the units tending towards sickness or have gone sick should be referred to the board immediately for nursing.
- To decide about the revival package for the rehabilitation of sick units.
- To co-ordinate with the central agencies so as to get maximum financial support etc. for the rehabilitation of sick units.
- To co-ordinate the working of different agencies involved in the rehabilitation process.
- To provide necessary management guidance and support to the sick units under nursing in the management of logistics etc.
- To recommend to the Government and different agencies the different steps need to be taken to strengthen the industrial culture in the state.

Be aware that. *"If the diagnosis is wrong, the medicines would be ineffective." "If the diagnosis is delayed, the medicines would be least pro-active. "If the diagnosis is time honoured and right, the medicines would be highly* effective." These above statements aptly fit in the relearn of industrial sickness. It is in view of these facts, it is said, that "Prevention is better than cure" and early detection is key to easy and complete cure. Here it is unfortunate to note that the present polices aim at curing sickness rather than preventing it or detecting it at an early stage. Lot of time is being taken to decide about the rehabilitation of sick enterprise which causes additional losses and more liabilities to absorb later on. Decision about the rehabilitation has to be timely, well calculated and encompassing all aspects of ill-health. Only potentially viable units should be revived and non-viable units be liquidated. Further, the industrial promotion in the state is being done in an environment of disbelief between the entrepreneurs and the financial and service organisations. They look at each other with suspicion and hatred. The different financial and service organisations are feared more than respected as their friends and counsellors.

On the other hand, the different organisation view entrepreneurs as incompetent, lacking entrepreneurial skills, confidence and doubts them with doubtful integrity. Unless and until the relationships between them is rewritten and closeness and confidence developed, the rehabilitation programmes are not going to bear the desired fruits. Many small and medium enterprises in the state are bogus and many have resorted to diversion of funds and many more units have manoeuvred sickness in order to obtain the benefits of rehabilitation. Therefore, purification of state level agencies from various forms of ill-health and obesity is to be done first.

S VII: Reforming State Public Sector Enterprises

As in the rest of the country, the state of J&K also emphasised on the role of public sector undertakings in accelerating the pace of economic development in the state. Accordingly, the state government assigned public sector a place of pride and went in a big way by establishing various corporations in different sectors of an economy like, industries, forestry, agriculture, tourism, transport, handicrafts, handlooms etc. In all there are 29 public sector corporations in the state, out of which 9 relate to industrial sector. Out these, five are manufacturing enterprises while the remaining four are promotional corporations. The total capital employed in these corporations stood at Rs. 448.09 crore as on

1996-97. The financial performance of most the public enterprises in the state have been extremely bad by all means. It is true to say that the performance of public sector enterprises can not be judged purely on the basis of profitability because such enterprises were also used as a vehicle to promote social interests. But making a modest profit or at least operating at break-even point in no case is an unrealistic expectation from public sector undertakings.

Contrary to this, almost all the public sector undertakings in the state have shown dismal financial performance. The cumulative losses of these enterprises as on 1996-97 are Rs. 650.27 crore which is more than their total net worth of Rs. 448.09 crore as on the same date. Except a few, these enterprises are dependent on the loans and budgetary support from the government, thus these enterprises are acting as a big drain on scarce government resources at the cost of other important developmental programmes. By now the social development role of these enterprises has got to be too thin to hide their commercial nudity. Given the precarious financial health of the state, the state is finding it extremely hard to bear the brunt of these parasites; as such there is fervent need to reform the public sector. Added to it, the changing economic milieu characterised by liberalisation, globalisation and privatisation has prompted to significantly reform the public sector. At the national level, the previous government had taken some radical measures to reform the public sector undertakings like, disinvestment, privatisation and granting greater autonomy.

However, the UPA government under the pressures from the left parties has decided not to privatise *'Nawratna's'* (Profit-making PSUs). The UPA government do recognise that disinvestment and privatisation are useful economic tools but it has decided to selectively employ these tools. Towards this direction, it has established Board for Reconstruction of Public Sector Enterprises (BRPSE) to advise the government about the measures to be taken to restructure PSEs and also to identify cases where disinvestment or sale or closure is justified. The declared policy of the UPA government is that no enterprise will be privatised but will allow disinvestment as long as the government retains control over the public sector enterprise and its public sector character is not affected.

In the past, the state government has made some modest attempt to reform state public sector by signing Memorandum of Understanding (MOU) with some public sector enterprises. But the government has failed to meet its commitments spelled-out in such agreements, as such leaving these enterprises in the same state of affairs. The Godbole Committee on economic reforms has recommended that 'wherever the units can not be privatised, have to be closed; the staff should be given an ex gratia amount equal to the last salary drawn sitting at home till their superannuation. The committee has opined that even with this liberal dispensation, the Government would stand to gain by the closure of such enterprises. Such a step seems to be economically a viable option but the political-will to adopt this radical measure seems to be missing in the state. As a matter of fact, the Godbole Committee Recommendation and the signing of Memorandum of Understanding are the two extreme ends of the same continuum with inherent limitations (Khan, 2003). In fact, we have to calk-out such reformative measures that are based on sound socio-economic goals and at the same time consistent with the changing economic realities fast emerging in the country. It is with this in mind, the following few suggestions are offered towards the reformation of state public sector enterprises:

- The policy of using general nature prescription should be discontinued with enterprise specific measures. Towards this direction, as a first step, a *'Core Group of Experts'* be constituted to study the different public enterprises for the purpose of identifying potentially viable and unviable enterprises.
- Closure of unviable enterprises would carry a great economic sense, however, closure of these enterprises is likely to create some sort of resentment among the workers of these enterprises which the political leadership may not be ready to

bear. So to minimise the socio-political fall-out of closure of public enterprises, option of 'Golden Handshake Scheme' or induction in related departments can be offered to the employees of the enterprises to be closed. For this purpose, the state would need to set-up 'Public Sector Renewal Fund' (PSRF) to provide compensation to the employees opting for Golden Handshake Scheme.

The potentially viable enterprises should be revived. For their effective and long lasting revival, the following measures need to be taken:

- Financial re-engineering which among other things should involve converting long term debt into equity. One time financial assistance is very much warranted to upgrade and modernise their manufacturing base and marketing network. But this should be provided only after signing Memorandum of Understanding wherein specific achievable financial targets are fixed.
- Since one of the causes for the poor performance of various public sector enterprises is over-staffing. Therefore, right-sizing has to be an important component of restructuring plan to take-out excess fat to make these enterprises fit to move on the track of growth and prosperity.
- Granting meaningful autonomy to these enterprises to free them from political interference would be equally important in the process of reforming the public enterprises. This would allow them to take their business decisions freely and purely on economic reasoning rather than on socio-political considerations.
- The policy of deputing bureaucrats to head public enterprises should be given-up in favour of appointing professionally qualified heads on permanent basis.
- Once these enterprises would achieve commercial viability fully, disinvestment of government stake and or partnering with some leading private corporate entities should be sorted out. This would allow the public enterprises in much needed

synchronisation in the areas of marketing, technology and management.

The implementation of above mentioned strategies to reform public sector enterprises would require sufficient funds. However, availability of funds can be no problem because the necessary funds to a great extent can be mobilised by disposing-off some of the assets of the enterprises to be closed. Many of the public enterprises in the state own some valuable land asset which can fetch sufficient amount of money. If the political machinery is resolute about the much needed reformation of public enterprises, then other problems notably of funds and of employees can be sorted out without much difficulty and discomfort to the staff. However, the state government now seems to have realised the immense utility of reforming the public sector enterprises in the state and has made a modest attempt by creating a corpus for Golden Handshake Scheme for public sector employees.

References

Aggarwal, M.L. (1999), "Market Freedom in India and Action Agenda" The Business Review, Vol. 5, No. 1 & 2.

Annual Report (2002-03), J&K State Financial Corporation, An undertaking of The State of Jammu and Kashmir, Srinagar, Kashmir

Butt, K.A. (2000), 'Modern Small Scale Industries and Industrial Sickness'. Anmol Publications Pvt. Ltd., New Delhi.

Butt, K.A. (2005), "Value Chain Management: A Small Industry Perspective", Vision, The Journal of Business Perspective, Management Development Institute, New Delhi,

Butt, K.A. (1998), "Rehabilitation of Sick Small Scale Industries in J & K State: Some Policy Decisions", The Business Review, Vol, 4, No. 1 & 2,

Daily Greater Kashmir, (1997), Wednesday, November 5., Srinagar, Kashmir.

Desai, V.V. (1988), " Rehabilitation of Sick Units", The Chartered Accountant, Vol. XXII, July.

Digest of Statistics, (2002-03), Planning & Development Department, Govt. of Jammu & Kashmir.

Economic Survey (1991), " Ministry of Finance, (Economic Division), New Delhi, Government of India.

Godbole, M. et al (1998), "Report on Economic Reforms for Jammu and Kashmir". The govt of Jammu and Kashmir

Khan M. A. (2003), "Seminar Report on the Problems and Remedies of J&K Public Sector Undertakings, J & K Institute of Management, Public Administration & Rural Development, Srinagar, Kashmir.

Mehta, P. (1996), "Fostering Creative Response, Innovativeness and Entrepreneurship: Some Thoughts for Discussion", Small Enterprise Development Management & Extension Journal (SEDME), NISIET, Hyderabad, Vol. XXIII, No. 2.

Naidu, L. K. and Padmavati, A. (1987), "Why This Growing Sickness in Small Scale Industries", Yojana, Vol. 36: 13 – 23.

Panda, R. K. et al (1992), "Industrial Sickness: A Study of Small Scale Industries", Ashish Publications, New Delhi.

Raju, B.Y. (1997), "Planning for Growth: A Small Industry Perspective" South Asian Journal of Management, April – June

Rao, N.K.A. (1996), "Entrepreneurship Development 2001" SEDME, The Journal of National Institute of Small Industry Extension Training, Hyderabad, Vol. XXIII, No. 1

Saini, J.S. and Sharma, D.D. (1996), "Entrepreneursing Technical Education Curriculum", Small Enterprise Development Management & Extension Journal (SEDME), NISIET, Hyderabad, Vol. XXIII, No. 2.

Samson, M. et al (1985), "Preventing Industrial Sickness in Small Scale Sector: The Role of Commercial Banks", Indian Journal of Commerce, Vol. XXXVIII, (142).

Annexures

Annexure I

Government of Jammu & Kashmir

Industrial Policy 2004

Introduction

Despite attractive fiscal incentives under the State's Industrial Policy (1998- 2003), the rate of growth of industrial! Sector could not be accelerated primarily on account of the disturbed conditions in the State. Competition from cheaper imported products, coming into the country as a result of the policy of globalisation and economic liberalization pursued by the Government of India, has also forced many local SSI units to down their shutters. With the problenl of unemployment, particularly of the educated, being high, the Industrial Policy 2004 has been evolved keeping in view the experience gained in the last five years and some new positive elements that have entered the scene.

Duration

Industrial Policy 2004 will remain in operation from 1 February' 2004 until 31-3-2015.

Advantage J&K

Some specific advantages enjoyed by the State are;

- Introduction of incentives for industries based on the package for the North- Eastern states in Jammu and Kashmir by the Government of India has created a new window of opportunity, This package of incentives is attached at Annexure-I.
- Centrally sponsored schemes available for development of infrastructure and common facility centres are fully utilized to strengthen and broaden the infrastructure base of the State in general and for industries in particular.

- Refinance facilities are available from the prime lending financial institutions.
- Infrastructure in the State for handicrafts and handloom sectors is being strengthened to further' hone the already superb craftsmanship available in the State by providing professional assistance in design, product development, quality control, marketing and human resources development with emphasis on active private sector participation.
- The State is endowed with rare agriculture and horticulture germplasm. The state has three distinct agro-climatic zones, each with its characteristic products, thus offering a wider choice for establishing agro-industries. With 57% of apples and 92% of walnut produced in the country being from The state, besides a host of other horticultural produce such as almonds, pears plums and cherry, the availability in terns of quantity and quality of a wide range of agricultural and horticultural products signifies good potential for value addition through food processing. Besides, the state is ideally suitable for growing aromatic and medicinal plants that can be the raw material for a wide range of essential oils and herbal medicines. A special package *of* incentives has been offered for this sector by the Ministry of Food Processing, Government of India. The State Government has also kept this sector in its thrust area.
- The State is endowed with rich mineral wealth of excellent quality Limestone, gypsum, quartzite, dolomite, magnetite and bauxite, besides. sapphire are available in the State.
- Technical, managerial and other knowledge-based resources available in government departments, universities and professional colleges. R&D\institutions like the Regional Research Laboratory of CSIR can be networked and utilized for the growth of the industry
- There is large scope for the commercial banks to push up investment within the state. The current credit deposit ratio is much lower compared to the national average
- There is a clear recognition by the state government of the

fact that the Industrial sector has a prominent role *to* play in its economic development and is an effective vehicle *to* reduce pressure on the strained employment opportunities in the government and public sectors.

- A perceptible improvement in the law and order situation, generated by the sincere desire of the people of the State *for* peace, has created a favourable atmosphere for investors. This has also created a new hope in the local educated youth.
- The state has a long history of excellent labour-management relations. Mandays lost due to labour problems are minimum.
- A wide network of roads, telecommunication and other infrastructure existing in the State is constantly improved. Railhead at Jammu will be extended to the valley of Kashmir by 2007.

Objectives: The primary objectives of the Industrial Policy 2004 are:

- *To* achieve sustainable industrial development in all regions for increasing
- the rate *of* growth, value of output, employment, income and overall economic development of the State;
- To strive towards balanced economic and social development in all regions of the State by promoting industrialization particularly' of the industrially backward areas.
- To encourage and sustain the cottage and tiny industrial sector which, with low investment, is able to provide employment to a large number of people in the state.
- *To* create a supportive environment with transparency and easy access to Information, technology and financial resources.
- To revive potentially viable sick industrial units .so as to put *to* optimum use the capital and other resources already employed In such enterprises.
- To promote the growth of thrust and export-oriented industries and encourage high-tech and knowledge based industries including information technology.

- To take necessary steps in the field of Human Resources Development to make available skilled/technical manpower as per the needs of industry.

Approach and Strategy

The strategy for achieving the objectives and the main elements of the Industrial Policy 2004 are:

- Providing improved infrastructure and support services, with emphasis on regular and uninterrupted power supply.
- Attractive incentives of the Government of India and of the state government,
- Single window clearance system for power, pollution control, land allotment and registration of industrial unit.
- Closer interaction with financial institutions and commercial banks to ensure regular and adequate flow of finances to the industrial sector.
- Rehabilitation of potentially viable sick industrial units.
- Improving competitiveness of existing industrial units by facilitating modernisation aimed at enhancing productivity, energy efficiency and better environment management.
- Enabling manufacturers of quality consistent products to augment their sales within and outside the state by brand promotion.
- Reorienting Industries and Commerce Department.
- Export promotional measures to augment export of products of the state outside the country.
- Permanent Grievance Redressal System to remove bottlenecks in Import and export of products to and fro the state.
- Environment protection, to confoml to state, national and global regulations.
- Entrepreneurship development in the state, to provide opportunities to educated unemployed.
- Encouraging Research and Development
- Focusing on thrust areas with natural advantages in the state and facilitating large investments in prestigious projects.

Improved Infrastructure and Support Services

The government will strive to improve general infrastructure of the state. In respect of infrastructure for industries, the policy emphasises the following:

- Development of modern industrial areas and estates, growth centres, Integrated Infrastructure Development Centres (IID) etc. will be done in a time bound manner. These focal points of industry will meet all the basic requirements of a competitive industrial environment. An action plan with specific implementation model and time frame will be adopted.
- Operational management of the major industrial estates will be rationalised, involving local industrialists through a suitable local self managed model both for development works and management of the estates including regulation of the estates including regulation of power and water supply
- The State Government will encourage private sector participation in infrastructure development and such private sector participation will be treated as an industry for the purpose of availing incentives. The Government will also facilitate acquisition of land for such private Sector initiatives.
- Efforts will be made to ensure that the power supply within industrial areas, estates, IIDCs, etc. is regular, reliable and of good quality.
- Private sector investment in generation and distribution of regular power supply in industrial areas, estates, IIDCs etc. will be actively encouraged. The government will provide necessary support for such ventures on a case to case basis to assure their sustainability.
- Micro-hydel projects are already open for private sector investment. A separate policy on the subject has been announced and implemented by the Power Development Department of the government.

Incentives for Industries

Incentives for industries provided by the Government of India arc presented at Annexure I. A revised package of incentives, offered by the state government, is at Annexure-II. Industries availing the incentives must always strive to plough back resources to constantly upgrade products and productivity, design and quality, so that after the incentives cease, they are able to survive on their own competitiveness.

Single Window Clearance System

With the objective of facilitating a new entrepreneur in getting necessary clearances within a short time, a Single Window Clearance System, for registration of the industrial unit, allotment of land. Clearance of Pollution Control Board for commencing construction and certificate of power availability, at the State and District levels, has been set up. ,A separate notification in this regard will be issued.

Institutional/Commercial Bank Funding

Industrial Policy 2004 recognizes that financial Institutions/ Commercial Banks have to play an important role in the industrial development of the State. An environment has to be created to arrest the present trend of flight of capital from the State. The procedures presently followed have not withstood the test of time. There have been glaring instance of delay and under-financing of projects resulting in cost and time over run. It will also be necessary to strengthen the state owned Financial Institutions. Moving in this direction, the government will adopt the following course of action:

- The present arrangement of credit flow monitoring through State Level Banker's Committee (SLBC) and State Level Inter Institutional Committee (SLIIC) forums will be actively utilised.
- State owned development financial institutions shall be reoriented to facilitate availing of refinance facilities from national level institutions optimally; and. encouraged *to* raise finances from the market. .
- Divisional and district level coordination committees will be

constituted to monitor expeditious settlement of the loan cases \within prescribed time limit.

Rehabilitation of Sick Units

An enormous amount of capital is blocked in sick/closed industrial units in the form of infrastructure and investments. Though industrial sickness is a wide spread phenomenon, its impact is comparatively high in J&K. The initiative for rehabilitation of sick units should primarily come from the concerned industrial unit, financial institutions and the commercial banks, the government playing a catalytic and supportive role. Government Order No. 47-Ind of 1999 dated 10-2-1999, currently in vogue, will continue. Besides, the Government will separately announce a debt relief package too. The sick industrial units shall have the option of taking advantage of either of the two packages.

Improving Competitiveness -Modernization

Industrial units operating in the state must realize that with globalisation and economic liberalization, the inflow of cheaper and better quality products into the country and eventually into the state cannot be halted. In order, therefore, to encourage such industrial units as are desirous of modernizing themselves with a view to increase productivity, energy efficiency and environment protection, the capital investment subsidy of the state will be extended to them all over the state. The procedure for availing this incentive has been separately prescribed.

Brand Promotion

With increasing competition in the market, manufacturers of quality consistent consumer products can sustain themselves only if they adopt an intelligent marketing strategy and build a brand of their own. In order to encourage efforts of such manufacturers who are desirous of developing and propagating their own brands within and outside the state, the government will extend assistance to them. Details are provided in the package of incentives of the state government.

Re-orientation of Industries & Commerce Department

In the liberalized economy, it is imperative that the capacity of Industries & Commerce Department and related PSUs is strengthened to meet the challenges of the new era. In the area of information technology, the process of computerization will be accelerated at the cutting edge level. Accordingly, the computerisation of the Directorate of 1 &C will be further expedited with a view to not only provide all relevant policy and information on the web site but also data relating to status of applications for registration, incentives etc. An investor and industry friendly atmosphere wilt be created.

Export Promotion

Exports have come to be regarded as an engine of economic growth. However, the share of J&K 'in the over all exports of the country is very low limited mostly to handicrafts and dry fruits processed by the SSI sector. the State has a vast potential for exports, both in traditional and non-traditiol131 items. With a view to promote exports of the State, two Special Economic Zones (SEZs), one each in Jammu & Kashmir Province, are under finalisation. An Inland Container Depot is ready at Bari Brahmana which will cater to the needs of the exporters. Various projects under the Assistance to States for Developing Export Infrastructure (ASIDE) Scheme of Govt. of India, Ministry of Commerce are under implementation in the state to strengthen export infrastructure. Air cargo complexes in Srinagar and Jammu will also be taken up in the near future,

Permanent Grievance Redressal System

In the past, despite provisions in the industrial policy, there have been many instances of consignments of raw materials, capital goods, fuels, etc. being detained in the entry point of the state, often resulting in delays and payment of fines and penalties. With a view .to ensure that the industrial policy is honoured in letter and spirit, an order will be issued by the Finance Department that no consignment for industries, covered by the industrial policy, will be detained at the entry point for more than 24 hours. In the event of any doubt, a notice will be issued by the concerned authority to the firm outlining the objections but the consignment will be instantly released. A Permanent Grievance Redressal Committee, consisting of Director Industries and Commerce, Commissioner Sales Tax and Commissioner Excise, to be set up by the Finance Department, shall meet once every fortnight to consider all such notices and pass orders which shall be final and binding on all concerned. In emergent situations, such meetings could be called at shorter notice too. This procedure is expected to check alleged arbitrary actions at the entry point of the state.

Environment Protection

Pollution Control and environment protection will be accorded high' priority. The Pollution Control Board shall give necessary clearances to new units to start construction only after satisfying itself that the required pollution control measures have been included in the project by the promoter. The State Government will assist setting up of Common Effluent Treatment Plants and providing sites of solid waste disposal etc. availing of the existing schemes of the Government of India as well as the States' own resources. Procedures for environment clearances will be streamlined to achieve speedy disposal. Environment friendly projects will be accorded greater priority. Incentive for procurement of pollution control devices has been provided in the state government's package.

Entrepreneurship Development

Lack of entrepreneurial skills of the local youth has been identified as an impediment for sustained industrial gro\\1h. J&K Entrepreneurship Development Institute (J&KEDI), a society registered under the J&K Societies Registration Act, has recently been activated to provide entrepreneurship training to youth of the state. Universities will be encouraged to include comprehensive entrepreneurial education in the course curriculum both at the undergraduate and postgraduate levels in the state. The State will encourage setting up of training institutions in the private sector, in the areas of Information Technology, Biotechnology and Communication. Educational and research institutions of international standards related to business/industry shall be provided land in industrial parks/growth centres at a concessional rate of 50%.

Thrust Areas and Prestigious Projects

The following industries will be the Thrust Areas of the government:

- Electronics (integrated circuits and micro assemblies)/ computer hardware and software
- Food processing including agro-based industries (excluding conventional grinding/extraction units)
- Floriculture
- Handicrafts
- Leather processing and leather goods
- Sports goods, articles and equipments for general physical exercise
- Forest based industry
- Processing of aromatic and medicinal plants and herbs
- Pharmaceuticals including bulk drugs
- Silk reeling, weaving, processing printing and made-ups, Yarn and yarn spun from silk waste
- Cutting and polishing of stones, gems and jewellery
- Precision engineering
- Wool processing, Spinning, weaving & finishing, woven fabrics of wool
- Woven fabrics of cotton
- Industries related to the promotion of tourism e.g. units manufacturing camp equipments, fibre boats etc, souvenirs for tourists

- Knowledge industry including information technology bio-technology etc.
- Auto ancillaries.
- Exploration of minerals.
- Green houses (only Ladakh).

The government may add new industrial activities lo the thrust areas from time to time. The industrial projects in these areas will be accorded priority in the matter of allotment of Land, sanction power and other clearances as also in the matter of grant of incentives.

With regard to Prestigious Projects, with investment above Rs. 25 crore, the government may consider a Special package of incentives, to be documented in the form of a MOU, on case to case basis on merits. Notification of a prestigious project shall be made by State Level Committee-l for granting Capital Investment Subsidy.

Research and Development

Encouraging Research & Development (R&D) in important economic sectors and transferring the results of these to the industrial sector are the needs of the hour. This is particularly necessary in agriculture, forest. Mining and mineral sectors, medicinal and herbal plants which provide a substantial base for value audition. Design cum Resource centres shall be set for supporting handicrafts/handloom sectors, Central government assistance for such purposes shall be fully availed. National level organisations of excellence shall be pursued to provide Support for these programmes.

Implementation

Effective and efficient implementation of the policy' must be ensured In order lo achieve this and also to provide for a regular interaction between the govt. at the highest level and the industry at large, the government will set up an Advisory Committee for Industries with the hon'ble Chief Minister as the Chainman. Besides the hon'ble Deputy Chief Minister in charge of Industries and Commerce and hon'ble Minister of State for Industries and Commerce, this committee will consist of all Principal Secretaries in charge of economic department, such as agriculture, consumer affairs, environment, forests, finance, information technology, planning and power development. Representatives of Chambers of Commerce of Industry and Federations of Industries of Jammu and Kashmir Divisions and also senior officials of the Ministry of Commerce and Industry, Government of India, will be invited to join this committee. Principal Secretary I&C will act as the Member-Secretary of the Committee. This committee will meet at least once in three months and provide a forum for timely discussion on major issues agitating the industry and arriving at prompt decisions, a dire necessity in these days of high level of competition among the states' for promoting industrialization.

Government of India
Ministry of Commerce & industry
(Department of Industrial Policy and Promotion)
New Delhi, dated, June, 2002

Subject: New Industrial Policy and other concessions for the State of Jammu & Kashmir

The Government of Jammu & Kashmir has requested for a special package for development of industries in the state on the lines for the North East Industrial Policy notified by the Central Government - Ministry of Industry's OM N0.EA/1/,2/96.IPO dated 24lh October, 1997. Discussions on Strategy and Action Plan for development of industries and generation of employment in the Slate of Jammu & Kashmir were held with the various related ministries on the issues inter alia: infrastructure development, financial concessions and easy market access,

Keeping in view the fact that the state of Jammu & Kashmir lags behind in industrial development, a need has been felt for structured interventionist strategies to accelerate industrial development of the state and boost investor confidence. The new initiatives would provide the required incentives as well as an enabling environment for industrial development, improve availability of capital and increase market access to provide a fillip to the private investment in the state.

The matter has been carefully considered by the Government and it has been decided to provide the following package of incentives for the state of Jammu & Kashmir.

Fiscal incentives to new units and substantial expansion of existing units

- New industrial units and existing industrial units on the substantial expansion as defined Set up in growth centres, industrial infrastructure development centres (IlOCs) and other locations like industrial estates. Parks. export processing zones commercial estates etc. as notified by the Central Government are entitled to 100% (hundred percent) excise duty exemption for a period of 10 years from the date of commencement commercial production,
- All new industries in the notified location would be eligible for capital investment subsidy @ 15% of their investment in plant and machinery, subject to a ceiling of Rs. 30 lakh. The existing units will be entitled lo this subsidy on substantial expansion. as defined,
- An interest subsidy of 3% on the working capital loan would be provided to all new' industrial units in notified locations for a period of I0 years after commencement of commercial production. This benefit would also be extended to existing units in notified locations on expansion as defined. as well as to Annexure-II Thrust Industries.
- the insurance premium to the extent of hundred percent on Capital investment for a period of I0 years would be extended by the Central Government to all new units and to existing unit on substantial expansion as defined.
- The present income tax exemption would continue as per the existing dispensation applicable to Jammu & Kashmir. The State govt. may consider extending sales tax exemption to the units which avail of concessions under this policy.

Development of Industrial Infrastructure

The financing pattern of integrated infrastructure development centre will change from 2: 3 between govt. of India and SIDBI 4: 1 and the GOI would be in the nature of a grant, so as to provide the required infrastructure support.

Other Incentives

- Design-cum-resource centre for footwear and leather industry, leather goods and shoes as well as of fur are being manufactured in the SSI/ Tiny sector traditionally in Srinagar and Jammu. The central govt. would make an initial contribution of Rs. 1.00 crore as grant for setting up a design resource centre and national leather development programme would provide assistance for machinery, training and salaries of professionals. Under the national development programme, exclusive assistance would be provided to market finished leather products of the artisans of the state in the form of buyer-seller meets and exhibitions.
- Ministry of textiles will extend their package of assistance as applicable to the north eastern region, to the state of Jammu and Kashmir on same terms and conditions.

Setting up of Jammu and Kashmir Development Finance Corporation

Jammu and Kashmir Development Corporation shall be setup by the central govt. with one time provision of Rs. 50 crore on the lines of North East development financial corporation. This corporation shall provide term loan, working capital and other infrastructure support in the state on the lines of NEDFI in the north east.

JKDFC would be designed as the nodal agency for routing the subsidies/incentives under various schemes notified under this policy.

The above concessions/ subsidies shall be available to all new/ existing industrial units on their substantial expansion, in the notified industrial areas by the central government. And thrust industries irrespective of location.

Ineligible industries under the policy

Cigarettes/cigars of tobacco manufactured tobacco and substitutes, distillation/brewing of alcoholic drinks and manufacture of branded soft drinks and its concentrates are excluded for the purpose of concessions under this policy

Thrust Industries

- Food Processing and agro based industries (excluding conventional grinding/extraction units) such as
- ✓ Sauces, Ketchup, etc.
- ✓ Fruit Juices & fruit pulp
- ✓ Jams, Jellies, vegetable juices, puree, pickles etc.
- ✓ Fruit Waxing, packaging, grading
- Leather Processing & Leather goods
- Tissue culture
- Silk Reeling Yarn and Yarn spun from silk waste Woven fabrics of silk or silk waste
- Wool & woven fabrics of wool
- Woven fabrics of cotton
- Floriculture
- Medicinal herbs- processing
- Green houses only Ladakh
- Computer hardware/Electronics (integrated circuits & micro assemblies)
- sports goods and articles and equipment for general physical exercise
- Auto Ancillaries
- Eco-tourism...Hotels, Houseboats, Resorts, adventure & leisure sports, amusement parks, cable car. Guest houses only Ladakh
- Handicrafts
- precision engineering
- Exploration of minerals

Annexure II

SIDO Schemes

SIDO operates a number of schemes for the SSI sector. At a glance these are:

Credit Linked Capital Subsidy Scheme for Technology Upgradation

Credit Guarantee Scheme - Collateral free loans up to a limit of Rs.25 lakh - for individual SSIs.

ISO 9000/ISO 14001 Certification Reimbursement Scheme - Incentive Scheme of Reimbursement of expenses for acquiring Quality Management System (QMS) ISO 9000 certification/environment management (EMS) ISO 14001 certification to the extent of 75% or Rs.75,000 whichever is lower.

For individual SISIs/Ancillary/tiny/SSSBE units

Participation in International Fairs - Full subsidy on space rent and shipment of exhibits of SSI units - ***for individual SSIs***

Purchase and Price Preference Policy - This is administered through the Single Point Registration Scheme of NSIC. Under this, 358 items are reserved for exclusive purchase from SSI by Central Government. Other facilities include tender documents free of cost, exemption from earnest money and security deposit and 15% price preference in Central Government purchases - ***for individual SSIs***

Prime Minister's Rozgar Yojana-PMRY (Scheme of Ministry of ARI) Subsidy for NE twice that of rest of India - ***for entrepreneurs. SSIs***

Small Industry Cluster Development Programme - For promoting technology upgradation in clusters for a group of SSI units of one industry.

Integrated Infrastructure Development (IID Scheme)

Mini Tool Rooms

Testing Centres

Sub-Contracting Exchanges

SSI MDA - The scheme offers funding up to 90% in respect of to and fro air fare for participation by SSI Entrepreneurs in overseas fairs/trade delegations. The scheme also provide for funding for producing publicity material (up to 25% of costs) Sector specific studies (up to Rs. 2 lakh) and for contesting anti-dumping cases (50% up to Rs. 1 lakh) - ***for individual SSIs & Associations.***

Assistance to Entrepreneurship Development Institutes - For strengthening training infrastructure in EDIs, assistance upto 50% or Rs. 50 lakhs whichever is less - *for State Governments.*

Scheme of Micro Finance Programme

Index

Index